JESUS SPEAKS

With the Disciples Who Followed in His Footsteps:
The Lost Years and Teachings Revealed

J. A. WRIGHT

DISCLAIMER

The information provided
in this book is only
designed to provide interesting
and entertaining info on the
subjects discussed. This book
is not a substitute for medical advice
of physicians. For diagnosis
or treatment of any medical concerns
or problems, consult your physician.

Copyright © 2012 J. A. Wright

All rights reserved.

ISBN: 0615544053

ISBN 13: 9780615544052

I dedicate this book to all Truth Seekers

Acknowledgments

First, my gratitude goes to Sharon for her guidance at the beginning of this endeavor. Thanks to Mike for his editing and Marguerite for her insights. My sincere gratitude goes to Ann, not only for her incredible support to me these last few years but for her selfless service to mankind, a true humanitarian. And I was fortunate to have the support of my extraordinary son who is a constant inspiration to me.

"Absolutely wonderful"

"Reading this wonderful book was like being given a key to the Vatican vault. I highly recommend this book, and I'm so glad I have it. I'm looking forward to J. A. Wright's next book."

Robin Landry,

author of *When I dream*

Top 500 Amazon Reviewer Vine™ Voice

"To say that this read is a controversial read is an understatement."

"Though controversial, Wright's book perhaps serves the purpose of only strengthening the beliefs of these Christians, who must take a closer look at their convictions and beliefs, while offering insight to those non-believers who are not yet sure what they believe."

Suzanne Gattis,

Pacific Book Review

TABLE OF CONTENTS

INTRODUCTION

Why is the Bible strangely silent about Jesus' life up to the age of 30? And what if I told you that those in power knew this history, but that it was so controversial that they conspired to withhold this information from their followers?

Well, now for the first time in over two thousand years Jesus and his disciples tell their side of the story to you, in their own words. The words of Jesus, you say? Yes. Several years ago I was presented with readings and lessons through trance channeling. During the course of these lessons I was made aware that I was to eventually bring these lessons to all of you, my brothers and sisters.

Venture with Jesus and his disciples, as you are taken through a series of lessons, events and travels, shedding new light and insight on the meaning of these events from their own perspectives. And seeing how many of the events are misinterpreted in the Bible. The twenty-one chapters contain the essence of Jesus' teachings, providing you with practical knowledge on how to renew your life, and awaken to your full potential.

Unlike in the Bible, Jesus and his disciples explain the exact meaning of his teachings including, *Physician, heal thyself* and *Seek ye first the kingdom of God within*. Which they say, ninety-nine percent of mankind doesn't really understand the meaning of and why they are even being spoken.

This book answers some of the most puzzling questions about Jesus' life from his early years to the Resurrection. With many original contributions that, to my knowledge, are the first of its kind; a treasure trove of profound knowledge, transcribed from scores of tape recorded sessions.

One note: The text is written in the conversational context from which it was presented. Throughout the book, Jesus and his disciples use the pro-noun "he" to indicate a man, woman or child. Also, they frequently switch between the first, second and third person (As in I, you, he and she).

For centuries people have searched for answers to the mysteries surrounding the lost years and teachings of Jesus. *Jesus Speaks* helps fill that void and is one of those extraordinary books for which the word *revelation* is not an exaggeration.

So, read, contemplate and enjoy!

J. A. Wright
May 2013

"Follow me my beloveds. Follow me. Let thy cares of the physical world fall away from your physical shoulders and let us find our presence in eternity. So let us walk into this beautiful garden of eternal expression. And let us walk to the rock that we have sat on before and let us take our place there."

Jesus

CHAPTER 1

We Told You the Way to Life is Life Itself

By Jesus

My dearly beloveds, once again I am privileged to come forth through this instrument that I might take just a little of that which you call your earth time to bring about, I pray, a degree of balance to your way of thinking. I was privileged to take hold of the instrument a week ago, and I shared with you some of the inconsequential things of my earth life, such as my birth date, when I was born, and various things.

What I wish to bring about now is of importance, for you see, I know you celebrate my birth date the twenty-fifth of December, and I was born in March. I spoke to you and said I was not put to the cross as it has always been given to you, and I shared with you various other conditions that have been part of a lost history. A history that was so lost they didn't even know I had been born in the Holy Land until three-hundred and fifty years after I had been born there, then that truth came out only in mid-Africa and India.

Therefore, there are many things that you have been sidetracked about but purposely by the money changers. You see, the money changers wanted these things this way so that you could pass your time arguing whether I was born in December or March. Whether I was put to the cross or in otherwise, or whether the year that I was born was the true year or whether the time of the conception of the so-called Christianity was in the year that you have established it. And many things such as this, in order to keep you from knowing the truths that I taught, these things are very unimportant that I spoke to you about last week.

Yet probably many of you spent your week contemplating these things. I wanted this to be said because I wanted to show you definitely how inconsequential these things can be and of no value to you on the pathway of life—of absolutely no value. Yet you would probably go on and argue these points out.

All that I wanted to share with you in my few years was the way of life—how to live, how to love. I was attempting to give you a way that would bring into your personal lives that which is the Brotherhood of Man, the Fatherhood of God. I tried to take out of your hearts the false gods that you are praying to, that you are lighting candles to.

These are the things beloveds that I have attempted—and did attempt at the time that I walked out of the temples of old. I only tried to give and to share with you the same God that I had, that is your God. I didn't try to change gods. I didn't attempt to make a God out of the gods that they had in the temples of that day. For you have done the same thing that they did in the days that I walked your physical earth. You have set me in your temples as the God, the flesh God. And all I wanted to share with you was how to live and to love each other. All I wanted to share with you was the knowledge that I was no different than you. That I was born of parents exactly as you were born.

But, what I was attempting to do was not what they were teaching in the temples of old, but was what the masters were teaching that were being falsely set forth as gods in the temples. What they had taught, which was, and is, the exact same teachings as I am teaching and was teaching in the past. Yet it is not being observed—you are not doing those things that I taught. You have put me on a pedestal as a flesh god—the son and the only one, of the Father. When I told you that you were the sons of God, when I told you that you were one in the Father and the Father is one in you. When I told you, you had to awaken the Christ within yourselves, as all of we masters did. We did not ever tell you that we were the only sons of God.

Remember, beloveds, that God and His creation is a finished creation, it's a complete creation, and what your creation is, is what you are making it. If you are building false gods before you then, of course, your creation is going to be one that is very disturbing—one that does not become fulfilling, one that does not fulfill the vibrations of love, and health, and inner peace, and awareness, and understanding—one that is going to be utterly confusing to you. I showed you that your God is the same God as I. Therefore, that when you spoke to your God, knowing, as I told you so, know, as I speak unto my Father, my Father has answered me.

But yet, you must be reminded beloveds that the God divine creation is a finished creation, nothing can be added or taken away. But you are lost in this vibration of a distorted world of your own creation. You have deliberately walked out of God into a world of the physical. Then you have deliberately built false gods, statues in your temples as they were in the temples of old. You have lighted candles to these false gods. You have done many things that are of no value towards life.

I say to you, beloveds, life was given to you and this life that was given to you—not to be taken away from you. But, that you were to fulfill that life and to reestablish that life, and to open up the energy powers of the universe that are within you. That you should awaken the Christ within you to fulfill that temple—that the furthest star in the universe is as close as your very breath. For you are the replica of this, your third-dimensional vibration.

So, I ask of you beloveds, why not take time to look and see what's taking place in your world? See what's taking place so that you will not attempt to go out there and say, "You're wrong. You are absolutely of no value." No. You are not to do this, but you are to be the example of that light life, that divine God essence that is the very function of this your temple. That you can then walk in the knowledge that I am the I AM; that I am one in my Father, that my Father is one in me.

Why do you need false gods? I cannot see the progress. For I find that you are very disturbed and that you are building on the quicksands—and these quicksand's may envelope you as they enveloped the great pyramids of Egypt. Beloveds, you cannot build anything on the fallacies of life. You see you were given these conditions, these fallacies, and you have not even attempted to look and to study the histories of the past. You have taken histories—re-written and where have they led you? Where? Where have the histories of the past led you? They have led you to the sword, to the atomic bomb, and to many other conditions of destruction.

Because you are doing the same thing as those that were the leaders of the past when they spoke and said, "I had a dream and God said for me to go and destroy those, for they do not believe in that which we believe in." So, they donned their suits of armor and their swords and went out and destroyed their brother man, because their brother didn't believe in the name of the Father of the universe, the creator of all things. What are you doing, beloveds? What are you doing to yourselves? You are destroying, you are destroying. . . I am looking here, beloveds—I am trying to straighten out the instrument here for a moment . . . thank you.

You say, I pray, I pray, I pray, but who do you pray to? What do you do when you pray? You don't even stop to listen to the answer. You pray to the many false gods. And, when you pray to your God and the answer doesn't come as you want it, you pay no attention to it. You wonder what's happening to your world. Why is this? Because you want to change it out there, instead of changing it here (within you), where God is and listening to that divine true nature that you are. That being that is almighty within you, that beautiful energy power that can never be destroyed, as long as you keep and maintain and sustain a balance of awareness of the Father.

That you can keep the spark of love awakened within your temple, and you will keep that spark of love that says, "I love you Father, but I also know that I must love and I do love my fellowman. I know Father that through that great love, the Brotherhood of Man and the Fatherhood of Thy divine nature shall become a complete and thorough awareness within me that I shall no longer, Father, doubt or fear. That I shall know, Father, that you are not going to come and destroy me, that you are not going to cause me to go into the hell and the damnation of my own creation."

"But if I listen to you I shall no longer know the grave. For that is the hell that I must face, but I do not face it any longer, for I know there is no such a thing. For I know, Father, you didn't create me to go that way. You created me that I may lift the temple of Thy love—that I recognize this temple as the temple of Thy divine expression. And as I recognize this temple as the temple of Thy divine expression, I shall never hold a false god before me."

(Author's note: These spirit teachers often use the word *temple*, not only in reference to a church or synagogue but also in reference to the physical body.)

So when you look at me, beloveds, and the masters of old, don't make gods out of them. But know that we reached mastery because we didn't hold any false gods. And that you, too, can reach that mastery if you will no longer hold false gods. But, listen to what we taught you, we taught you the way of life. We taught you to love under any given condition or circumstance. We never taught you to destroy, to kill, and to maim.

We told you the way to life is life itself and to recognize life—to recognize it as a total part and parcel of your being, that every fiber, cell, bone and tissue of that temple shall respond to the divine nature of the Father and that you, through His divine mind, can make your temple respond to your every need. You will listen now when you speak, "Father show me, I will walk."

Peace be with you. I am your brother Jesus.

***

Unfortunately, the previous lesson of Jesus referred in the first paragraph, at the start of this chapter, was inaudible. However, it is all covered in accompanying chapters.

There are a few points that Jesus speaks of below from this chapter that you may be unfamiliar with that I can assist you in understand.

Jesus begins the lesson by saying, *"My dearly beloveds, once again I am privileged to come forth through this instrument..."* Jesus and these teachers have, as far back as I can recall, referred to the channeler as the *instrument*. I understand, not only referred to this channeler as the instrument, but also to other channelers they work with in many other countries.

Jesus' reference to *"The Brotherhood of Man and the Fatherhood of God"* is not a passage from the Bible as I initially surmised. As I understand it, the Brotherhood of Man pertains to our peaceful co-existence with our brothers and sisters. And the Fatherhood of God is all of mankind's mental, physical and spiritual kinship with God. This phrase was often used by religious liberals in the 1920s and 30's and may still be used by the Freemasons.

Then, Jesus states in paragraph six, "*I was born of parents exactly as you were born.*" Jesus is saying here that he did have a biological father and that through his father's intercourse with his mother, Jesus was conceived just as all of us. Not a virgin birth as it is presented in passages of the King James version of the New Testament, such as in Matthew 1:18 and Luke 1:26-35.

In later chapters Jesus and the other teachers will explain this further and the reasons why religion hid this history from their followers and the world.

Also, in the same paragraph Jesus states, "*When I told you, you had to awaken the Christ within yourselves as all of we masters did.*" Jesus and these teachers believe the word *Christ* has been misinterpreted for centuries. Below are two brief explanations from other lessons:

(27-602) "The Christ consciousness is not Jesus. The Christ consciousness is the consciousness of knowing my oneness in the creator or the Father, and that belongs to every soul in the universe." (Eterna)

(12-205) "Christ means God consciousness, but man puts Christ as a man. How often do you hear people say, Christ this and Christ that, and they're talking about a man called Jesus? Christ is the consciousness of the living God within this temple. That's the Christ consciousness." (Akim)

Then, in paragraph nine Jesus said, "*You have deliberately walked out of God into a world of the physical.*" To help explain this, below is an excerpt from another lesson. This will also be discussed and explained in detail in later chapters and which will also refer to Adam, when he first entered into the physical.

(25-703) "When this identity man entered into this body he lost something because of the density of the animal. Because he had identity of the freedom of the love, of the realm of joy and the pleasures of God, and the capability that God had given unto man to have dominion over all of His creation. Now, he entered into this physical body or the hu-body and it now became a prison as it were to him." (Unnamed teacher)

And in the last paragraph Jesus says, *"But know that we reached mastery because we didn't hold any false gods and that you too can reach that mastery if you will no longer hold false gods."* Although mastery is explained fully in forthcoming chapters, below are two brief explanations.
(11-171) "Now mastery only means that I no longer have to go through physical death. That is mastering life. Understand?" (Kuthumi)
(11-123) "So, now let us take a look here, mastering means rising above the last enemy called death, which it speaks of in your Revelations." (Kuthumi)

To summarize, Jesus and these other master teachers are saying that it is not necessary for us to die physically. And we should be able to master life or ascend, as they did, in this, our present lifetime.

CHAPTER 2

He Lived the Word and the Word Was Life

By Unnamed Teacher

Peace. Peace. Peace. Dearly beloveds, once again it is my pleasure that I have the privilege of taking hold of this instrument that I might come forth and share with you those things that may have value in your personal lives. I know we have taken the facets of life's expression or the diamond of life, as it were, and we have attempted in every way possible throughout the years to help you to help yourselves polish the facets of this diamond of life.

But I find, as I look to this your physical world that there is a great deal that yet is needed in order that you will be *ready* to fully understand that which the Elder Brother attempted, in every way, to share with you. Even as he traveled in the various parts of your world, he attempted in every way to help his brothers and sisters to realize that he, as a teacher, was attempting to reach the mastery.

Now, I am speaking, at the time now, when he had left the Holy Land and traveled in the various parts of the world. This was before he had attained the mastery. But yet, by the same token, he had reached a high vibration in the physical expression. And that which he was receiving, by doing, as he shared with each one that he met upon his way—sharing that which he had received, himself, in order to not only embellish and renew and reestablish *his* world around him, but to also help those that were following or attempting to follow in his footsteps. That they too, if they would attempt to know themselves more fully—that they too would be well upon the way to reaching that which is not the higher ground but the *rock of life*.

Because, you see, even at his early age, even when he spoke in the temple this young man at the age of twelve years had so completely reached within himself that he understood—even though he had not yet reached the point of awareness, that he was not to play the part of history that was being taught in your physical world, at that time—yet *is* your physical world even as of this present day. He knew that there was something more to life. That there was something greater to life than just the existence of a few years, and, of the negations that came out of those that were teachers in the various temples, in the various places upon your physical earth—yet, even though, they are supposedly believing upon the same one God identity, the same God creator.

So when he moved into this your present, the country called America, he then was of an early age. He was about fourteen years of age at that time, when he reached here in America. And, he did have not children as his disciples, he had chosen well those that were to walk with him as disciples. So, there were those that did master, that were with him at the time that he traveled through the Americas—not only the North American country but the South American country.

But let us take a look, here, and see what took place. Now, of course, in this your country at the time that Jesus traveled there were those known as the Indians. He chose well to have certain ones that would walk with him. They were wanting to learn. They were wanting something to know more of what life was all about. So it was that his teachings were very, very simple teachings. He had no bible, but he had God. He had the divine essence of awareness. He knew that in his contact from within that he could get the answers to any problem that was necessary to be answered, that had anything of validity in order to maintain balance; to create joy, pleasure, of peacefulness, of love that was not threatened by the selfishness or greed, doubts, fears and so on and so forth.

So his choice was very good because there were those that came to him that willed to walk with him and to go into the various tribes. So it was that he made a good choice of the Indians of the North American continent in order to travel into all parts of the continent. He and the Indians worked very closely together. They sat in meditations quite often, and this was not a processed meditation. It was not a meditation that said you've got to meditate in this way or that way. The meditations were such that was for them to try to know themselves more fully. Because he knew that if they knew themselves, they were going to know God. You see? They couldn't know themselves without knowing God. Of course they also knew a great deal *more* than just themselves, because they knew as they entered in they could, eventually, understand they were capable of seeing the dimensions of life—the dimensions of life that had transpired since that which was the creation.

So it was that he remained for some time in the country of America—I'm saying this here of your country because he traveled here in this part of your world for three years. But many of the Indians when they heard of his teachings came, also, to listen to him from various parts of the country. But then he left his disciples here to carry on his work.

Those of you that have any contact at all with the Indian tribes, I'm speaking not of the Indians you see today. I am talking about the Indians of years ago. If you had any contact with them and I'm talking about those Indians that didn't travel in the cities, but lived in their own world. If you contacted them you would find that they were teaching of the Great Spirit or the Great White Spirit. You see? They were not teaching of the man called Jesus that traveled with them. They were teaching how to greet to the Great Spirit of eternal life. Because this is what the master Jesus was teaching, even though he was not a master at the time.

But he was moving and having his being on the premise of knowing within himself that this was the way to mastery. Because he knew, as he had studied some of the histories of the masters of the past—even though he was but a young man, it was enough to help him to realize and to recognize that he had to know himself.

Then, he traveled into South America and India and Africa, as well, and Australia and other places. But, now, all of his teachings could be put down very simply. There was very little to his teachings, it was summed up in the essence of knowing the self. But then, of course, when he began to know the self, he began to discover that he was not bound by borders, he was not bound by the conditions of the physical world. He was not bound any longer—and he felt and he knew that there was something beyond that which is the physical.

But he knew also that he had to reestablish himself in the divine essence of the universe by bringing his temple into a high vibration—a vibration that was not traveling in the essence of the conditions of the past histories of man. But that's when he became acquainted with himself, he became aware—as his temple began to quicken that he could evolve and move and have his being in many expressions of life without having any physical vehicle, of any kind, to move himself about; that he could move and have his being just through the element of that which the Father had established and set into motion and so he began to evolve.

If there is a land that could have been called the Holy Land, the country of America should have been called that, if there was any Holy Land. But you see this is not true; there is no Holy Land. You take a look at the Holy Land—what you call the Holy Land and you find nothing but strife, you find nothing but destruction, you find nothing but bitterness, hatreds. You find doubts, fears. All of these things are multiplied many, many times in that part of your world. But it's also registering, in like manner, in all parts of your world.

Even though, you may find in your own country that man isn't at war or destroying, he is but in the depth of fear. He is doubtful of his brother. He is ready to destroy if he sees any excuse to destroy. So, you have a very loose destructive world that is supposed to be bound by the teachings of your Elder Brother Jesus.

So this should be saying something to you—you that are here and hopefully to learn and to rise above the Last Enemy, that the elder brother Jesus was trying to teach you and I. It should be telling something to each one of you. It should be telling you that—in that which is bound by the conditions of limitation—then there is something wrong.

In his travels, of course, he eventually ended up in India with the masters there of the Far East and stayed with them for quite some time; studying, but mostly being in the meditative moods of life by attempting, at all times, to discover himself. To discover, to see what was necessary in order to help all of mankind, this was his goal. He hoped to be one that would evolve to such a degree that he would be able to help all of mankind. But his hopes became rather shattered because he found that the masters before him—when eventually he had reached the mastery, he found that the masters before him had not been very successful. That they ended out as pomp, the little gods in the temples. Therefore, then, reality was lost, the flow of that which was balance was completely lost.

So, then when he finally decided after reaching the mastery, to come back into the part of the world where he had been born, he found that he was rather disenchanted with many, many things that took place. Everyday there were disenchantments in his life, but no bitterness, he had learned well. But yet, by the same token, he knew that he could not limit or put any thought of limitation of that which he had to share. That he would put it out, give it to man and hopefully they would accept and would move into the greater expression of life.

But, of course, you know what took place, there were constant disenchantments. There were threats to his life and all of these things that abounded there. But, what were his main teachings? What was he attempting to do? What was this man really wanting? Of course what he wanted was hopefully that all mankind would understand where they had came from, out of what dimension of life they had moved and had their being. Out of that dimension where did they move? What did they do? Did they go upwards or downwards? Did they go backwards or forwards? Of course he knew that man had not gone forward, but had gradually moved down into other vibrations; but had not gone forward excepting very few, that had remained and stayed with the vibrations of that which they were established and created in.

Then, of course, it is well known in the history, and yet, it is never given to man that it was over three-hundred years after Jesus had left the physical world expression, three hundred years later—they didn't even know where this man had been born. Yet, the country that he was born in today is called the Holy Land. You see how very narrow and very unthinking man is? He is not attempting—he is just moving. He is like a zombie on the ball called earth, because they are not capable of rising above their dogmas and doctrines that they have accumulated through the many, many years.

It is no different today. It's not an excuse but it's yet not a bit different than when it was at the time that Jesus taught in that place called the Holy Land. They too were dense. They too were like zombies, and they too would become bitter and hateful. Or they would just turn about face and say, "Oh, this is not what I have been taught and so I'm not going to try to attempt to follow anything such as this." And many will say, "I will not change this condition, I don't care if it kills me" and it does kill them, of course. Because they don't attempt to move up the ladder of life, they don't attempt to find the pleasure and joys that God gave and created for man. You see?

Where is man now? Do you see man in the joyful, creative, loving, pleasure loving, dancing, singing, peaceful and not filled with doubts and fears and so on and so forth? You don't see any of it. Everyone is caught-up in their own little world. They have spun a web, a web around themselves. They have been not only the spinner of the web, but they have been the spider that bound themselves. They only bound themselves. They didn't bind anything else but themselves. Although they attempt in their various religious backgrounds to cause man to move in the various directions with the knowledge that states, "This is the way to walk. This is the only way and your way is not of any value."

So, it is that you have the difficulties that you do have, and the fears and the doubts and the anguish that follows as you go on into the years. And as the years approach you keep on saying, "Well, I'm not as young as I used to be. I've got to expect these kinds of things because of my age. I've got to do this, I've got to do that, I know that that's the way and so it is *all* that there is." That's the way it was at the time of Jesus and so there were very few that even got the word.

So, this is the way the conditions of your earth are. You're born in that which is destruction; yet, it is under a holier-than-thou pious hypocrisy that all of this is given. So, the teachers and the priests and the rabbis and so on, they play on your sympathies. They try to create a sympathetic vibration. They reach in with the beautiful words that are so empty that they have nothing to hold to. They are just the quicksands. But you move right into them and you become a part of that degenerated vibration.

So it is that this is the way your world is and very few on your earth feel even comfortable if they are at "loose ends." That is, if they don't belong to something that binds them, "I've got to belong. I've got to be bound by this." And so they join, and then, they become a part of the doctrine that is brought in. Then they are fed the dogmas through these indoctrinations. So, it is that there is very little accomplished in the realm of the physical world.

But here was this man that was so generous with everything and was one that never attempted at anytime to bind anyone. He never wanted anyone to become bound to the living dead and the dead. You see? He was trying to work with those, those that you and I would call in your present day the *living dead*. Those that are yet moving around on your earth, but yet they are dead because they are not aware of the divine essence of a God unlimited. How few in a world, as filled with as many souls as there are on your earth, and very few are knowing to any degree, at all, that they are moving in a degenerated history of the past. And, know not that they can rise right out of that condition or those conditions, by simply knowing themselves—by simply contacting the withinness.

Yet Jesus walked with all mankind in his day. He didn't only give the word, but he lived the word and the word was life. The word was God. The word was eternal. But as he gave the word and he told man, "Ye are Gods," they turned their back on him. Because, you see, they had already established their gods. Their gods were in the temples already and so they turned their back on him. Now, today, it's the same thing. You talk of God the creator—which is not the way to go, you can't go anywhere until you go through this man called Jesus. And so it was written in that which you call the Bible.

But what have you really looked at and studied about that book? How real is that book? Is it as real as you hoped it would be? Does it have all of the answers? No. The answer you are going to get to life is when you enter within. Beloveds have you ever stopped to realize that that which you call your Bible, that which you say is the King James version, that word "version." That word alone should cause you to cringe a little bit. It is King James's way of thinking that went in there, his way of keeping you under his way of suppressive vibration.

So, his version was put there—he was a man with a great deal of authority. Of course his authority ended as he attempted to bring to you those things that would bind you and cause you many, many imbalances in your lives—through illnesses or through bitterness's or hatred or doubts or fears and so on and so forth. Therefore, certainly we do know there are many books on your earth that have a greater capability of giving you the keys to life than the Bible has. We certainly know this. But, Jesus also knew in his day that there were many things and books and many writings that were— if man would look into them, that were much greater than that which the religious orders of his day had and were teaching.

So, beloveds, isn't it time that man really realizes who he is? How unlimited he is? What his purpose is? These were the things that Jesus was attempting to bring to you. He wanted you to know your purpose. He wanted you to know that you were not limited to a few little years of expression filled with fears, filled with doubts, filled with illnesses, filled with all of these conditions that are destructive. He *knew* that this was not the way of life, as it was being taught in the temples, that you had to suffer, you had to give everything that you had and more. If you could move towards buying your way to that which would help you—when you let your body become filled with disease and die. You see? They didn't care as long as they got all that you had while you were there. But, also, while you were there, those that were close to you were also being indoctrinated in these conditions.

So, this is the way your world is and it is yet this way right now. There are very few today that can truly say that they are functioning in a manner that they are thoroughly honest with themselves. This is what the master was teaching—he wanted man to be thoroughly honest. But you see there's no honesty and there's no physical punishment for dishonesty in your world of today.

So, you find that those that are in the high places—suddenly find that they have lost their lives—suddenly something has happened to them. They have moved out from that which is, supposedly, among the living at a very early age. Supposedly, those that are the leaders of the world in the spiritual teaching—that all of the religions of the earth look to them for what they are to express in—you find right in there the politics and the destruction of life doesn't mean anything. So, if I don't want that person, all I need to do is destroy them and no one will ever know because of the hierarchy that keeps them all under their thumb. So, beloveds, this is the world you are living in—that is, existing in. If you are happy with it, well, alright, go right ahead and stay with it. But eventually, of course, you are going to find that the conditions of negation are going to take over and you're going to end up as you have done through countless incarnations.

I would like to share with you tonight the thought, the thought that is so terrific and so beautiful. That you can use it without any strain of any kind, without any of these pious vibrations, without any of this hypocrisy that is said to be a part of your religious world. Let's let go of hypocrisy. Let us let go of these things, let us let go of religion per se. Let us know that God didn't create that in the first place. So, let us then begin to realize that, even though, I have bound myself, even though I have taken this physical body—I can yet be free. Even though I feel I am bound in this temple—but in all truth, no, you are not bound. You are learning lessons and everyday is a lesson and every condition in your personal world is a lesson.

So, if I just take hold of myself and recognize me as the I AM power of the universe, that I AM power *is* my identity. My identity is that which permeates all of the creation. I should just stop long enough to take time to meditate, to enter in, especially the hours that I am walking this physical expression of earth, busy with that which I have contracted to do. By asking for a job or a position or whatever I have asked for, I have contracted that. I have been the causation of it, in other words. So, in order that I fulfill that cause, and balance it out I've got to know how to do it. I've got to work from within. I cannot do it perfectly from without because there are too many interferences by the zombie negations and the frustrations of man's creation. So, I see these things and I know that I am in that expression. But I know, also, that I am beyond having to accept that. I know that I am that which is the I AM, that which is the God expression within my being.

Therefore, I enter within and I say, "Now, look, here it is, Father, it's there. I know somewhere—I don't know how, but I know somewhere along the line I have brought these things upon myself. But I want to balance them out. All I want Father is to be shown. That's all. Just give me an answer that I can really travel on. Open up that central avenue of eternity. All I want is the answer." You don't have to cry to anyone. You don't have to do any of these things at all. All you have to do is ask the Father, just to be shown. Not that God should do it for you. No. "Just show me. That's all, Father. That's all I'm asking for because I want to walk with you. I don't want to walk in this density. But I can walk in this density *with you* and this density will have no hold over me." This is what the master Jesus was teaching, how you and I could walk in the deepest negations of even our own creation and not be flustered or not be destroyed by them—that we could rise above them.

So, while I'm working I just lean back and say, "Thank you, Father. I just know I have the answer. I know the answer is." Because, beloveds, it's here and now, and you'll never get the answer out of the *Book*. I don't care which book. You've got books, as I said before, that are more balanced than the Bible in every way, more reality in them in every way than the Bible has. Because you have on your earth today, the approach of the fulfillment of the age, and you've got many that are capable of reaching in now, and putting into word form that which is of value to you to reach the mastery, if you are seeking *life*.

But, all of it put together, every word spoken, every key given, if you don't use it, what value does it have? If you don't put it into action in my life today, I have nothing. I have no more than I had yesterday. In fact, no, I have even less because I know and I've got the key and I refuse to use it, so I create havoc within my temple. This, beloveds, is why Jesus said, "Bring the children to me. Bring your children." You know why he asked that? Because they were yet unspoiled, they were not yet indoctrinated. They were not yet poisoned by their parents, by the churches and the temples and so on and so forth. That's why he asked for the children, so that he could—not indoctrinate them but to tell them the truth.

To let them know how simple it is to live and to love and to turn their cheek. To be loving, to be peaceful, to be able to say, "I forgive." To be able to say, "I'm sorry," I did this or I did that. You see Jesus said, "Confess ye, one to another." He asked man that. Why did he ask that? He knew that you could not go into the temples as they were hearing your confessions in the temples of that day and as they are doing it in some of the temples of your present day. That it was only leading to a great deal of destruction. He knew this.

But, he knew that if I hurt him, that I should go to him and say, "I'm sorry. I did this, and after thinking it over I know that it was not as it should be, but I'm very sorry, I'll never let it happen again." Alright, now you have balanced out, even though that person—if you went to that person they would say, "Well, you can ask forgiveness, but I won't forgive you." That person there is the only one taking on—not only their negation but they have doubled it or tripled it. They have caused themselves a great deal of harm, themselves, not you. Because you have asked forgiveness—they didn't forgive, you forgave. You see what I mean? You have forgiven, you've forgiven yourself and you have asked forgiveness. What more can you do? You know I've learned my lesson well. I will not be repetitious in it. This is the thing.

But you see, confession as you are finding it in your world today gives you a license to go and confess and be forgiven by that individual, a priest or a rabbi, whoever. But then you are given the knowledge that you must stay pure until you have received what the temples call the sacraments. God didn't create any of this. Who wants sacraments? Who needs sacraments?

I mean, they are of no value. They are not a part of living. They are only a part of the hypocrisy.

Then once you have received the sacraments you walk right back out and go right back and do the same thing, again, that you just went and confessed. So, then, you go back again later on in your hypocrisy and again confess the same thing. You may have hurt somebody else, but yet you've done the same thing. So, you see, beloveds, how hypocritical the whole picture is; how it really is the demoniacal conditions of the churches that are destroying your world? They are the demons of destruction. That is actually what it is.

Now, Jesus also told you, you are a healer, to heal yourself. Alright, well, we haven't attempted to do that. We've always tried to run to someone else to get the healing. Rather than knowing that out of my Father that healing *is* and it is *fulfilled*.

Alright, now, then they came to Jesus that the demons be chased out of them. What are these demons? They weren't demons that God created special to come and take hold of you. They weren't those devils that man has wanted to say that there are, that God created a devil and so on and so forth. There is no truth, whatsoever, to any of it, yet it is written as truth. These demons are your own causations. These demons are your letting yourself become so low in your thinking that you open up your temple to the low vibrations; earthbound creatures and they take hold of your temple, that's all.

But that's enough, because sometimes there are many that take over; one after another that will take over, because there are many earthbound creatures that have let themselves die in their filth, so they come back. They want a body and when they can leech onto a body that let's themselves move in—they are mostly in the lowest thought patterns. You may be moving fine otherwise, but your thinking may be right down there in the lowest of the gutter. That's when that demon or that earthbound creature takes over and there you are.

Your institutions are filled with them, loaded with them. Many of them are due to the fact that some of your religions have helped them to reach that stage and especially that which is called spiritualism. Why? Because they try to open up your centers of awareness (chakras) and they work with one center and another center and pretty soon you got them out of balance. That's just when you're so out of balance that the earthbound creatures come in. (Author's note: The master teachers advise opening the chakras or centers of awareness all together, in balance, not one at a time. Opening the chakras one at a time can throw the whole body/mind/spirit out of balance) I call them creatures because they are not human. They are almost what you call, a soulless vibration. So, anything can take place once you let one of these earthbound creatures come in. If that one that came in is one that is destructive, then he is going to take command of your temple and you're going to lose the little mind that you do have and you move in that destructive condition.

So you see, this was the thing that Jesus was showing man, how he could and should never allow himself to move into any direction that could be destructive. That's why he wanted man to be sure to know themselves. To know that I am the influence of eternity, I am life. I am God in motion in the physical expression. I am that which is the I AM power of eternity. I am one with my Father. My Father is one with me. I am one in my brother. My brother is one in me. I am capable of doing all that is of value for myself and my fellowman. Why not accept this? You've been doing it the other way, haven't you? I can accept everything that is of no value—I can be bitter. I can be hateful. I can be doubtful. I can be fearful. I can be selfish. I can be greedy. I can accept all of these things and destroy myself. Why should I accept them any longer?

Why not accept God and let God be the word? The one word within my divine essence is my Father guideth, standeth, walketh and *is* the very center of my being. Now is this anything to cast out of myself? No. This is what the master Jesus attempted to teach you and I too—and that's why he wanted children to come to him, so that he could help them to realize, to know God. To know that they were walking with God, that they could see God in motion around them. Have you seen God lately in motion? Have you? Have you seen God in motion lately? Or have you just seen the destructive powers around you and accepted them as something that you could do nothing about? What have you accepted?

Alright, beloveds, God is and now. You and I can walk that avenue of eternity together, but I've got to know that I no longer entertain these things I once saw around me and said I could do nothing about it. I take myself out of that by raising my sights unto the Father. I walk and I find pleasure now. I find inner peace. I find that suddenly I'm shedding all fear and doubt. I find myself shedding all that is of no value and I'm putting on the Coat of Eternity. Believe me, beloveds, it's simple. I ask of you enter within, please enter within. Take the time to pleasure yourself. Take the time to pleasure yourself, because the only way you're going to get pleasure is through God. God is the happiest of all happiness. God is the joy of all joy. God is the peace of all peace. God is the love of all love. *God is, all in all expression.*

This is what the master Jesus was trying to bring to each one of us. Certainly he was sad—oftentimes there were times he could almost have become bitter on his way up to the mastery, when he saw how people turned their backs upon reality, when he saw how they would not accept. Yet what they were doing they knew was destroying. They knew it not only was destroying that which they were functioning in, but themselves also, yet they would not change.

You have heard those around you that possibly have said, "I'll do it, if it kills me"—and it does. For I am going to say to you, why don't you change that word to, "I am going to do it, if it does give me life eternal. I am going to do it in spite of myself. I'll do it even if I live into all eternity. I'm going to do it. I'm going to walk with my Father. I'm going to be the very expression of the entire creation. I am going to look at the creation. I am going to see its beauty. I am going to function into it and I am going to move and have my being in it. I am going to be that creation. I intend, even if I live forever, I am going to do it." Why don't you turn your thoughts this way rather than to say, "No, I'll stay with this if it kills me." You have done it through countless generations.

Brothers and sisters walk with us, will you please? We are entering into a greater dimension, that which is a fourth-dimension. Are you going to move back again into, and be rolled up into that dimension (Third-dimension) that you have been repetitious in? Or are you going to move into the greater dimensions? With that greater dimension you will find the doors are open to the countless dimensions in the Father's house. Peace be with you, beloveds.

Now, let us for just a few moments, let us just for a few beautiful moments cleanse our temple out. Let us for a few moments look into the glory and the beauty of our temple. Let's look from within and see the glory, the Shining Armor of Eternity that is manifesting in every fiber, cell, bone and tissue of my temple. I'm looking at my entire being. I am not seeing a skeleton. I am not seeing a body that is distorted. I am looking at a body—and I am looking at life, because I see God expressing in and through this temple. I see God from the top of my head to the bottom of my feet. I see God in the divine essence of eternity. I see God in peace and joy, and I see God moving into all expression. I see God—and I am God.

For I feel the very presence of His being moving in and through my entire temple. I feel Him moving in the bloodstream, I feel Him in my nervous system. I feel God moving in the very essence of my entire being. I feel God in every breath. I feel God in all that there is. Oh, Father, God, we thank Thee. So, let us now feel that energy and that presence, that divine presence that is yours and mine.

(Author's note: Meditation for eight minutes)

Feel that energy and that power, that love. Feel it. It is permeating your entire temple. You are going to feel this energy and this power now throughout the whole night. You are going to feel it. You are going to sleep with that power of love, that power that opens the door to eternity. It helps you to see, helps you to see through the singleness of life. To help you to see that, even though, there are scattered forces, I am the single force of eternity. I no longer scatter my forces because I belong to the one identity God. I belong to that which is the creation. I belong to that which moves and has its being *in* eternity.

This is where I walk. This is where I have my being, this is where I belong. I belong to life. I belong to peace. I belong to the Brotherhood of Man. I belong to the oneness that is the Fatherhood of God. I belong to only that which is complete and whole, that which is finished and is good and very good. I belong to that which does not have anything added or taken away. For I belong to my Father, yet as I belong to my Father I am not bound in any way—for I am free now. Free to move and have my being. To touch and feel the glory of God in everything that I can feel, see, touch or image. Let that peace reign eternal in the very center of your being and let it move outwardly into all eternity. And, whatever that beauty touches to and to whomever, that person will know that God is the victor. Peace be with you.

[Unnamed teacher]

The teacher near the end of the lesson expressed, *"We are entering into a greater dimension, that which is a fourth dimension. Are you going to move back again into and be rolled up into that dimension (Third-dimension) that you have been repetitious in? Or are you going to move into the greater dimensions? With that greater dimension you will find the doors are open to the countless dimensions in the Father's house."* There are many references regarding "dimensions" in the forthcoming chapters. I noted three examples below. Also, I think, it is interesting to note that they consider the word "dimensions" synonymous and used in the same context with the word "mansions." As it is referred to in many bibles, for example in the New Testament of the King James version, in John 14:2: *In my Father's house are many mansions: if it were not so, I would have told you. I go to prepare a place for you.*

Below are three brief explanations from other sessions:
(12-208) "Like he has said, In the Father's house there are many mansions or in the Father's house there are many dimensions." (Akim)
(21-139) ". . .you are in that which is the third-dimension, you came forth certainly since the creation. You have reached out of the first-dimension. You have reached out of the second-dimension. You are in a third-dimension and are seemingly though many incarnations are in complete repetition of that which is your own limitation." (Follower of Jesus)
(17-801) "That takes you fully—not on the fringes any longer of the fourth-dimensional world, but steeped right into it. Moving now towards a greater and a much more beautiful dimension because you have these dimensions in the Father's house—here are many dimensions, many. You have written it in your Bible as mansions—alright, what's the difference, dimensions. Your dimension is your mansion, the dimension of consciousness that you are in—that is where you are." (Salamar)

CHAPTER 3

Your Elder Brother Jesus Knew This Only After Many Years of Study

By Estonia Mercury

Peace. Peace. Dearly beloveds, it is my pleasure that I take hold of the instrument, that I might come forth and share with you this evening those things that may be of value to you.

It is of great importance now that man recognizes that he is no longer bound to the earth, that he is beginning to awaken within his own being and beginning to really understand that he is no longer subject to the conditions of the density of his own creation. So, in this awareness he begins to move more fully, more creatively, and feeling that which is the boundlessness of God's eternal gifts.

So, beloveds, it is well that you and I as, let us say, brothers and sisters, individuals, yet only one in the divine essence of the universe, realize and recognize that it is a very important part of living that we become aware more fully of our capabilities; of our recognizing within our own selves, that we are the subjects of the unlimited vibrations of the Father. Through His divine gifts that unlimitedness became the very essence of our being. Yet, through the generations of our movement from the first- dimension of creation, into that which we called the second-dimension of creation and, then, entering within the third-dimension we sort of went downhill in a sense—downhill to recover and renew ourselves in the creation.

Your Elder Brother Jesus knew this only after many years of study; from the time of his, let us say, twelfth year through his various travels as he moved about and went into the various parts of the world, especially after the age of sixteen years. But yet, those four years between the age of twelve and sixteen were not lost years. They were years during which he studied a great deal. Not that which was being expressed in the temples, but he studied that which he could find through those that were functioning in a manner that was constructive in their way of knowledge, of no expression of limitation being their part of life.

So it was this young man moved and had his being. So, as he began to awaken and open up his centers, the centers of his being, he then at the age of sixteen was able to release himself from the complete densities of the physical world. For he no longer allowed himself to function in that density. He had opened up his centers to the degree that now he no longer allowed himself to even *think* in a manner of limitations. When he caught himself in thoughts of limitation, he immediately changed his thoughts. He immediately expressed that which was the unlimitedness of what he knew the Father had given unto all mankind to find expression in.

There were a number of sages in his day that were mentioned by the master Jesus, but, of course, were not accepted by the temples. From the moment Jesus had released himself from the density of the physical world these things were scattered. They were no longer allowed to be a part of his teachings. So, you have, my beloveds, very little of the teachings of your Elder Brother as far as your temples of today are teaching. It is almost nil, for you see you are actually being taught that which the money changers were wanting man to know—and to be held in that suppression through their teachings.

So this, of course, did ire your brother Jesus and it was no small matter to him. For you see, he knew every facet of what was necessary in order to establish greater identity in the Father. Even though he had not yet reached the mastery, of course, at the age of sixteen years, but yet he recognized himself as a master of his own self, not of his fellowman. Understand? He recognized himself as the master of his destiny. You see? Not a destiny that was set into motion by God. But, he knew that God didn't create destiny, but that he had to establish his destiny. That if he was going to move and have his being, his destiny was in his mind's eye, that he had the complete expression of God unlimited. You see? That was what he was establishing as his destiny; unlimited vibrations of love, unlimited—everything that had to do, that had value for himself and his fellowman.

Then as he traveled and moved into other expressions of life he found that God was in all—all in all. So when he came into this part of your world there were those masters, here, in this part of the world. You call them the Indians, but they were not, all of them, on a low vibration. There were sages there, those that had reached into the highest vibrations. Some of them, in his day, were many years of age as far as the earth function was concerned, but they had great understanding.

So it was that he adopted from these great sages those things that had great value. But, also he found that there were limitations in their awareness, so he also was able to teach them. You see age doesn't mean a thing. You see, what he had to share was not just of what he had learned from the time he was born in this, his present incarnation. Understand? But his past incarnations as he had set forth his temple and built his temple in the various parents—mothers that he had through these various incarnations. He had taken all of the wisdom that he had attained and had reached in his awareness through these various incarnations, and set that forth into his temple.

But a sage, a true sage is one that is filled with the divine essence and the wisdom of the universe, without taking the physical body into that consideration—excepting to recognize that that physical body was a part of that which he needed to return. For he, actually, in a sense had taken that body as though he had actually stolen it from a part of God's creation, even though it didn't have in it the recognition of God identity—as *he* had God identity. He, in this sense, as he took hold of this physical body had given it a greater identity than it did have, at the time of his taking it over. But yet, with the limitations that he had born within himself, had created within himself, through leading the highest of identity in the first-dimension and into a density of the second-dimension; by letting his mind dwell more fully upon that which were the conditions of the identity of the animalistic vibration that he would want to, let us say, be born to experience. That's really what man has done, you and I, as well as the Elder Brother Jesus. And all of the masters—no matter who, everyone that is experiencing in the physical realm has done the same thing.

But yet, there is something that should be recognized and that recognition should be—no separation. If you can identify yourself with all mankind, then, you're going to find yourself being able to delve more deeply into reality; that is, knowing yourself, knowing yourself as the master. Jesus attempted to teach the knowledge of knowing your identity in all that there is. Because how can I know God if I only know certain expressions of identity? If I limit myself to that which I am functioning in, then I cannot know God, fully. To know God I must know every member of my being. Understand?

So, I say, I am one in you, you are one in me, as the master Jesus said. The master said, "I am one in the Father, the Father is one in me." He was moving and having his being; knowing himself as he was looking upon all of his brothers and sisters, all of the divine creation, as a member of his temple—as a member of this body. I am one, I am one. You see? Because the same identity within you is the same identity within the instrument here—within each other is that same one divine eternal identity that is pure and alive that can never know death. It cannot know a lack of function through the mind if man will allow universal *mind* to express entirely in and through his being. That is, universal mind that did set forth into action that which you are calling, my identity God.

Now, if you let this divine mind move and have its being in this identity, then, you can see where I am; feel that which is the I AM. You can then know that when I see that certain person out here that seems to be beyond my reach, who is doing things that are of no value to me, then, I must recognize that who I am unhappy with out there are a member of my body. See, there's only one in the entire universe. There can be nothing else but that oneness. So, it's a member of my oneness or my temple—my body, that body of creation that is not pleasing me.

So what do I do? I don't do what they tell you to do in the temples—destroy it. Because the Bible tells you, if a member of your body, your arm, let us say, gives you trouble because you have misused—and so the Bible says to get rid of it. If a member of your body gives you trouble, destroy it, if thine eye—pluck the eye. But you see that is a misinterpretation of reality. Actually, if you followed that through you would find your temple rather massacred in a very short period of time. Wouldn't you? You'd be without arms or legs or eyes or ears or whatever. But that isn't it. I am one in you, you are one in me.

So, if you are doing that which is out of proportion to my way of thinking I sever. But how do I sever? I don't go and kill you. I sever by lifting myself, moving and having my being on a higher vibration of awareness. And so my member is no longer giving me any trouble. I can walk and have my being, and I can still see my member but now I look at my member with a full quota of eternal love. You see? Not looking at my member with bitterness and wanting to destroy them. I am looking at my member, now, with love, fully aware of love. I see also the condition there, but that no longer is interfering with my love, I have raised my thoughts. I have raised my awareness into that expression. I see my temple in perfect order. I see my capability and my capacity of moving and having my being, unlimited, in the divine oneness of the universe.

So, beloveds, we have got to simplify the world that you are in. You must do it. I cannot do it for you. You cannot do it for me. But we can do it for each other by taking dominion over—and knowing the conditions of that which is no longer functioning in limitation. I function no longer in any sense of limitation.

So, this is the reason why your Elder Brother Jesus moved and had his being through this part of the world and was meeting up with those that were aged and had been teaching for sometime. Although, they were physically aged they were yet not aged as some of mankind today. Because of the fact that some of them were a hundred and twenty-five, a hundred and fifty years, two hundred years of age, but didn't look any older than some of your fellowman at fifty and seventy-five years; and so, were on the right path, but yet had not recognized that death should not have been a part of their evolvement.

So this is where Jesus came in. He was able to see and recognize that there was no such thing. That which man was doing was destroying that which he had accepted. So, man had taken over and allowed that condition to control him rather than the I AM expression, God within him, controlling that expression that he had taken over. So, this is what Jesus was trying to show man—how to rise above that which was the lower animal vibration that he had taken over in a manner of destruction. So, what he saw was the limitations of the animal, after he had taken over this hu-body. He had allowed himself to move and to express as the animal expressed and saw.

Of course the animal was now building up fears because man was taking and destroying some of the other animals. So fear began to build up in these conditions and so death began to occur. And man, of course, followed suit because this was all he understood.

But, the brother Jesus in his evolution—and devolution as it were, in a sense, became aware of that which was the endless expression of life. That his cause now—in order to become, again, that which is the free moral being in his creation, knew that he had to give back this temple in the perfect order that he had taken it. When man took that temple it was a part and parcel of God's divine creation. And, he was now using it in a manner of distortion, and he had to now bring it back into its own and give it back.

So, that is the reason why man has gone through countless incarnations, because he has been told by the money changers, throughout the generations of life, that there's no other way. If man would only stop to think. But, of course, who am I to speak? I did the same thing time and time again. I didn't stop to think. I didn't stop to realize that what I was doing—that the only causation of death was because of my impropriety. It was because of doing things that were not as they should be done— the little bitterness, hatreds, doubts, fears and so on. And yet God had established everything in its perfect order and I was distorting that perfect order. So I had to, then, just as Jesus became aware—I had to bring that order back into this temple.

So that's what he did. But, he had to do it in a manner of opening up his centers to awareness, that there is no limitation and that there is nothing but oneness in the whole entire entity of God. God created man—He didn't say millions of men or humans. He said, "Man." But that same identity, man, scattered its forces into all facets of expression and now we've got to gather those forces. We have got to bring that force back into that sole identity in the Father. Then, we can rise above all expression. We can take that temple, we can cause it to move anywhere we will in the great galaxies of life that God has established for us—until we want to let it go and give it back into its perfect power, perfect energy and perfect peace unto all of God's creation.

So these are the things that we are hopeful of bringing to you, in such a manner, that you are going to find that you can no longer separate. If you are in condemnation of anything, then, you are separating your member. You're condemning a part of your member. Because that is just like saying, "I hate this member of my body, I hate this part of my being, I dislike this or I love this part of my body." So, I love only part of it and until I love it all how can I return it to its own identity? So, I've got to love it all.

Therefore, when I say, "Love your fellowman," know that we are one in the Father. The Father is one in you. I am my brother's keeper. I am the brother of eternity and so how can I be my brother's keeper? I have only to be my brother's keeper by identifying that which is imbalance within myself. When I look at it being demonstrated out here and so, then, I raise my expression beyond that imbalance. So, I am my brother's helper. For I have set myself as an example of reality, an example of pure life, an example of love, inner peace—of pure awareness and understanding. So, the more I function in this manner, the greater becomes the health, the energy and the power within my temple.

Believe me, beloveds, you can get to the point where you have no feelings of tiredness, you can move and do things that would tire even a youth—because he is unhappy by doing what he has to do. Because he contracted for it and after he contracted for it, he dislikes it. So he destroys slowly but surely his temple. He gets all worn out. He gets tired. You see young people—right in your world today, they are tired. They awaken in the morning they are dead, they don't awaken, they move like zombies. They are working on the job for two hours before they realize that they are at work. Then, when they realize that they are at work, they wish that they are through.

So, I'm saying these things to you. Why? Because look at what's taking place in your earth; your earthquakes, your destructions that are greater every day. Your member is dying all around you, but don't die with your member. If you will recognize this, you will know what Jesus meant when he said, "Let the dead bury their own dead." He knew he was living. Every one of his members that were seemingly dying out there were balancing within his being, because he knew no distortion of his own oneness in identity with all of creation. So he knew nothing, actually, is dying. Nothing is distorted in his own awareness. Only that which out there wants to distort but he wasn't a part of that. He saw it. He was moving around and through it, but none of it disturbed his being, because he was the physician and the physician knew how to take care of all expression.

He traveled through the various countries, and, then, finally into India. Then up into the mountains, and he studied there with the various masters that had already reached the greatness of that which was their identity in the oneness in the divine universe. So, alright, he studied with them and this wisdom grew because he had to keep after himself—you know the great thing about this master Jesus was—I know the things that they talk about, the things that he did and so forth. Please give it no thought. It is absolutely not as it's told. Not in the least was it as they told. This master Jesus didn't run to God every minute asking God for this and that because he knew God is. This is God. This is the way the Father is functioning in and through me. The Father's permeating my temple. The Father is the very essence of all of the creation.

So all he was doing was taking dominion, as the Father had asked him to do—take dominion over yourself. Command yourself to perfection. Command yourself to move and have your being where you will to have it—in a thought, that's all. Jesus moved and had his being in the universal mind, or the super consciousness of the universe. So he functioned in this manner, and so whatever he was doing he did it without any struggling. He did it in the very simplicity of action, most of it just through thought. I need to be there, so he—that's where he was, because he saw himself in that image.

So each one of us, you and I, can move and have our being—we can do all of these things, and yet even greater expressions in the Father's house.

The reason why the master Jesus was speaking in this manner was because he knows, and he knew then, that God's creation was on the move. It was finished. It was perfect; moving and evolving, cycling and recycling and renewing. Because, beloveds, if it wasn't that way there would be gross unhappiness, even though you would return, let us say, to that expression or identity of God without shape nor form. If everything remains the same, it would be rather boring. Wouldn't it? Very boring. Even on your earth, here, if you see things the same every day you would say, "How boring life is."

So, eventually this is what takes place, actually, because you get to a point that you say, "Well, I'm not as young as I used to be. I'm not as capable of doing things like I used to." So, I exist in this sort of an awareness that, finally, you do get bored with life. You pretty soon say, "I wish it was all over," and you have already committed suicide. You see? You have actually asked to commit yourself to death. Thinking that you're going to get out of what you're supposed to be doing—and find yourself very disappointed. But try to tell this to the average person, "Oh, no my mother died and I know—she was such a saint, she is way up there. She has a special place with God. My dad was the devil—oh, I know where he is. He can't be any other place but in hell." You see that man has established such expressions because the priests, the rabbis, the ministers that want to keep you under their thumbs and keep you giving—big business and all through holier than thou pious hypocrisy.

Beloveds, the day is soon that all of this is going away like the great empires of the past. This is why I am saying to you that you should function properly in the divine essence of the universe, knowing your oneness in the Father, and all expression in the Father and not partake of that which is limitation. I will not run away from anything because I'm not fearful and I'm not doubtful. I just know I am in the right place at the right time because I am no longer distorting my member of my body. I look at the members of my temple. I see those conditions of distortion there, but I am not bitter against my temple or my member. And I must make that member pure light awareness. I must purify. I must be the identity that is my true self in the oneness of the universe. So, I move in that awareness and none of it, now, is disturbing me. For I find the member of my temple being purified because I have established the purification within my own being.

So I simplify my world and this is what the master Jesus was talking about because everything works together. There is nothing that can function properly, separately. Everything was set into motion with a divine and eternal purpose for you and I, to *enjoy* every moment of it. That is where you and I must function. We've got to move and have our being in the countlessness of God's divine evolution. The gifts of eternity are ours, now.

So let's move and have our being through the super conscious identity of God within my being that is functioning and having its full expression in every fiber, cell, bone and tissue, every avenue of love expression within this temple. I am functioning in that completeness of God within my being, so I am not functioning in hypocrisy. I know, now, that God is enjoying every moment of expression through this temple. Knowing that the super consciousness of God is permeating every avenue of my being—then my oneness I AM is enjoying everything that I do. I am giving that which is my Father's delight back to Him because I am accepting His countless gifts.

So, I am making my Father happy. I am making every member of my temple happy. You see? Because no longer am I separating, I am one in the divine image. I am one in the Father and the Father is one in me. What I do, it adds to it, it lightens my burden that I carried through from past incarnations. It lightens everything because the member of my body becomes lighter and lighter.

That's why, as I move and become more understanding of this divine oneness, then, I only need to think one thought—I need to be there—I want to go there—and I am there. I am not going and taking something out of myself to be there. I am taking the whole temple into that expression, and you don't have to be a saint to do it. You see? You don't have to be a master to do it. It is on your way to mastery that these things begin to take place because I am taking command, dominion over myself. Not over my members out there of my temple, but I am taking command here, that which does purify, cleanse the members of my temple without changing anything out there. It is a very simple expression and yet, man has to become aware of that one thought within his being. When he knows his oneness in eternity within his own identity, then the Brotherhood has been reached and the Fatherhood is, and has always been, of my being—able to move and have my being in the acceptance of those countless gifts that are forever changing.

Never am I accumulating anything. I am no longer subjecting my temple to accumulation of any condition or things that have been said are needed. I can rise above all expression, including physical death because that is the only member of that which I have taken over, out of God's divine creation that must be returned. The mind is already, and it shall ever remain. The spirit, the identity God cannot die either. So the only thing that I have distorted is the physical brain, or the lower brain of the animal that has accepted death. Walk in life and the more you do this the greater shall be the identity of man returning unto the divine essence of the universe—that which he has invaded.

So I want to leave those thoughts with you tonight. And I am going to ask you, besides this, whatever you meet up with in your daily life don't try to live tomorrow, live now. Give no thought to tomorrow. Today is the day. Then make today—this day that I live in, that divine essence. Therefore,

I make this day as simple and enjoyable as I can possibly make it, because I know that in my Father nothing is impossible. Therefore, I am that identity and so, I know my Father gave me nothing less than Himself.

So, beloveds, remember this and life becomes most pleasant and enjoyable. Life becomes that which is beautiful and pleasant and joyful and happy. And whatever I do, now, I see no longer anything distorted in it. Because what I do, I do because I feel happy and joyful and God is enjoying everything with me. I do it because my brothers and sisters would also enjoy the same expression in the Father. Letting that energy and that power flow beautifully and knowing no longer any separation, but seeing just one beautiful expression, and that is God moving and having His being within me.

For you see God created nothing of evil. If you and I express evil then it must be that which is self-destruction because I have subjected myself to that condition of limitation. I say to you, live with God and there is no condition of distortion. There is nothing that I can do, in any way, shape or form that will cause my fellowman any hurt or any harm. What I do now is only express peace. I only express balance and so I can no longer distort anything. So, I move with life, I don't move with that which is self destruction.

Simplify your world and you will have no time to say, "I don't like you, I don't like what you are doing. I hate that. I dislike this." Even saying, I hate something in a way that you are really not actually hating, you are yet putting a condition there that is out of balance. So, it has to have its toll upon you physically, mentally and spiritually. It will have its distortion, because it closes the door to certain expressions of reality. I hate not. Love all that is God's creation. I love all because God is the very fountain of eternity and I move and shower and have my being in that fountain of eternal life. I am going to leave that with you my beloveds.

So now, my beloveds, I shall take my leave. I am one known as Estonia Mercury and I shall return one day and we shall walk together.

Peace be with you.

CHAPTER 4

I Asked You to Enter Within

By Jesus

Peace. Peace. Peace. My dearly beloveds, it is my pleasure this evening that I have been called upon, out of the Father's house, that I might reach then, unto the dimension that thou art expressing in, that I might more fully share with you those things that once were given unto me in the expression over two thousand years ago.

Yet, my beloveds, as you and I know, I was not the first to come forth to give and to teach a way of life. For you know, beloveds, the great teachers of the past were also eventually enveloped into the money changers' law. And yet, you and I know that they taught as free moral beings, as I taught. But, after they left to go beyond, into the greater dimensions or mansions in the Father's house, to follow the greater teachings and to share—not only with those in the expression of the mastery, but also with those that have left your physical earth at that time—and were seeking the greater knowledge in that which you call the world of the spirit, they went forth to teach and to help those that would seek that help.

As you know, beloveds, as you are sitting here this evening in this dimension, you know that there are those surrounding you from the unseen side of life that are preparing themselves to return to the physical world of your third-dimensional expression. They are hopeful, this time, of learning and of receiving that which will help them in their future to reach that which is the mastery of life, that which we call the dimension through which you shall endeavor to rise above, and that is the last enemy called death, my beloveds. These were the prime teachings that I gave to you in that day. But also, everything that I attempted to share with you was that which *you* could benefit by, and your fellowman could also be helped by being lifted out of that rut of negation that the money changers have accepted as reality.

You see, beloveds, you and I cannot condemn those that are in the temples of your present day, no more than I could condemn them in my day because they knew not what they do. They knew not and they know not today what they are doing. For if they attempted, though, to realize that which is yet expressed in your physical world of the teachings that I left with you, there would be no place there for anything other than that which is what God gave you, *life*. You see what I mean? But man is not in that expression. They are not in that avenue of awareness and, therefore, have accepted only a minor expression of that which you call *life*. But we, of course, of the spirit know that it is only a very poor expression of *existence*, because it envelops and takes on, in its vibrations, the countless false gods that man has established.

You see, when I spoke unto thee, and when the great masters before me spoke unto thee, we asked of you one very specific expression out of each one of you; in order that the Brotherhood of Man and the Fatherhood of God can be and will find expression in those and only those, beloveds, who will function in this manner—and it is not through me, it is through the Father. I know it is even written in the *Book* that no one will reach unto the Father excepting they come through me. Beloveds, this is the moneychangers' version. I never spoke those words.

Beloveds, it is only reasonable, if man would only stop to reason, that I said unto thee, "Seek ye first the *kingdom* of the Father and all things shall be revealed unto you." And I said, "Where was that kingdom?" and I said, "Within." Understand? I attempted in every way to make your world the most beautiful and simple expression of life that I possibly could, but, no, you have adopted everything else.

You have taken my family—my mother, my father, my brothers and you have made gods out of them. You have made a god out of me. I mean, *super gods*. But remember, beloveds, in the realm of my family, even unto this day, I am the only one that mastered life. Yet, the religious orders of your earth have set my mother on the throne of God. They have made her the mother of God because I was supposed to be this unique son of God. These are all conditions that take you away from reality. These are only things that can lead to limitation and ultimate physical death because they do not express the Father. They do not give you that which is the ultimate that you are seeking, or should be seeking in this your third-dimensional world.

You see, beloveds, on one hand I was supposed to have said, and which I did say, "Seek ye first the kingdom of the Father within and all things shall be revealed unto thee." But then, I have also been accused of having said, "Unless you come through me, you shall never reach the Father." You see? Beloveds, I never spoke of these things. I spoke to you of being capable in your own selves, of reaching in and evolving through that which is the revelations out of the Father. I didn't ask of you to go into the Old Testament—and yet, look at what you are doing. Very seldom do you read out of the New Testament. You mostly bring whatever is to be taught behind the pulpit out of the Old Testament.

I bring this to you, tonight, beloveds, because you are now reaching the end of what you call your year. You soon shall be celebrating my birthday, which, of course, as you know was not in December. But, beloveds, I accept your gift of remembering. Yet, beloveds, I also would like to ask of you, rather than to celebrate my birthday as you usually celebrate it, that you would celebrate it in the manner of attempting to recognize that which I attempted to share with you; that which is *a way of life*, and, that which I have attempted, at times, coming through this instrument, and the master brothers and sisters that have also reached through this instrument to teach that which is of value, that which is the Gem of Life, that which would help you to polish the facets of that which you are, the *Gem of Life*. You are the Gem of Life, and if you will just attempt to recognize and realize that I am the atom out of my Father, which you call Adam.

You see, God just established man identity, I have attempted, and did attempt in my day to teach which never has, ever, been put into print in your Bible. If it had been put into print you would not have Genesis as it is written today. You would have Genesis as it was in the expression of the

Father. You would not have Eve as one that was made from the rib of Adam. You see, beloveds, the Father didn't have to create something else. His creation was finished when Adam was created, man. Understand? When Adam—the atom of His world, His creation, which is in each and every one of you—this was the end and the fulfillment of His creation. There and then He said unto the atom, man, "Nothing, my beloveds, nothing can be added to my creation or taken away."

So, Adam being alone sought companionship and that is after he entered into that which you call the hu-animal, now, which was the only animal at that time that stood erect. Then, Adam became aware of the density and lonesomeness of being there. So, he took unto himself another one of the hu-animals, the female unto himself. From there the atom burst into what is known today as humanity. It was the splitting of the atom. That is what the masters, every one of them, wanted you to know about these things. I attempted again through my teachings in the Western part of your world to teach this—that you are all the sons of God, every one of you. You see?

You have today in your physical world split the atom again, but this time you have split it in creating a monster—a monster greater even than those of you that have moved out of reality. But, you see, who created the monster? But the monsters are those that are functioning in your physical world as the beast. They are Godless souls. They have no remorse. Have you noticed, beloveds, that there are around you in your present day those that can destroy life? And I am not talking about the animals. I am talking about, there are brothers and sisters who have no remorse, not the least bit of remorse. What are they? They are out of that which has been the Godless world that man has established.

You move and have your being from day to day—how many of you realize that you couldn't move a finger without the divine energy and power of the creator, that which gave life unto thee? So, this is the reason why I asked of you to be aware, to be more fully aware that—look, I am man. What I see beyond myself is that which is functioning and I am unhappy with it, for I see what? My brothers and my sisters expressing in negation and all I am looking at is myself. I am seeing myself, because there is but man, one identity in the divine essence. That identity is split up into this which you and I became out of Adam—when Adam took that which was the hu-animal and became known as Adam.

Now, then, do I have to try to assemble myself by taking each and every soul of the five billion souls upon the earth to reestablish myself? Of course not, this is quite the opposite and this is what I attempted to teach you when I walked your physical earth. I attempted to show you—look, out of the Father is the answer; there is no other way to reach that which is the ultimate, the eternal expression—life, to rise above now that which is the hu-animal, in other words, death—to bring that human, that dense human to that which is the fulfillment of the age, to bring that into a quickening, so that it can be returned to the elements from which you took it—when you built it within your mother's womb.

Now then, you have fulfilled, you have returned, you have evolved. And you now are in the essence of that which you are aware of, now, to take dominion over all of that which the Father established—for man to take part in and to enjoy. So, you have got to be reminding the self, then, that this which I have established around me was established through my becoming selfish, greedy, doubtful, fearful and so on—and greedy, very greedy. Through my greeds I created my false gods, through my wanting to, let us say, be the leader of suppression and having everything I want. Through my greed I felt I needed to suppress those that were around me, to keep them feeding me that which my greed demanded.

So, this is what you have in your temples. You see it all around you. And so, they are praying to me. Beloveds, never did I ask you to pray to me, nor to any of my relatives, nor to anyone other than the Father. I didn't ask you to *pray* to the Father. Then, I asked you to enter within that you would know yourself, and said that once you knew yourself, you would know the Father.

For you see, the identity God is the very center of your being or the atom which is the divine essence of God, the Father. I tried to simplify your world. I tried to make your world something worthwhile. But, no, you insist on becoming involved in everything that surrounds you. How often do you think of the Father? Have you asked yourself this? How often do you recognize the fact that I am that which is the I AM, that which is the very essence, the motivation, the power, the light, the love and the expression of all that is good within my being? Understand? Have you attempted to realize this? Then, do I need false gods? Do you have to go to John, to Peter, to Matthew, to the various ones that you call saints and those that you have elevated through various instrumentalities of your physical world, to take you away from the reality?

Beloveds think of these things. Think of these things. They are very important. You have got to realize, I am ONE. And, if I see my brother in distress, I am seeing the conditions around us distressing me, and I am seeing my need of elevating myself. So, I elevate myself out of the condition that is distressing, that is bothering me because I see my image there. Beloveds, it's simple. It is so simple; the mathematics of life I attempted to teach, but I haven't seen a word of it put into the Bible, in the manner in which I gave it to you.

Can you not see for a moment, beloveds, when I became aware at a very early age as to that which was very disturbing to me? As a child that went into the temples to attempt to awaken the teachers in those temples, those priests that I attempted to share with them through my many incarnations. I came forth and was able to put it together, and attempted to share it with these priests and rabbis in the temples, and they would not accept it.

I traveled your world, as you know, and it is rather a pleasure to me that wherever I went, at least one mastered life, of the disciples that I had grouped around me. Beloveds, John in his mastery never attempted to ask anyone to pray to him, anymore than I asked, or any of the masters ever asked you or me to pray to them. All of them taught one divine essence of life, God essence. This was the way it became the expression of my fulfillment of that which is rising above the last enemy, or what you and I call the mastery of life.

If you wish to reach the mastery, you don't complicate your world. You do not complicate your world through all of these various gods that you have created. Has it not sufficed you that you have made your world difficult for yourselves to earn a living? Which is, again, one of the most unnecessary expenditures of energy there ever was, and to group around yourself all of the things you think you need physically, when I showed you how it could be attained without difficulty by entering within, and knowing yourself, and knowing your God through entering within the self, seeking first the kingdom of the Father within and then all things that are necessary would be revealed unto you.

Therefore, then, I walked your earth and I walked all over. I was in every part of your earth, beloveds, and I didn't struggle. I didn't earn any of it by the sweat of my brow, but I did accept the countless gifts. I didn't accept all of the gifts of the Father, they are countless. But I accepted only that which was necessary to benefit myself, and you that were with me, and to benefit you now. I accept only that which is necessary to come forth and to share with you, and that is the way to *life*.

Beloveds, never did I one time refer to any of the masters of the past, other than to let you know that they were teaching as I taught; one God, one creator, one divine atom of awareness that is dwelling within each one of you. To bring that together; I'll never do it, and I'll never attain eternal life, and I'll never rise above the last enemy, if I don't function in the one divine essence that will let me know how to raise this temple into its highest order and to give it back to the elements from which it came.

My teachings, beloveds, were always utter simplicity because I had no gods other than my Father before me. I asked of you to enter into the garden, but where is the garden? The garden is that place you call heaven, within the self. Because once you know the self *everything* becomes utter simplicity, beloveds, utter simplicity! There is no need any longer to struggle. You may do much the same as you were doing today, but you will never feel the urge that it is something I have to do, I am forced to do and in order to maintain and sustain life within my being, because you will see that it is absolutely unnecessary.

I know, beloveds, you may make many excuses. You may say, "Well, brother Jesus, you didn't live in this place. You see there are almost five billion people on my earth today. There were not that many in your day." And I would say to you, it is absolutely true, but, I will say to you the density was as great. Why? Because when you have entertained, the false gods that your temples of your present day are doing, and the many other vibrations that are expressing these false gods—pouring them out and all that it is doing; take a look beloveds, those that are the leaders, or the head of these organizations are living off that which you are feeding them.

But, they are not living, really. They are only existing, because they in their fallacies are only reaping that which is the abundance of a dense physical world. That's all. They are not reaping the abundance of life. They are not reaping that, which when you assimilate that abundance out of the Father, encompasses all things; it permeates everything in your earth. Therefore, the needs that you have, whether you call them physical, mental, or spiritual, you will find that all of it is out of the Father.

But that, which you personally are functioning in, is the misuse of that power. Therefore, it becomes the destruction that takes place in the physical temple, causing the temple to slowly but surely shrink away, which causes age, wrinkles and bitterness, the aches and pains. Then, the atom moves out of it; the atom of divine awareness, the atom called man, that atom which is the identity out of the Father.

Remember, beloveds, life in your dimension became the full expression that you call, the soul of man. And, in the Bible, Adam didn't know life. He was made of clay and he didn't know life until God came and breathed in his nostrils, and then what does it say? "He became a living soul."

Well, beloveds, when you know the truth and when you in your Adam awareness of the Father entered into that which was the physical or the hu-body, that hu-body became a living soul. Why? Because now it became aware of God, and you have been repetitious ever since you let it shrink and die through various ways. Sometimes you died without pain because you functioned in greater protection, such as when you would look into your Bible of your present day, that man did live a thousand years. It was because he had not yet established the greed's and the selfishness that you have established today. So man lived a thousand years, but once the greed's began to take place, and those there that had lived a thousand years decided they wanted to suppress others, and then the age began to diminish you, and so on through the centuries.

But the consciousness of death was there before you were born, because you built your temple, many of you, with a limited expression of life. In other words, you put into the thoughts that went into the system of the atoms, and the cells of your body—you put in them the thoughts, you put into the sub-consciousness of that temple the thoughts that I am coming back to the physical world to accomplish such and such, that you have become aware of in the unseen side, and I am going to fulfill those thoughts. And, I know this is going to lead me to a greater expression in the world. So, once I come back and once I have fulfilled this, there is no longer, many of you feel, any need to continue to live. So you will yourselves to death at that period that you have accomplished what you came back to accomplish. Therefore, then your world seems to end there. But, you find that it doesn't.

So, beloveds, this is the reason why I came forth when I did, in that awareness, to help you to help yourselves to know that there is not one thing in the universe that you cannot change. It is entirely up to you personally. Not I, nor any master, nor any false gods, can change this for you.

We, the masters have come forth and we gave you the keys, but, we had to master our lives, first, before we could truly be of value, by letting you know how you could approach reality in your own lives by recognizing God within yourselves. Knowing it doesn't take incarnation after incarnation to master. It only takes your knowledge and the awareness of that knowledge that I am the one that can change anything. Even though I came back and I put in every cell or in my subconscious mind—in that little temple as it was being formed in my mother's womb—that it was to accomplish *only* certain things, then, after it was accomplished, then, I would give up that body to a "heavenly realm."

Beloveds, once you have entered into the physical there is *nothing* that you cannot change. Even though you may have said this and have put into that which is within the cells of your body, within the subconscious world—you know, beloveds, that out of the Father there is nothing impossible for you to accomplish, because He gave you no limited avenues of expression. He gave you everything that He set into motion and He asked you, even, to use it all. Whatever was needed to use it for—for your benefit and for the benefit of everything that was needed. So you see those that even die at a very early age because they came back with that sort of awareness and never attempted to change it. You may say, "Well, they were too young to do so." Well, certainly as one that would come in as a child and pass as a child, thinking that was all they needed as an experience to pass into the heavenly realm.

But, many children in your present world of today, even at the age of five or six years have much greater wisdom than many in your physical world of fifty and sixty years. Sometimes, even, in my day there were those of very small children that I knew had greater wisdom. All they needed to do was to be just directed a little bit. And I asked the mothers and the fathers to bring their children to me because I knew they had greater wisdom than their parents.

So, beloveds, when are you going to let go of all these false gods that you have collected around you? When are you going to look to the future, knowing that this future, this universe, this world, this entire expression of life, is mine? It is absolutely mine. I need not store a thing away and need not put anything aside. I need not do any of these things. For when I reach within, deep within the expression that I call the I AM, and which is the atom of life expression within my being—I open a universe, the universe of my Father's creation. I open the door to that creation and no longer is there any thought that "I cannot do it," by going to the so-called mother of God, to the so-called Saint Peter, to the so-called Jesus that is the only son of God, to the so called this and that. Beloveds, you'll never reach mastery in this manner. But you will reach mastery when you move into that which gave you life, the Father eternal, the one and only creator of the universe.

That creator didn't need any help. If He had needed help He would have created that right at the beginning. Beloveds, He knew what He was doing and He'll always know. He has not slept and He is not dead either.

You have a living God, if you want that living God. Or you have a God that is on one hand, that which I was supposed to have said, "A God of love on one hand and a God that you were to fear." And I never, ever, gave you a God of fear. If you have that God, it is your adaptation, not mine. I never gave it to you. Never, ever did I give you but the living God. And only through the keys of life that you open up—by knowing I move and have my being in one God and I fear not where I walk. I move and have my being in that one and only divine essence that is perfect life and abundant in all things.

So, once you move and do enter within the self to open up these centers of awareness, you will find that eventually, that which I am doing becomes simpler. But, also, I find that I need to make some changes now. So I move into the greater vibrations and the greater powers and energies—not to suppress. I move into the greater things. I set forth into motion out of myself that which is of greater value to me and my fellowman. That is the way to life. Then, beloveds, you will move before too long out into the beauty of the galaxy, not only through the mind, but you will move in any way that you will to move and you will find a land within this temple, that you call me.

So, all that is necessary in order to experience every beautiful part of God's divine creation is to understand that it is all mine, for it always has been, and it is still. For, beloveds, you haven't gone through many and various incarnations without having, at least, done something in the improvement of the animal that once was called hu-man.

I am going to leave this with you, my beloveds. I will be with you to celebrate the day of my birth. But I hope that when we celebrate it together we will celebrate it in the love of our eternal Father. Celebrate it because we have become awakened unto reality. We will celebrate it because we are, for the first time, at peace with one another. That we are looking at each other and seeing man—knowing that which is the oneness, the I AM presence. I am one in my Father. My Father is one in me. Peace, beloveds, be with you.

I am your brother Jesus.

CHAPTER 5

Jesus as He Walked the Plane of This Continent of America

By Golden Eagle

P eace. Peace. Peace. My dearly beloveds, it is my pleasure this evening, that I have been called upon to be of service unto you in the eternal light of the Father, in the thankfulness of my communion with our Elder Brother through the generations of life, as we once walked together upon this the plane of your physical earth. As I moved into other avenues of life expression, due to the fact that as we commune with the super consciousness of life, we are capable, of course, of moving in many and varied directions—and, of course, to be of greater service unto ourselves, as well as our fellowman.

Now, beloveds, I have a great deal, of course, to be thankful for. For as one of the disciples of our brother Jesus, as he walked the plane of this continent of America many years ago, I was one that chose to be one of his disciples, and work diligently with him through several years of travel in

47

various parts of this, your continent that you call North America. I learned a great deal from my brother and I'm sure my brother learned a great deal from me, for I had moved into the mastery before my brother Jesus came into this country of America and I had yet remained in the physical expression of life.

But I chose to walk with my brother because we sat together many, many nights and many days, and we communed with one another, and we communed with our fellowman in the various parts of the continent. It was a glorious experience not only for myself, but to see the progress that your brother Jesus was making from the age of fourteen years to the time that he left the continent of America—approximately, a little past the age of seventeen to move into another continent called South America.

I share this with you tonight, because being that we have come into the part of the year that you call the birth of our Elder Brother and are celebrating it, I would like that you and I would do something a little different this year; rather than celebrating the birth, that we might celebrate the mastery that he attained. But, above all his teachings—this, my beloveds, is very important. The birth as to that which you have understood was not as it is written. And, of course, it was not even at that time of the year. His birth was, as you know, in the month of March, right on the cusp around the 20th or 21st of March.

So, beloveds, I've often thought why did they change this? Why did they not leave his birth date as it was? But I find that the reason for this was that it didn't fit in with that which they hoped to establish as the story of his birth. You see at the end of March the weather wasn't cold enough and it wasn't bitter enough. So they had to move it back in order to make it a bitter cold for the Elder Brother, to make a story that would kind of make you and I feel a little bit sorry for him, and for his parents, for having had to sleep in a stable. Beloveds, he never slept in a stable. I have a feeling that I have to believe Jesus rather than those that have written the story of his birth.

Beloveds, it doesn't make any difference, of course it doesn't. It doesn't make any difference at all. It is that which the man gave you and I. He gave me priceless love. He gave me identity even to a greater degree, even though I had reached the mastery of the early fourth-dimensional expression. But I even furthered that with this beautiful soul, because of the fact that his moving within his being—he lived in the garden of life, actually.

He did not exist in it, he lived in it. And he had such a profound love for all mankind. It was not something that he forced himself to become aware of. He let God's divine nature permeate his very being and in doing so he reached out; not always calm, not always as he has been depicted as a person almost of a feminine vibration. No, beloveds, he was far from being of a feminine vibration. He was a man, thoroughly, and he was a very profound person. He was a man, that when he had something to say, he said it and he didn't attempt to pacify those that may not have been of the same vibrations of awareness that he was in. He attempted at all times to shock you, to stir you. To make you think, is what he was attempting to do.

You see, beloveds, his day was very similar to your present day. Those that were the leaders of tribes, in this our country of America, and those that were the leaders of your world in the various parts of the world where your Elder Brother was born, were suppressed. The leaders of many tribes were suppressing those in their tribe, keeping them thoroughly subject to their way of thinking; so were they doing the same thing where your Elder Brother Jesus was born, keeping mankind under suppression, fearful of making any changes. This is what your brother Jesus was opposed to.

Of course, he didn't come back to this earth without having gained many expressions of awareness through his many and varied incarnations, and having been one to help to build the pyramids. He had come back with a great deal of inner spiritual knowledge. He had come back with a purpose because he had expressed that identity within his being, as he had made the choice of his father and his mother in this physical realm and put together that which was his knowledge.

So, in his early youth he was rather a very bright and intelligent young man, even though in his early youth he was misusing the powers that he had. But, he was not aware that he was misusing them until his mother showed him how to use them properly, letting him know that destruction was not of any value. So, he was capable of reversing everything, and he did so. Now, he could have rebuked his mother and his foster father that he was with at that time. He could have rebuked them and said that he was going to do as he well pleased, which many are doing in your physical world of your present day—and did also in the day that your Elder Brother was walking the physical plane of earth.

But, my beloveds, he *chose* to be of service to himself because there was something that he identified with. And what was that something that he identified with? That something that he identified with was that which established all mankind, that has entered into the mastery and that is *life*. He identified with life. He identified with life because he saw that the conditions of his physical world at that time—the avenues of expression that were of little or of no value to himself, or to his fellowman in any facet of expression from his brothers or his sisters. So, he felt that this—he had to question, he questioned and he kept on questioning. But, in the early part of his years around the age of ten, this is when he began to question, nine and ten and eleven.

He began to question things, and he seemed to remove himself from the others around him, especially those that were the children around him. Not that he was opposed to them, but he had to do some thinking. And, when he saw what was, let us say, what we—you and I, and all mankind, saw happening around him, he couldn't believe that this was natural. He couldn't believe that a God, a creator could create a world so immoral, so destructive, and of such little value. So it was, that this was his purpose, because he had established that within his temple prior to his death.

This is why we are not opposed to those of you that go through the physical death. We are not opposed to it, but we know it is needless. The only thing is we know, it's needless, but yet, it is of value if man is not going to attempt to try to better himself in this incarnation, and to reach the mastery in this incarnation. Then, he's better off to go into the spirit side because he can after a time—especially after he looks things over, relax and find himself without a physical body. But yet, finding himself not having taking care of his responsibility, then he knows, and sees now what his purpose is, to a greater degree. And if he continues to study and stays in the spirit side *long enough* he can come back—like the Elder Brother Jesus with a greater awareness and a greater capability.

But, there are those that go into the spirit side and come back within a matter of just weeks, and they have attained little or nothing, and find themselves, oftentimes, in a very destructive condition of physical—the body is not a complete physical body (disability). Or, you have not remained long enough to attain anything of value, to take out of the subconscious those conditions that brought you into this physical death, and so on. You see, all of this is working together, but yet it also is separated because the mind has been taught to separate. So, the master Jesus went into the expression of no longer separating.

But what he found in those years, early years, in those years from ten, eleven and until his twelfth birthday, and I stop there because there's a reason for it. He found that man in his day was not productive and what they did produce was not constructive. Even though they called it progress, it was actually not progress; exactly as it is taking place in your world of today. But, he found out the reason early, for this, in himself. The reason was that man was first physical. He worked from that which is the physical. He worked outside of himself almost constantly because he put value on his brother, for what his brother had obtained physically, never looking at what anyone attained spiritually. Always, it was looking as to what he had, or she had attained in a physical manner. If he had a beautiful home, he had plenty of money, he had all the wherewithal that was necessary to live a joyful, happy life, he was considered somebody.

Even though, if you would have looked into that person's life you would have found a very unhappy group of people in that environment, because it was all of a physical nature. Therefore, the temple also was suffering for the lack of spiritual identity or awareness. So the body was not fully functioning properly.

So, he saw this. He saw now, that man was working and *struggling* for what he knew, there was no need to struggle for. He knew that everything in the universe belonged to each and every man, woman, and child. So there were those that were experiencing and having a great deal around them and there were those that had little, and those that had nothing. It all was in the way they were thinking, and sometimes the one that had the least seemed actually, in a sense, to be happier than the one that had the most.

So, all of this did not confuse Jesus. It didn't confuse him. It just made him stop to think more deeply. Then he said, "My brothers, my sisters are functioning backwards. They are not functioning properly." And so, this is when he went into the temple at twelve years of age; to try to show the priests in the temples what their teachings were doing to the people. They were worshipping the various masters that had mastered life and had moved on, like what was going to happen to Jesus later on, being put in the temples as a God. You see?

So, they were worshipping them, but that was not really what the trouble was even then. The trouble was that the master Jesus—what he was telling them at the age of twelve years of age—he was not a master, but he had reached that point of awareness that he was able to talk to these priests because he was considered a man at twelve years old. Understand? In that part of the world when you reached the age of twelve you were considered a man in the temples. Understand? This was in the Hebrew temples that he was considered a man.

Alright, all he was trying to do was to tell the priests and the rabbis in these temples, everything that is being taught is purely on a physical basis. You are working out of the mind. You are working out of the physical. You are asking for the physical wherewith, but where is God?

This is when Jesus understood, seek ye first the kingdom of God within and all things shall be added unto you. In other words, you become aware of them without struggling—the needs. You're not going to try to gather all of this around you, because you're going to find that there is no need for it; only what I need for myself and my fellowman to be comfortable and to move—because it's all here. It's mine and it is forever. I'm living in the foreverness of eternity. You see? I'm living in that which is what God set into motion, which is the evolvement and the evolution of man.

Now, I know many of you—I know that there are those in some of the greatest religions on your earth that don't believe in spiritual or even in physical evolution. They deny it. Beloveds, what you call progress, what is that? You may look at it as progress or evolution, evolving, moving into greater expression, but you find that everything that you have established has caused you what? Fear, exactly the same as it was in the time of your Elder Brother Jesus. Everything that was brought into action was brought with selfish motives, with greed and with fear attached to it, and so it was of absolutely no value, excepting to those that were of a higher vibration of awareness, because they knew no fear and they knew that those things were there, and they could accept them or reject them according to their own way of expression.

So, what Jesus then attempted to establish as he moved on into the years—when he finally came over here to the country of America at the age of a little past, I believe, the fourteenth or early fifteenth year of his life. All that young man did was to move and have his being, in God. All he identified with was his oneness and the more he functioned in the power of God within himself—and this is not holier than thou hypocrisy. He wasn't doing like they said in the temples. Jesus wasn't falling on his face, like it is often said, and crying to God for this, and that, and the other, like they're teaching you to cry to God or if you have an ache or a pain, ask God to take it away from you. God's not going to take anything away from you.

He already gave it all to you, and you accepted what you've got or else it wouldn't be there—remember this. You accepted what you have or else it wouldn't be there. In other words, you caused it to come to you and you can take it away—it's that simple.

So then, Jesus started to live first—*first* out of the inner sanctum of his being. Everything that he did was identified out of the Father, and so his every action, his every deed, his every move was of value, and what he did touch to, stayed. It stayed what, over two thousand years, hasn't it? Even though it has been molested in your temples of today—really there is but just a minor, a fraction of reality of Jesus' teachings in the temples today.

So, beloveds, if man will only attempt to realize this. You can wake-up everyday of your life in the future—everyday—I'm not saying one day, everyday of your life in the future, you can wake-up in the morning and you can know that this day is the best day of your life. You also can know that whatever my needs are today, are already taken care of. Also, not only are my needs taken care of, but everything that is necessary for me to be of absolute balance and service to my fellowman; in whatever capacity that I am given the awareness of, because I'm asking only for that which is good for me and *good* for my brothers and sisters. That's all I am asking for, only that which has value for me and my fellowman. That's all, and believe me that's everything.

You will find that you will go through the day—you will rise above all sorts of conditions of, let us say, suppressions, limitations, and negations. It makes no difference. You will see them all. You will not miss any of them, but they will strengthen you now rather than weaken you. You see? Because you will see them, you will rise above them—they will no longer have any hold upon you.

You will have strengthened yourself to cope with all situations. They will not cause you to turn to several of these negations and condemn them or turn to your Father and say, "Father, look at all of this here—help me, and give me this, give me that and the other." No. You have set your pace and you have asked, in this sense, to move into the evolution of God's divine energy and power, into that which He set into motion, knowing that what He set into motion is the perfect power and energy. So, you move into that each day, because whatever I do, I am working first out of God's divine creation, out of His energy and His power. So, what becomes my awareness, I know has to come out of the right action that I have set into motion, and so, I am evolving.

So, now, I find whatever I have begun to do, I have done it out of the Father. First spiritually, then to the mental level, and to the physical and I find all of it is just one. I am no longer separating. You see? I come through the super consciousness, to the subconscious, to the conscious. You see? The super conscious, to the subconscious, to the conscious—now, I am conscious of what my actions are. They are of value. They are building that which can never be destroyed. I am not falling on my knees. I'm not crying. I am only thankful for everything that is. And I know, now, that as I move in this direction, everything has to balance out.

So what happens? My temple is responding, also, it responds because it has better health, because—seek ye first the kingdom of God within. You see? Then, I become aware of all of the gifts of life. There's nothing dying here, now, it's *life*. I am moving into and with life. Therefore, I am evolving according to the universal plan of life, that I was created in.

So, now, I am not putting my temple into destructive vibrations, or motions, or identities, or fears, or doubts or any of these things—I have discarded them. I have uprooted those conditions. So, I am now moving as the Tree of Eternal Life. I am beginning to bear the fruit of reality. I am beginning to see what God created. I am beginning to see what He created in the reality, in its true beauty, because there's nothing in it that is obliterating my vision. There's nothing in there now that I am seeing, that is looking through a glass darkly. You see what I mean? I am looking now through the lens of life through these eyes. These eyes are now beginning to show life in them. They have reality. They have color and they sparkle. They identify with that which is my identity or the soul of my being.

So this, beloveds, was what the master Jesus was doing even at an early age. He traveled until he went into, of course, as you know, eventually, in the country of India with the masters of the Far East there, and worked with them and they with him. This, of course, is where he eventually mastered life in that expression, there with the masters in the east.

But it's so wonderful to know that here was a man born with a degree of obstacles in his early life—not per se on his, but his mother and his true father, there was that which you over look today, because most of you are seeing things in quite a different way than you used to in the expression of life—because you find that much of that which is being expressed in your physical world today is only and purely man's creation. So, it is identified with man's creation. It is identified also with, let us say, a tax motivation—something to take in a little extra money, such as, a license for marriage, such as, a marriage service to pay someone to say to you that you are married, and so on.

We are not opposed to this, but we also see the negative, or the side of it that is rather disturbing to us, because we find the holier than thou's, those that go to the temple once a week and feel that they have done their duty towards God—they don't have to think about God the rest of the week. They went to a service. They went to church. That's fine. They went and got married by a priest, or a rabbi, or minister. That's fine. So, they are looking down on two people that say and feel that they love one another, and so, will to be with one another and are living a very beautiful, creative life. But, that doesn't make any difference because they are living in sin. What sin? The sin that man created. Not God. You see? They put a license fee there and they put somebody there to say that you are married. Now, then the other one doesn't do that. He or she feels they are living in sin.

Now, beloveds, let's take a good look at these things, because every one of them, we know, are man made. Now, what happened in the day of Jesus then? It was the same thing, exactly the same thing, excepting under a different expression. In the day of Jesus, two people that loved each other would have a wedding feast. That feast was the marriage. There was no one to say to them, "Do you take so and so to be your lawfully wedded husband or wife." No, there was none of this. All they did was come together and put on a wedding feast, and that was the marriage service. But, if there were those that didn't do that they were looked down upon.

That's where your Elder Brother Jesus was looked down upon, that is, his parents were—his mother and his father. But, of course, also, he was looked down upon because he was born out of wedlock. But, in order to cover it up, Christianity said he was born of a virgin, and so that would cover-up the story, or the *real* background of your Elder Brother. It covered up the whole thing, because they got rid of that, and five hundred years had elapsed anyway. So all of this was forgotten. So, now he was born of a virgin, and so that is why he had a foster father, because Joseph was supposedly feeling sorry for that which was being said, and so on. So, he took her then, and married her. Then the child was born and was supposed to have been born in a stable in the part of the world called Bethlehem.

Now, beloveds, these are the things that kind of stir mankind up, because man is continuously looking down, or functioning in a manner of wanting to look down on someone else, or to down someone else, thinking that by downing them, they are elevating themselves in a purer vibration of expression. In other words, me, I am that holier-than-thou hypocrite, but I don't want anybody to know it. So, if I can put my brother down, my sister down, and set them lower than me, then I am sitting on a pedestal. I am functioning more creatively and I am a pure being.

So, beloveds, these are the things that Jesus saw throughout his early life, but, he let none of these things disturb him. Although he spoke of them, and he called them hypocrites, that were functioning in a way that would down rate their brother and sister, because they didn't do the same as they had done. So, beloveds, the master Jesus looked down on no one. No one. There wasn't a soul that Jesus touched to that he downed.

He spoke to the woman, and spoke, and talked to her—that woman of ill repute, and his disciples downed Jesus for having stopped to talk to such a woman of such an evil character. But Jesus didn't see any evil, because Jesus knew that evil is only in the heart. If my heart is evil then there is evil. But there can be no evil, where evil is not given any energy or power. So, when he spoke to that woman of ill repute, he wasn't seeing evil and he wasn't seeing that this woman was putting anything—any actions out, to be of evil, or of hurting anyone. She wasn't doing anything to do anyone any harm. Her motivations behind what she was doing were not of a destructive nature.

He saw only that which was her motivation, her identity, and he saw that which was the God within this beautiful soul. So, he treated to that which was the higher self of that person; not saying you are evil, not saying to her anything of that character. He was only talking to her on that which was the higher self within that woman. Of course she changed her way of life because he was not seeing evil and he was not treating her for evil. He was treating for the good that was, and is, the very identity of all mankind. You see? There's a difference.

So, beloveds, let's you and I treat for the good that is in all of God's creation; mankind, that which is the Brotherhood of Man, that which is and is known as the Fatherhood of God—that which is known as the expression that leads to the divine essence of the mastery of life, that no longer are you caught up in doubts and fears. No longer are you caught up in anything that is beyond your capability of finding the greater expression, the evolution of it—the motivation of something that is character in the divine essence of life.

Yes, beloveds, one might say that Mary made a mistake. One might say that Jesus' father made a mistake. One could down rate both of them. But, I say to you, there is no room in the heart of Mary, mother of your Elder Brother, other than that which is love, and I mean of a greater love than the average person today, that stands before a rabbi, a priest or a minister and marries. Why? I'll tell you why, because most of them, a great, great, all too great percentage of them are prostitutes. You say, "What are you talking about? Getting married and you are a prostitute?" I say, "Yes," because some of them are married three, four, and five times, and all they have become is legal prostitutes—both of them, men and the women alike. That's all they have become.

Yet they would turn to their neighbor that is living with love, and peace, and quietness, and progressiveness, and joy, and all that is good, and down rate them because they didn't get a piece of paper that says they are married. I mean man has no mind of his own, only that which has been prostituted by the rabbis, priests, ministers and all of that which is known as religious orders. There are the great prostitutes. Jesus called them just exactly that, religious prostitutes and that's what they were.

Beloveds, isn't it time now that you and I begin to look at our world, and know within my own heart that I love my fellowman, and that I'm not going to look and see whether my brother has a piece of paper that says he is legally this, or legally that, according to the laws of the physical world? You have seen the laws of the physical, and they have destroyed the greatest part of your physical world.

Beloveds, I was born in my last incarnation before I mastered in this your country of America, born an Indian known as Golden Eagle. Yes, beloveds, and I've seen your country go down, and down, and down, as far as its conditions of evolvement. Beloveds, everything that you have established, you are fearful of. You are fearful. You are afraid of tomorrow. You are doubtful of yourselves, of your capabilities and your capacities. Yet, beloveds have you asked yourself the reason why? Beloveds, you know you have created many, many religious orders in your physical world. You have set them into motion, and they have caused most all of mankind to be incapable in their physical minds, of being in control of themselves.

Yet, there is a change, and it is beginning to take its place, and you are going to see the youth of your tomorrows possibly take their stand. There are millions of those that are walking in a greater avenue of spiritual awareness, because they are doing what Jesus did, walking out of the temples and they're contacting God. They're contacting, they're sitting, and they're becoming aware of a divine truth that they never knew before. They are at peace with themselves more fully then they've ever been. They know that there is value in all things—if it is in the spirit of good for me and my fellowman.

So they are looking, and moving, and having their being more fully, not in a false god, or any false god, but in the divine God in themselves—that identity that is the motivating power unto eternity. This is where they are. They are going to prove this to mankind before too long. This, my beloveds, is something worthwhile looking forward to.

It makes no difference what dimension you were in before you entered this one. Remember this dimension is the one that you have to function in, and to move, and have your being in the greater essence of knowledge and awareness of one God. And, once you do this you will evolve beyond this dimension into the greater dimensions of life in the Father's house. Yes, there are many mansions. There are countless, and the avenues are many. We ask of you, walk in that light and you will enjoy every avenue of expression from this day on unto eternity. Peace be with you, peace.

I am known as Golden Eagle.

CHAPTER 6

Now These Three Expressions Out of the Master Jesus All Were Intertwined

By Ashtar

Dearly beloveds, it is my pleasure this evening that I take hold of the instrument and bring forth that which is the will of the Father unto each and every one of us, that we may, through the expression of that which is given, find our path lighter and more abundant. Yes, my beloveds, we know that the future holds a great deal for each and every one of us. Because, if we function in that which is the peace and the control of our being, we shall find that we shall have pleasure, we shall have joy, we shall have inner peace, and we shall awaken to greater awareness, and to greater understanding. Therefore, of that which does not want to walk in the light, we shall give no thought to. We shall function within the expression, "I am in it, yet I am not of it."

So, beloveds, be aware of this so that you cannot, in a sense, divorce yourself from the conditions of destruction, but to be no part of that destruction. Let that which does not want to find balance, let it flow in its own direction, and walk in the greater light. Move into that which is the garden of life that the master, or Elder Brother Jesus taught you and I to function in.

Now, beloveds let us relax for just a moment or two. Let us find that we are cleansing our temple. Let us feel that beauty of God's divine power and His divine energy—that beautiful peace and love that is the expression of God's divine action in this, our physical world. Now, for the moment, let us feel the prana of life as it were—that energy that cleanses and purifies, renews and reestablishes the body. Let us feel that energy flowing through the entire temple, feeling it move in and through and out of the temple, through the feet. As we feel this energy and power flowing through we release the conditions of thoughts, possibly, that we have had today, those thoughts that have not been, probably, as well balanced as they should—without being bitter or hateful or being even sorry, actually, for having allowed ourselves to flow in that; but, to feel that I am happy that I have become aware—aware that I need not entertain these things, because, they have no value for me, nor any value for my fellowman.

So, I am releasing them from my thoughts, from my expressions, actions, and deeds of the future. I release myself to the perfect energy, the power of love, the power of healing, the power of inner peace, that power that opens the door to untold awareness—that which is greater understanding. Let us feel this, as the prana of life flows though us, that we are also being fed by the manna of eternity, the manna, also, that feeds the temple from the unseen—so, that which is of great value to each and every one of us. So, let us feel this as we become very quiet for a few moments.

(Author's note: Meditation for eight minutes)

The master Jesus spoke and said, "Greater things than I shall you do." Also, he was known to raise the so-called dead. Also, he said to one that had been with him for some time—when he came to him one day, and said, "Master, I cannot be with you today for I have to go to a funeral." Someone in his family had passed on and the master said to this beautiful soul, he said, "Let the dead bury their dead."

Now these three expressions out of the master Jesus all were inter-twined. They were not separated. There was all of that which the master had been expressing throughout the years that he had been teaching in the Near East. And, of course, this had to do also with his teachings when he was teaching in the country of India and other places as well.

But, nevertheless, we've got to look at what the master spoke of, and when he said, "Let the dead bury their dead," he also said, "We live. We must move on into life." Of course, this was difficult for some to under-stand, and when he spoke of these things, and the reasons for his teachings in this manner. He had spoken quite differently than they had given unto him and unto his fellowman in the temples, because, he found that as he attempted to talk with the priests and the rabbis and the ministers, he found that they did not want to teach as the word of *life* had been given.

They had not accepted life, but they were accepting only that which was leading mankind to the limitation of a few years of expression in the physical realm, then, to the conditions of the limitations that lead man into death.

But, also, they did not attempt to realize that man was cycling himself in just a limited expression of awareness. They were not aware as the master Jesus attempted to speak to the priests in this manner. To let them know, "Well, then what future is there to the conditions that you are teaching? What future is there to that which limits you to a few years of physical expression, with doubts and fears that you teach your children? You teach them from the beginning that they have nothing much to look forward to, excepting to earn their living by the sweat of their brow and then to turn about and go into the earth." Then when the Elder Brother spoke unto them about that expression—and also telling them that that sort of teach-ing made your children very doubtful, fearful, and also wary of their God. They were very wary of their God.

So it was that he was also going one step further with them, and of course, this was not accepted in the temples. And, he told them, "Now, look, you go into the earth. You let this body deteriorate. The only reason the body deteriorates is because you have misused God's energies, God's power, God's love, God's inner peace, God's awareness and God's under-standing. You have not accepted love and the brotherly expression of living. So, this is the causation that you have brought upon yourself that destroys the physical body." He said, "The spirit cannot die, for the spirit is that which is the divine identity of God within your temple."

So, then, he said unto them, "You must then, move about in the spirit, until you have found yourself ready to return, again, to the physical realm. So you, then, make your choice of parents to come back again and do it all over again. So where is that which you are teaching about? Where is that heaven and where is that hell?" So, the master said to the priests, "Heaven is now within you and so too is the hell."

So, it is up to you, either to establish yourself in the realm of that which is the beauty of living, the joy of life, the joy of sharing, and the joy of knowing peace, and love, and awareness of greater understanding. Or else create for yourself that which is the condition of destructive motives. Using the energies and powers of God in a manner that establishes in your being those aches and those pains, those fears, those doubts that destroy the physical body—and again you must go into the earth.

But, we the masters teach you this is not what God gave you and I, for He gave you and I that which is the dominion over His creation. When He gave you and I the *identity* of life, He gave us that which is the entire universe, that which is the entire expression of His creation, for you and me to take, and enjoy, and find love and peace in it, but we have not accepted this. So it is, that we go through these conditions of changes of bodies for generation upon generation.

I would like to delve into something else that has to do with this condition a little further, but I will leave this for another time. But it is rather strange—it is in your Bible, and it is written there, and it is telling about the visitation of your imbalances, or your conditions of sin—as the Bible calls it, "...upon your children, unto the fourth generation." I would like to delve into this a little more fully because it has a great meaning that could help you to help your children to realize, that they need not go through the physical death, that they need not find it within their temple, any condition of illness *whatsoever,* and I am going to delve into this with you at a later date.

I know, beloveds, we the masters do teach here on your physical earth either through an instrument such as this, or we have our various places in your country. We have various places, especially in the Himalayas and in the eastern part of India. That is where we find ourselves moving in, and teaching, and helping our fellowman towards that which is the mastery of life. All too few are seeking this, but beloveds, the great saying has always been: "When the student is ready, the master appears."

But let us also go a little further, because God is, and God has never let His children down. God has never brought about, or threatened you or I, in any manner. No matter how remote a condition of imbalance may be, God never ever caused this, never gave you and I that expression or condition to accept. He never threatened us. The divine energy power is love. That energy power, God, is pure identity of love. It is pure identity that expresses within my being, your being as you enter within, and discover yourself.

So, beloveds, God never at any time created anything but life. So, therefore, then you and I must accept the fact that if there is acceptance of death physically—I am speaking of physical death, because there cannot be spiritual death, I can only speak to you of that which the Elder Brother Jesus spoke of. The only death there can ever be is the death of the physical, not the death of the spirit. Because spirit is eternal, it cannot die. It knows not death and never will know death.

So, then it is up to you and I to establish ourselves in such a manner, in our physical world, that we take out the conditions of destruction that we have been the cause of. Therefore, in this present life we are discovering the effects of the causations of what we have done—not only in our present actions in this physical realm, but also some of the lessons or karmic conditions which you call karma from that which was lessons not learned in the past.

So it is that you and I must move on. For you see when God established us and He gave us dominion over His creation, He did not establish any condition of limitation. So, having then the freewill to find our own expression, and to deliver unto ourselves and our fellowman, that which has value to myself and to my fellowman; then, it must be done as an expression of awareness that is known as *cause*. I *cause*. Also, then, discover in my causations, the effects thereof.

So, the master Jesus in his teachings often said, "One must pleasure in life. One must pleasure." He cannot function properly if he is unhappy. Yet, I know that in the temples you are being taught—not only in the temples of old, but you have absorbed these conditions in your temples of your present day. You have lived by the cross. You have lived by the blood, and you have lived or existed—I cannot say *live* because that is not living. Because you teach your children to live by the blood, to live by the cross—to go forth and say, "I do all of these things until I die" and so on. Understand? This is absolutely destructive because your children from the very early years of their lives have nothing to actually hold on to or to live for. They have a God that is love on one hand but also a God that will come and take their life on the other hand. What kind of a God is this? You see?

So, beloveds let us begin to realize that today we live. Today we let go. We let go of those things that bind us. Let us not say that in this day and age—and I hear this so often, not only in your country here, but I find it in every avenue of expression upon your physical earth. Wherever I make contact—and I have students in the country of India that I find this with—even as I have taught them for some time, are yet holding onto that which they feel that in this day and age you cannot get away from the conditions of selfishness and greed, that are being put upon us in the various ways from the leaders of our countries, on down to the expression of our working element. So, I say to you this is not true. You need not be a part or parcel of this. You need not be in this. In other words, like the master said, "I am in it," but he also expressed his awareness that he was no part of it, "I am not of it."

You must realize, beloveds, that there are those also that are saying, "Well, yes, but you are a master, you don't have to be a part of this." But, beloveds, what are you here for? What are you expressing for in the physical? Are you not attempting or moving through these incarnations towards that which is the mastery of life? For if you are not doing so then you are only making small cycles. That is all you're doing, and you're being repetitious, and you have done that. You and I have done that through countless ages, since we found ourselves, or moved into this third-dimensional world.

Isn't it time, now, beloveds, that we begin to realize this, and to move into the joy and the pleasure of living; to not allow ourselves to be concerned about what my fellowman says outside of me, what he thinks about me and so on? I should be concerned first of my true self, identifying myself with that which is my identity in God. Then, as I find and move into my identity, then I find that I am not a small part of any condition in this your physical world, or for that matter, in the universe, but, I am one in all that is, in the expression of life. You see? Because this is where I was created; I was created in that divine expression, in the very identity of God, in that which is the absolute identity, man, in the divine expression to take over and move into the creation, and to accept the countless gifts that are mine.

So, therefore, then I must cleanse my subconscious world. I must take that subconscious world and take out all of the rubble that I have put there, because all of that rubble is limitation. It only serves me to that which is the expression of physical death. That's all that rubble does. It binds you.

In the time of Jesus they had their laws, just like today, and this is what Jesus was condemned about because he would have no part of this. They had their laws and he would not take any part of it. They wanted him to become a part *of* these conditions and he would not attempt to move into them, at all. He was there, and he did what was of value, and he did only that which was good. Because he felt that when I love my fellowman—I cannot love only those that belong to this group here. I must find that God is the expression of the entire universe.

Therefore, whatever there is in the universe and all of my fellow-man—wherever—I must love also. Thus he loved from the very bottom of his heart. There was no condition of limitation, saying you belong to that country, I belong to this. And, so I cannot love you because you don't belong to my way of thinking. He kept no condition. No barriers. He put no barriers around him. He opened wide the gates of eternity from the flow of the superconscious mind of God, to that which is his fellowman.

He also said to you that you were exactly the same as he, because he said, "I am one in you, you are one in me." You see? He didn't try to say that he was different than you. He said, "I am one in the Father and the Father is also one in me." Therefore, I am one in you. You too, are one in me. So, that made you one in the Father and the Father one in me and you. You see?

So you see, beloveds, we've got to release and we've got to take out limitations. We've got to release ourselves. We've got to move that mind. Move it into the reality of that which is *life,* as Paul said, "Renew the mind." Of the disciples, John was the only one that mastered. The rest of them returned to their negations. But John was one that went quietly about, and he moved into, and he taught, and he established around himself those that would come to him, and to teach them how to be children of the universe, rather than children that say, "I belong to this group, or to that group and to this condition of dogma or to this condition of doctrine, or limitation." So it was that he mastered. Paul also mastered.

(Author's note: Paul was not an apostle, he was a disciple. However, many considered Paul the thirteenth apostle.)

So it is, that they taught exactly the same teachings as Jesus taught, because they were hopeful of teaching man to become involved in reality, to enjoy living, to find health in their temple; the only way you can feel and know—there is no other way you can find out whether you are on the path of life, or on the path of self destruction. The path of life you find yourself experiencing more and more health. You're experiencing more and more beautiful energy. You're experiencing more and more of the divine power.

Now, this power is not a power that is destructive. But, the power of God can only be destructive when I take that power and misuse it, when I take it and put it into some action that I know is not valid, that is not balanced, that is going to hurt me or it's going to hurt my fellowman. And, no matter how little that hurt may be, if I continue, let us say, using that power in a manner that is not balanced—even if it doesn't hurt anyone greatly or doesn't even hurt me greatly, but, as long as I keep using it, it keeps on slowly but surely eating away upon my temple. So my temple then slowly but surely deteriorates and it grows with fear, it grows with doubts. It begins to get denser and denser, and I get to the point where I cannot think.

Have you not had persons, your brothers and sisters somewhere in your physical world that have said, "Pray for me. Pray for me. I can't pray for myself. Pray for me. I can't think anymore?" You see, beloveds, they have let themselves become so completely dense—never probably having done anything real harmful or hurting. They have probably been their own worst enemy, probably been throughout their lives—they have been unhappy with themselves and disgusted with themselves, and so on, and so forth, but, never did attempt to make any change, just remained in that category of awareness. Even though, if someone would have attempted to help them, they would have probably become a little bit angry at them. They might not have been happy for that advice.

So it is, that man allows himself to move into something that is only an expression that eventually is the unhappy condition of physical death. So, it is not always—I don't want to misguide you. It is not always an unhappy expression of death, because there are those that are definitely happy only when they are sick. Now, I know you must have known those that cannot speak enough about their illness. They go from one person to the other, day in and day out and just steep themselves in their aches and their pains. They're seeking pity. Then, eventually they get to the point of where they say, "Oh, I'll be happy when the day comes when I am released from this temple." So they are not really unhappy about going into the death penalty. But yet, they have not moved into or gotten anywhere, at all, on the ladder of God's divine and true evolution.

Now, then, there are others that will say they are ill, and they will not attempt to do anything about changing their way. They have not attempted to listen to what the master Jesus said, "Physician, heal thyself." You're the only one that is going to do it. The doctors aren't going to do it—you know this. The doctor cannot heal you. He can take away the outer scar. Understand? He can take the outer scar away, but, until you renew your mind, that scar can break out again into another condition of illness, and eventually self-destruction.

There are those that say they want to heal themselves, they don't want this illness. Yet, they will not attempt to do anything to change, or to even endeavor to go into the withinness of themselves, to find out, or attempt to find out what the causation of this condition is—how it started. What have I done to cause this? Then there are those that say, in self pity again— as they're getting up in age and they say, "Well, I'll be glad when the day comes and I have to leave and go to my heavenly reward." Hypocrisy! But, nevertheless, it is there, and then with the first little ache or pain they run as fast as they can to a physician. What are they running to a physician for? They said they'd be happy to be released from this body and yet, they are running to a physician to be healed. What are they doing? They are being absolutely dishonest with themselves.

Of course, if man would only stop to realize, and to think even super-ficially, let us say, off the top of your head, you will begin to see, and to realize there is something wrong with that which is the expression, and the teachings in my physical world. You will begin to move into a greater depth of awareness as you discover the reality of life. You will begin to recognize the fact, that being that I am the cause, and I am also experienc-ing the effects of my causations. Then that which is the expression within my physical realm, my physical world, *is* my creation. Therefore, as long as I maintain the thoughts that I am expressing, then I am expressing only that which is limited, and therefore, my world that I create, is a world that has only a time limitation, and so it moves into that which is the death expression.

But the more I delve within my consciousness, or my subconscious world, and into the superconscious world, which is the divine world of God's creation—now, then, I begin to see that creation. I begin to see that which God is—is that which never knows destruction, never knows imbalance, never knows anything but inner peace, contentment, and understanding.

So, as I move into that expression, I am yet in this. Understand? I am yet in this, but, I am no longer now functioning of it. I find my world becomes a much more beautiful place to live in. I become contented with myself. I love myself and I love my fellowman. I may not go with everything my fellowman does, but, I yet find myself not condemning the condition. Because if I find myself in that condemnation then I become a part and parcel of that condemnation—therefore, I am then again in the limitation of my own creation.

So, then, I would like to mention another condition here that the brother Jesus so often spoke of, and he said to all of us. He said, "Give no thought to tomorrow. Live today." So we should do the best we know how to *live,* and I mean *live* today—not exist, to move into something that I am enjoying today, and I'm going to make my day the best day—*this day,* the best day of my life. I'm going to recognize the fact that if there are any conditions moving into this day that are out of balance—that I know that in my action, so far this day, I didn't cause it today—so, I see then that it's a karmic condition, or a lesson that I must learn. So, I do all that I do with love, in order to bring about a balance to that condition that presented itself in this day.

So it is that the master attempted—when he was speaking in this manner of "Give no thought to tomorrow," he was trying to show you and I how we could most definitely master life by taking care of today—just taking care of today. Knowing another thing—and this may strike some of you rather strangely, but the master taught this, and we have always attempted to teach to those that have come to us. When that day—what you have said is a day—you have put so many hours, you have said it starts at this and it ends at this, and so, it's another condition to a degree of limitation, but nevertheless, it's there, and you call it your day. Attempt to keep yourself under as much awareness as, "I have dominion over myself, for my God gave this to me." This is mine, and no one—nothing in the universe can take this away from me. I have dominion over myself, for my Father gave me the freewill to do so. He didn't say dominion over my fellowman. I'm talking about the self. In other words, control over my being, over my own being. Understand?

Alright, now my day is done I'm going now to lay myself down. I'm not going to say a prayer of limitation such as, "I lay me down to sleep. I pray the lord my soul to keep. If I should die before I wake. . ." Now, right there, a limitation that you teach yourself and your children. All of these things are conditions that are destroying. Eventually it's going to destroy the world that you created, and those that are yet in that world of that creation are going to be destroyed with it. In other words, you're building a Tower of Babel, and it's going to fall on you, and it's going to destroy you.

So, let's take a look—so what do I do? I lay myself down, and I'm thankful to the Father for a beautiful day, for the strength, and the energy, and the love that He has given me, and the capability of seeing into this beautiful day. I know that His world is a world of love, and peace, and so, I'm thankful for it. Now then, though I don't make a long story out of it to the Father, the Father is not expecting all of this. He is only happy when you accept His gifts. This is when the Father is the happiest; when I accept His gifts, His eternal gifts, and I walk into the path of what He gave me, the path of life, and accepting His gifts. This is when God is happy and contented, because God is the very energy and power within my being. So my being has to respond to it as well. Understand?

So, then, I lay myself down and say, "Well, I'm going to sleep now, and I'm looking forward, and I'm going to awaken"—I don't *think* I'm going to. I'm not going to lay myself down doubtful as to whether I'm going to awaken in the morning. I *know* I'm going to. I know. I know I am going to awaken to a better, and a more prosperous and beautiful day, a day of greater love, and inner peace, and awareness, a day of greater understanding. I'm going to awaken to that energy and power of being able to be of great service unto myself, and wherever it is needed in my fellowman's expression. I'm not going to try and push myself, or try to put myself on somebody, and tell them how to do this or that. No, I'm going to be ready though, to be of service to my fellowman, if that is necessary.

So, I move and I lay myself to sleep with those thoughts, that I'm going to awaken to a much more beautiful, creative, and energetic day. Alright, then in the morning you'll awaken, and you'll know right away, "Father, you and I are walking together today. You and I are walking side by side. I know that whatever my needs are they are already taken care of. So, all I'm doing now, Father, is moving with the joy, and the love, and the peace, into your beautiful creation. I begin to realize, suddenly, what I really am, inside of me—that I am that fountain of life, because God gave me that fountain to renew myself with, He gave that fountain of eternity to me, and I'm moving and having my being. Not in just a world, but in a whole universe. I'm moving in that universe. I'm beginning to feel and know the greater expressions that my brother Jesus talked about, about moving and having my being in the most beautiful and creative energy power of God."

You know, beloveds, the reason why I bring this again to you—I brought part of it to you before, but I had to add a little to that, because of the fact that you are in that time. Understand? You can be of greater service—not to your country alone, not to just a few, but to all of your world—to everyone, because your brothers and sisters are in all parts of this beautiful globe. Remember, God created it all. God is the essence, and created all of this beautiful universe, and I'm not just going to experience this little globe. I'm going to experience everything. I'm going to stay and enjoy living with my Father.

Remember the little story that is told, and I believe the instrument's wife has told it several times, also. But it has a great deal of great truth to it. This person was walking, and every day he would find himself with another set of footsteps along his side. So he eventually knew that these other footsteps were God walking right alongside of him. But one day it seemed as though his little world fell in upon him. So, now, he is looking and he sees only one set of footprints and he says, "God, oh God, when I need you the most, when I need you the most, you are not here." And God responded, He said, "I am carrying you."

So, beloveds, remember this; God is always now. God is always ever and beautifully expressing. So let that divine essence be the energy and the power of your being. Believe me, beloveds, then, when you smile at someone that smile will not be a strained smile. If you say, "I love you" to someone, it won't be because someone said to you, "Tell them you love them." Understand? Should you wait for someone to tell you—to tell someone you love them? It wouldn't be coming from the heart. It would only be coming because someone told me to do it. But, when I find the super consciousness of God and His divine expression in and through my being, I permeate this and it comes out of every pore of my body. It comes out of the very essence of my being. I look at my fellowman and I say, "I love you," even though they might not be on the same rung of the ladder of evolution that you are on. Now, you're beginning to recognize it more and more.

So, you are at the ready—not to try to pull that person up on that same rung, but your being there, and present, and your actions, are sufficient. Your aura is spreading out around you, and its color vibrations are beautiful, and that person may be—you'll walk near that person, and that person feels that beauty, and the love that is in that aura, that energy, that power that surrounds you now. They may turn around—even though they're not on the same rung of that ladder—they have felt something. They want to know what that is. They turn to you, and they ask you, "You're so beautiful and you look so happy. You look so contented with life. What are you doing? I'd love to know."

They have opened the door, and now you can extend your hand out there, because, beloveds, remember, now they have stepped up on that rung of the ladder of God's divine evolution that you are on. Watch. Sometimes they might surpass you, and get on another rung, and you have to reach out your hand to get their help. This is the way it is supposed to be to move ourselves back into the realm of God's divine evolution, to move and have our being in that which is His creation, and that creation is the creation that is eternal, and never is out of balance.

As we move into the super consciousness of God's divine essence and we accept the energy, and the power of His prana and manna of life, and all of the countless gifts—and especially, knowing that all of my needs are already taken care of. So, I am not going to go to sleep tonight thinking and worrying about, "What am I going to have tomorrow? What is my need going to be tomorrow? What if I should be sick, or this or that?" Because this is what you have been indoctrinated in—to fear these things, and to prepare for those conditions. But, why not do what Paul said, "Renew the mind," and now prepare for the greater expression, the greater deeds, the greater fulfillment of life. You see? Now I know I'm moving there, and wherever my brother reaches his hand out, I'll be there to help them—also to enjoy this with me, because I am living, because God lives in me.

Also, we find that there's a general change taking place. There are those that have left the limitations of what they call their religious backgrounds. They left them. Now, they were not bitter, nor are they bitter at all against what they were taught in their religious backgrounds. They're only looking at "Alright, it was a step that I took, and now, I don't need that. I know all I need is to know what I am, in my God. All I need is to know what I am in the absolute expression of my Father, the creator of all that is."

So, they are not in self-condemnation because they were held back—seemingly through their own acceptance of certain dogmatic expressions, and doctrines, and so on. As they are leaving these situations, they are not bitter, nor are they bitter against those that are yet steeped deeply in it. But, they are moving and finding within themselves, that they are capable, now, of doing what the master Jesus was a teacher of—he was a teacher of a way of life. He taught man how to heal himself. He taught man how to love, and he taught man how to be at peace with himself. He taught man all of the nice, beautiful conditions that are of value and priceless to reestablish and renew—and lifting you into a much more joyful, happy consciousness.

The master Jesus was a wonderful teacher, one of the most wonderful teachers out of the ones that I had the pleasure of knowing, because he was so light hearted, and he was such a *happy* sort of person. Laughter came easy to him, and he shared the joy and pleasure of living, but never attempted at any time to force any situation upon anyone. All he did was, actually, put himself in a position—such as this instrument. He puts himself here for us to take over and those that will to come, come. Those that are not in that consciousness, that are moving into their own consciousness, and don't feel that they are wanting to hear anything such as what we have to share—and they go their way. They're not forced to come. They're not told, "Now look, if you don't come you're not going to make it." It's that which you are, within your own consciousness, which is going to be the results of that which is the life, and the living expression—that God is within your temple.

But, the results are beginning to take place; the changes. And, just in the past six-hundred and some odd days on your earth, we have found that there is returning, in certain parts of your world, on some of the continents, the renewal of that which man has destroyed—forests, and so on. In a new way your earth has slowly come back, some, upon its axis. Upon that expression there, your earth, your continents have slowly started to now move in together. All of this is causing what you are experiencing.

And it seems as though as we are saying to you, "It's for the good of every man, woman, and child concerned on this planet earth, if you are in the proper consciousness." But, you would say, "Well why, if it is getting better, why should all of these terrible storms take place, and the ocean rising, and the tornados, and so on, and so forth? Why should these take place if it is getting better?" Because, it's a very simple answer. If you've ever tried to uproot someone, a person out of a certain density, you will find that that person is going to be very difficult. Even in your own self, making a change, you seem to be so comfortable in your misery that you hate to make the change. But you know, deep down inside it's the best thing I could do. But, oh, I am so comfortable in my misery, "I hate to make a change."

So, this is the reason you are finding these storms, these miserable storms that you are having, because, there are millions of souls that are comfortable in their misery. They're seeing things change and they are feeling it. They are feeling it within themselves, but, they are just absolutely reluctant to try to make a change, and that mind is doing it, causing this disturbance. But, in the disturbance it is renewing, reestablishing, and rebalancing your earth.

So, you're going to find, if you will look, and you will listen—if you have ears to hear, use them now. See the things that are changing and feel them, and know that I am not at all reluctant to make the change. I'll make the change anytime it is necessary. I feel within myself that if it is of value to me and my fellowman—I am going to do it. Watch and see how your world is going to be most beneficial to you, and how much simpler it is going to be for you to attain whatever you are hopeful of attaining—yet, being very capable of sharing, in every manner, every facet of expression that meets up to you in your daily lives.

Beloveds, don't think that there's anything else in your physical world through thinking; whether it's thinking densely, thinking something of value—whatever you're thinking, whatever kind of thoughts that you put into motion in your lives, is the result of that life. Don't blame it onto anyone else but your own self. You are the alpha. You have accepted the omega. But, believe me God gave you the whole picture. He didn't give you a part of it. You are that eternity, and so be conscious of this.

Recognize, now, that I am no longer the omega—I am the alpha. I am the alpha because I am that which is the expression of the eternal creator of life. He gave me life and He didn't give me a final expression in it. He did not give me the omega. The omega was accepted by man himself and he has made his own grave. So, let the omega alone and open the door to the eternity—the alpha, the beginning. You are going to find that all will be absolutely most abundant for each and everyone.

So, beloveds, you will find yourself so clear in your thinking, and the cells in your body will actually seem like they speak to you. They will be so clear, and so vibrant, and you will feel and know what it really does mean—that you have misused the word *living* for so long. You will know, now, it is *great* to be alive. It is *wonderful* to be alive. There will be no more thought then, in the minds of men, that are moving towards that eternity of old age. There will be no thought of that. That limitation, there, will be taken out of your consciousness, because you will not feel age. You see? Man feels age because he has established it that way. He has said, "Well, if you reach seventy, seventy-five, if you've gone seventy-five, you're already on borrowed time." You see? So, you will not be functioning in that kind of a consciousness. You will be moving and having your being in what truly is life or living.

I'm going to leave this with you, beloveds, and believe me; God lives in each one of us. I want to see the day—and I am hopeful of it that every one of you will be on the same rung of the ladder of life that you were created in—that divine essence. And as you pass me up, I'll put my hand out that you will help me, also, to move into the greater expressions of God's eternal universe. Believe me beloveds it's wonderful what the Father set into motion. And that it doesn't remain the same because it continues to move into greater and greater expression. Oh, this is the most wonderful thing, to just realize that God has established a universe that is ever greater, ever greater. So, let us begin to experience that beautiful universe.

Peace my beloveds, peace be with you.

I am Ashtar.

CHAPTER 7

Once Again I Shall Open the Book of Truth unto Thee

By Jesus

My dearly beloveds, I come unto thee this night, that once again, I may share a few moments with you, as I did once in the long, long past. Yet, I come once again dear souls, and I come unto thee, that I may share with you the light that so beautifully glows from the Father—unto this the light of eternity, that shall once again bring forth the melody of the garden of everlasting life unto thee.

Therefore, I ask you this night, that you follow me. Let us go forth into the garden once again, together, as we did once in the long ago. This night shall we sit upon the rock, and look up at the beauty of the stars, and feel the depth of the powers of the divine Father, as it flows beautifully within each and every soul of us.

Once again, I shall open the book of truth unto thee. For this book of truth is the book of eternal life, and I would ask you this night that you would release yourselves of the cares and the woes that you have so deliberately allowed yourselves to be filled with, that you would look to the skies and the heavens, and know that all is as it was in the beginning, and shall ever be. If only you release yourselves from the cares that you have burdened yourselves with, by finding yourselves, once again, knowing your brother, knowing your sister. The only way you can find this awareness within you is by turning your eyes within, and knowing yourself, and when you have known yourself then, so too, do you know your Father.

These words are not idle words, my beloveds. They speak of eternity. Release yourselves of any bitterness, any causations of imbalance. Release yourselves of the density that seemingly crowds you in your physical world. The way to release yourselves of this density is forgiveness, forgiveness of all conditions that seemingly crowd you. Conditioning yourselves, then, to become aware that there need never be fear in your hearts, that there never need be doubts in your hearts, that you could speak whatever words of balance that would come unto thy mind and speak them with authority— knowing as you have spoken them, that no man could cast these words asunder by denying them unto thee, but they would be not just words, but awareness from within thee, that you would know immediately, as you have spoken them, that they are of the Father, "I fear not, nor shall I cast any doubts before me."

It is spoken often, that I spoke unto myself, and that I had entertained the devil or demon. Dear souls, I was no different than you, and therefore, the mind would become cluttered with those conditions of the lower physical self. Remember, dear souls, that you are no different than I was, that these same conditions befall you and that you too should entertain them. Entertain them until you have released them, yet, not fulfilling them as they would will to be fulfilled. For there are wars, and constant wars, but these wars are the greatest that are within you. The lower self trying to dominate the higher self—this was the demon that I entertained. Often times, did I speak aloud, even though I was by myself. And always, did I stand with this demon of the lower self, until I had reached the awareness that the higher vibrations of the self had won out.

Too often you are being told that you are evil, and the good seems to be constantly trying to find its place within you. But, my beloved brothers and sisters, it is not at all that way. For predominately, you are good. For it was through good, through balance, through love of the Father that you were created. Therefore, that which is known unto thee as evil is only of your own creation. If you would recognize this, it would be much simpler for you to gain the balance that your true self, your Father-self, your

Mother-self attempts, at all times to maintain, and which tries to sustain these things.

It is well, beloveds, that you know that which is evil, and that which is good. There is a difference, for if you would be reminded, once again, that in the Father, all is good, then you would enter within the self recognizing this. You would then set aside that which is evil with much less difficulty. For there is evil in all that is good, and there is good in all that is evil. By this I mean, beloveds, that which you all too often speak of as evil is only evil in your mind's eye, but in God it is not evil.

All too often you have been taught that certain actions, certain deeds are evil, and yet, under certain circumstances or conditions you find that they are not evil. Yet, your brother may look in your direction, and yet, say that you are evil. It is you that must take the condition, or the mote, out of your eye. For, if you do see that evil, then that evil cannot be that which is outwardly presented, but must be that which is within you. There are many other conditions that are said to be evil, but if you were to take out of you—strip yourselves of the dogmas, the indoctrinations that you have falsely been given, then you would find that you would have taken out of your own personal life many things that have been considered evil.

In God, the Father, you are not bound. You are only bound within yourselves, and when you have reached this awareness you will have found this to be true. The only way to reach this is through entering within— reaching constantly and daily within the self. This need not be a ritual, but if you are going to find your true self, then fight that war. Do not go forth into your daily lives saying, "Well, there isn't anything I can do about it."

I left you the key to life eternal, physically, mentally and spiritually. And the only way you can accept this key, my beloveds, is by fighting the war, the war within yourself. Not fighting it outwardly as you have all too often been doing. For when you see this, or that, or the other, beyond your-self and you have cast the negative thoughts, the negative words and sent forth negations outwardly you are destroying the temple—you are clos-ing the light within it. You are shutting out the power and energy of the Father. Fight the war, but fight it from within. Speak loudly unto yourself, if need be.

One of my disciples, one time, did not know that I was close by. I entered into his little room. I stood there watching him and he was speak-ing very loudly, and he was seemingly very angry. Ay times I saw him take

77

and pound the table that was before him and eventually a smile came upon his face—for once again he had conquered.

Yes, beloveds, take time to fight the war, but fight it from within. For within thee, within this temple, the Father resides, and always recognize that you can, if you feel yourselves weakening, turn unto Him. He shall gratefully and gracefully bring forth those powers, those teachers, those masters, those guiding influences unto you, to help you. No, they will not do it for you, but they will be the power behind it that will help you conquer the enemy—that demon self, the lower self.

I speak unto you this night knowing that the years that are before you are the years of fulfillment. They are those years that I once spoke of as the vintage years. They are the years that the wine of life shall then be aged and fulfilled. Therefore, I ask you, those of you here, present, be reminded of this, that you will look forward to those years; that you could turn to your brother man, and under any given condition say unto him, "I go forth in my Father. I fulfill these years and I know that no power shall prevent me from doing so. For I am the I AM, and I stand in this awareness that, I am that which is the I AM. My Father and I are one and, again, I repeat no power shall prevent me from fulfilling." Peace be with you.

I am your brother Jesus.

CHAPTER 8

The Master Jesus Gave Forth the Lessons of Life

By Kuthumi

M y dearly beloveds, it is my pleasure at this time, that I have taken hold of the instrument, that I might come forth and share with you that which may be of value to you. Each and every one of you are individuals, and you cannot be receptive to those lessons that we share in each and everyone of you in like manner, because, it is something that you set into your consciousness, pretty much to the tune of that which has been the pattern of, let us say, your upbringing and your background in the home environment.

If you have been, let us say, indoctrinated to some degree in various religious backgrounds—even though you may not be attending other religious orders of any kind, there are dogmas and doctrines that, oftentimes, remain in your consciousness. That which you are receptive to in the teachings that we give, then, are accepted and made to blend in with that which your background has accepted throughout the years.

But, we are hopeful, and we attempt as the master Jesus gave forth the lessons of life—he attempted to share with those who were there listening to that which he had to give, and to share those lessons. He was attempting to share, hopefully, in the minds that were there, a way of being able to release themselves from any previous connections that they had. Not that he was saying to them, "You have to let go of everything that you've ever learned or ever accepted," or that, "You cannot go to any religious temples of any kind." No. He never asked them to release themselves from these orders.

All he was asking was that they maintain in their consciousness the capability of being able to put into motion, into action, in their lives those lessons that he taught, in a manner of absolute freedom, freedom from any situation or condition that was previously limited. This is what he was attempting to share, because he didn't feel—or want a person to set into motion in their lives, that which he was sharing, in a manner that could be blended in with other doctrines or dogmas, because each and every one of them were conditions of limitation.

That which he was sharing had no dogmas. There were no doctrines there. There were no conditions of limitation set there. It was absolutely a free morality that he was attempting to give to each and everyone that was present, and listening to that which he was teaching.

But, of course, as you know in his doing so, oftentimes, he was rebuked by those that were out there, because they failed to want to let go of their limitations, their doctrines, their dogmas; not only churchianity, it was also the home environment, the conditions in the home that were so thoroughly put upon the children, and they carried that through their lives, fearful of making changes. It's surprising how many in your physical world today are functioning in like manner. They are functioning in actual fear that they are doing wrong if they let go of some of these limitations that they have been accepting through their lives.

Then, of course, the home environment was not free, although, it is freer today than it was back in the time when the Elder Brother was teaching. Limitedness, fears and doubts cause conditions of inner anger and doubts, that establish and create that which is, eventually, brought back to that individual in the manner of illness and unhappiness, expressions that eventually cause people to become incapable of properly releasing themselves to a condition of health, beauty and self expression—and knowing, full well, that they were created free moral beings. Even though they may even express that they are free beings saying, "I can do as I please." But yet, you will find that if you follow that person and see what that person is expressing, for a few days, you will find that that person is definitely bound by her own acceptance of dogmas and doctrines—conditions of limitation.

So, it is well that one asks one's self every so often, "Am I really and truly free? Am I actually expressing in my world, freedom?" Even though I feel in my own self free, what am I doing that can be deteriorating or destructive to my brothers and sisters? Am I expressing in such a way, that I am establishing a thought pattern of limitation to those that are close to me or are dependent, in a sense, upon my actions and deeds? These are things that are necessary for one to function more creatively and abundantly in.

Your world has been very, very repetitious. Every twenty years doing the same thing over and over, so not much progress being made. Of course, you have noticed, I'm sure, upon your earth today, that man is getting further, and further, and further away from reality. He cannot seem to be able to put things together anymore. The only way he can see his way out of his dilemmas that he is creating, is self destruction. The only way I can express it—he is hell bent to that self-destruction because all of it is done through greed, selfishness and fear.

So this is what your Elder Brother Jesus was teaching—teaching you how to evade those things because he saw only one thing that was going to take place. He told it oftentimes, he said, "Look, you are going to self-destruct. You're building the towers of destruction. You are building that Tower of Babel that is going to fall upon you." And thus he was hoping to reach a few that were yet not in the same density, that had steeped themselves further into the animal vibrations of the hu-animal. So, he was hoping to reach those, and to establish, at least, in them the awareness that they could bypass these conditions of destruction. Which, of course, they did do, but it was only the few that attempted to find expression in this.

Now, you find today that your great religions of the earth are abiding with all of this animalistic vibration. They are accepting it. They don't care about their children. They care not about this at all. They don't care one iota about this, all purely of the lower vibrations. And so, their children are as intricate a part of the density as the parents are, because it is, even at times, that the expression in these vibrations are lower than the animal that they were supposed to be in dominion of. You see? But, this is only the beginning of the great destruction. This is the beginning, now, of the downfall of the empires.

This is why we cannot come close enough to you—or were hopeful of coming close to you to let you see what is taking place. That you will not attempt to walk in it, nor will you attempt to change it, in any way, but that you will keep yourself aloft from these things. Because, if you don't, and you become a part of it, by discharging bitterness and hatred towards these conditions, then you become a part of that condition and, therefore, can be destroyed with it.

But we are wanting to hold some of you—we cannot forcibly do this. We don't want to be forcing anyone into anything. All we can do is to let you know what is taking place, and that once this begins to move, it's going to move awfully fast. You're going to find that those that are occupied, and preoccupied by those densities, are going to be rolled up into them, and destroyed with them. It is just that simple.

I know that there are those that came to Jesus and said, "Well, my brothers are all involved in this. My sisters are involved in this. My mother, my father is involved in all of this." But he said to them, "Who is your mother? Who is your father?" You see? Who is your mother, who is your father? But, you see, they don't put these things together so you will understand them in your Bible. You see? Why isn't it there so you can understand it? It was there—it was there by those that spent their first thousand years with God, and with love, and peace, and with awareness, and with understanding.

Even though they had fallen from that which was the pure identity of the Father, they still had that love. They had not entered into all of these densities. They wrote the Bible, but that Bible that they wrote was not that which you are seeing today. You see, God didn't give you countless things to do. All He told you to do was "To do unto one another as you would have done unto yourself." He asked you to be unselfish. He asked you to just do that which pleased you, and hurt nobody else. He asked you not to interfere with your fellowman, not to try to dictate to your brother man—to make your brother man do what you wanted him to do. You see?

This was the way they lived at that time. So, there were times that I'm sure that, through those thousand years, that there were neighbors that, let us say, in the tribes of that day, that didn't do the things that the other one cared for. But he didn't interfere with him and his brother. They didn't try to tell each other what to do until the greed and selfishness came in. Then, they chose sides and started now to suppress each other. They were not happy with each other's suppressions, and they tried to destroy each other, and this is the way it is in your present day.

So, this is what we are hopeful of; your becoming so thoroughly aware that you will no longer have the least bit of doubt as to what tomorrow holds. But you cannot do it, not one of you will ever do it, until you have entered into your own secret closet. Not one. There can never be one soul upon the beautiful earth, or anywhere in the galaxy, that can know God, until you have entered in the secret place within your being. In other words, getting reacquainted with yourself, and once you get reacquainted with yourself—that being called the I AM presence or identity God.

Now, then, and only then, can you ever hope to move into the higher dimensions in the Father's house. It cannot be done, nor will it ever be done and it has never been done, other than one has to do it themselves. We cannot do it for you. Jesus attempted, in every way, to show you how—the masters prior to Jesus attempted to show you how to do it. But, all that happened was the minute they moved into the greater dimensions, they took them and made them gods, rather than to take the teachings and abide by those teachings.

So, this is the reason why you've got such a great turmoil upon your earth. Your Bible has been so distorted, that man doesn't realize what is taking place. Except, the lower animal man is getting one great jubilant expression out of it, because he sees the pornography of it, and so is abiding by the lowest of vibrations that has been put in there by his fellow-man, not by God. So, this is a very destructive thing. You have almost made a beast out of your Bible rather than to make it something to live by. You see?

So, your new Bible is going to give you that which is a way to death, rather than to life. But, then, it has been gradually going that way ever since man has decided there is no way to rise above this condition of self-destruction, excepting one in millions that have recognized that there is a way. The way is simple. It's just not to abide by those conditions. Have you not that God within yourself? Then get acquainted with God within the self. You don't need that *book*. Where did the first book come from? It came through the mind of man—not man, but hu-man. Understand? It wasn't written by man prior to his taking a physical body. That Bible was written after man had taken the physical body, that which was known as hu-man, and it was written in your Bible as hu-man, HU hyphen MAN.

So you see how man has allowed himself to be invaded, his mind so cluttered up that he has accepted these things, all blindly, not allowing God to speak through him, when every man, every woman, every child is born with that privilege of reaching that awareness. Excepting those that have been set forth into motion upon your physical earth by the beast of man, those are the ones that are not understanding, and don't understand, and you've got them in offices. You've got them in the high places in your world, and they can sit for days, sit for years and argue one point, and never get an answer. These are the people you have put into offices.

You have your attorneys. You have those that are in your highest courts, that don't know what pornography means. They don't know what is evil, and what is good, and they have proven to you that they don't know. They have argued for years, and have yet to come up with an answer, because they are so steeped in the animalistic vibrations of your earth that they actually don't know. You wouldn't have some of them in your cellar, let alone in your living room. If you knew how they lived you wouldn't have them in the pig pen. You won't put them with your pigs because you'd be afraid that they would destroy your hogs. Those are the ones that you have that are the leaders of your world.

There may be one here and there among them that has the "know how," but do you think they even hear that person? Of course they don't—they didn't hear Jesus either. They milled around him and he spoke for hours to them, and there might have been one in the group that knew what he was talking about, yet he was using just plain language. This was a simple man with simple teachings.

What do you want, or what are you looking for? Have you asked yourself what do I want, and what am I looking for, and what is my purpose? That's why I have asked you—enter into that private place within your own self. When you have entered there and you have truly communed, you're going to find that what we have told you is true. You are going to find time nor space does not exist, nor did it ever exist. And, it will probably be the first time since you invaded the human body, that you have found that there is no such thing as time nor space.

Then, once you have entered in, and you have communed with God within, you are going to find that you are one in everything in the universe. Because you are going to know that universe is not out there, but it is here, and it is now. We have told you that time and again. Jesus told you that over two thousand years ago. The great masters before Jesus attempted to tell you, but only a few would listen. But, when you have truly entered into your little private closet, you'll no longer stray out here. I mean enter in, and know the beauty of God within the self. You will find that you will be able to cope with all situations. There will never be a situation that will arise upon your physical plane that you cannot handle with balance. There will not be one thing difficult from that day on, not one thing will you do, that you will not find joy and pleasure in expressing in.

But yet, you will believe that you were created to suffer—you want to believe those things. You want to believe that you were created that you cannot earn anything or have anything without having to suffer to get it, and to fight and struggle for it. This is due to the fact that you have taken the gods of the money changers—not the God that your brother Jesus attempted to show you. Not the one and eternal God that all of the great masters attempted to show you. No. But, you cannot do anything without fighting and struggling, and being self destructive, and destroying others in order to attain it.

I say, again, once you will enter in the center of your being, you'll no longer be involved in any such turmoil. You will find that you will move and have your being in God, in the one God—just one, divine and eternal God of balance. And, whatever you will do—you may be looking at your world with these physical eyes, but you will express it with the single eye. For you will only know how simple it is to have everything, and all of the gifts. For they are right here and now. They are all right here and now; the heaven, the hell, the balance, all of it is here now—right within, because you invaded this temple. But, you did not lose your identity, if you will go in there and take a look at it, that identity is exactly as it was the first time you recognized God.

I know that Jesus spoke of this, and the masters spoke it time and again, that God gave you everything that's needed. It's all here and now. He didn't put it in the hands of somebody behind a podium. He didn't put it in a book for you to read it. He didn't do any of these things. God never did any of these things. God gave you identity, perfect balance, identity of that oneness in all things in the universe, and use it in balance—and that's all there is to it. It will never destroy, but if I want to live, and live generously, and hopefully, and gloriously, I've got to know my identity. That is the only way.

I say, not a one of you can reach into a greater dimension, not one, including the instrument, not one of you can move into that greater dimension, until you know your God within. When you enter into that private closet, when you become aware and quiet within that closet, then you're going to know. You're not going to have to cry. You're not going to have to shout. You're not going to have to fall on your knees and pray. All of these things are man established.

You know. Play God once, your own self, and see what it's like. You're His child, why can't you play God? See what you would do, were you to create a world. Would you put all of the turmoil that you have in it now? Would you establish sickness, and illness, and death? Would you establish people that have no control over their own beings? Would you establish a world filled with bitterness and hatred? Would you establish a world filled with conditions of telling your children to build for destruction of one another? Your Bible tells you that your God did do that; because they have gone and they have prayed, and then they've come back and they said, "Well, God told me to tell you to form an army and go and destroy your brother." This is what your Bible tells you. You say, "The Holy Bible" and then you turn around and say, "The Holy Land" because Jesus was born in a certain place. But, you don't stop to realize that God is the permeating expression and life of everything that is upon your earth and in the whole universe.

So where is the holy part? Only where you walk in balance, that's where the holiness is, that's where the peace is, that's where the love is, that's where all the genuine expression of the universe is, and when it emanates from you with a genuine beauty and a joy, with an inner peace, that is God in expression. There can be no destruction there. That's why they couldn't destroy your brother Jesus, or they couldn't destroy the masters prior to him that they put, also, in the temples. Where is the church and where is God?

So, why can I point and say this piece of land over here is holy, and yet, everything is destroying itself there? But yet, it's the Holy Land because someone was born there. You see how dense man has become? You see how dense the animal in man is? That he has not allowed himself to see his identity in the divine essence of the universe.

Until I have put that which I heard into action in my personal world—that I have walked into the garden—picture yourself, if you have to, walking into the garden. I'm walking into the Garden of Olives right now. I'm walking there, and there I see my brother Jesus standing tall among the olive trees. I hear what he's saying to himself, to the self, to the higher identity, which is the God divine vibration of life within himself. He calls it, "Identity God divine expression." He calls it, "God, the divine atom of life," because this is what he knows himself as. "I need an answer, I need to know something. I am putting it out into the ethers of eternity." When he says, "I am putting it into the ethers of eternity," he knows that within his being is the sum total of all there is. This is why he said to his fellowman, "I am one in the Father. I am one in the Father."

You see, he knew no separation and he turned to you and he said, "I am one in you. You are one in me." You see, he knew no separation. He knew that the sum total of eternity was right here and now within his being. He would look with the physical eye upon the world that he was surrounded by out there—yet he saw it, and realized it, and recognized it, because he knew that he had been part and parcel of the creating of that expression, but he was no longer of it. You see? That is why he said, "I am in it, but I am not of it." You see? Because now, he knew he had cleaned out that which was his part of the action that had formulated the dying expression of his world. Now, he knew he was in the living world. He was back again with the divine essence of eternity, the creative energy powers of the universe.

So, no longer was he of that dying expression, and nowhere would you find, at anytime, where the master was ever in need. Never was he in need. He always had a place to lay his head, and he didn't have to lay it just any place. He always had a place to lay his head in comfort. Jesus always had what he needed and, of course, the food that he needed. But beloveds, you see, he didn't need food. But yet when he was invited to sit at the table, he sat at the table, and he did eat, because he wasn't going to separate himself in anyway from that which was his environment. He was in it, but he didn't have to be of that expression. So, he did what was necessary to maintain and sustain the balance. He didn't try to say, "I am better than you. I am different than you." No. He was only trying to show you, man, his brothers and sisters, that he was no different.

What he had attained was because he had evolved into or reached within, and moved then, into the expression of life. And, he was hopeful that everyone that would hear his voice would also do likewise. He asked them to do that, didn't he? He said, "Do ye likewise" and then he said, "Do ye greater things than I." And you're afraid to do something different. "No, I'm in this rut here and I don't want to be disturbed." But, you pretend you want to be disturbed, so you scatter your forces in every direction of your physical world, running from one thing to another.

What are you doing? You're running away from yourself, running away from reality, running, running. If you would only stop to look at yourself and say, "Where am I going?" What would you do? You would see the scull and crossbones right there in front of you, and you would see your grave. You would want to go over and kick the scull and crossbones into it. That's what you'd want to do, because that's what you're doing. You say, "Well, I might as well get it over with." You're not walking into the reality. You're running to that which is your own destruction. Because you're running as fast as you possibly can, "Get out of my way. You're stopping me from getting there."

It's so simple—every bit of it is so divinely, creatively simple, and so much pleasure. Look, you haven't realized what pleasure is, what joy is. You have found momentary pleasures in this thing, or that thing or the other thing. But when it comes to pleasure, I mean joy, something that isn't way up here and then down here the next moment. No. This pleasure is something that is continuity. You move into it and there is no more doubt in your mind, there is no fear in your mind—"I just know where I'm going, that's all. I just know that my dimension is eternity, my life is forever. My expression is the service of myself, unto myself." You see?

Now, this may sound a little bit selfish when I say, "My service is of myself, unto myself." The master said that too, Jesus said, "I am one in you, you are one in me." He was saying that which is of the beauty of my being, I share with you, for you are one with me. He was hopeful that you would pick it up and use it your way. He wasn't trying to say to you, "Look, use it the way I have said it to you. Look, if you don't listen to me. . ." No. He didn't say that. He said, "Look. Just enter within. Find your divine essence."

Your divine expression, your creative energy powers are here, and they are unlimited. No shortage of power, no shortage of love, no shortage of peace, no shortage of contentment, and the whole thing is here and now. Not only that but it goes on and on. It becomes more and more beautiful each and every day that you live, not exist. I said, "live." Try it. Try it, beloveds, and stop scattering yourselves, and your forces.

Well, beloveds, it's been a pleasure once again having had the privilege of being with you, and now I'm going to take my leave. I've got a little trip to make tonight. I go down into Argentina. It is going to take me at least thirty seconds, your time.

Alright, beloveds, I am master Kuthumi.

CHAPTER 9

Beloveds Awaken—for Paradise Awaits You

By Jesus

Peace. Peace. Beloveds, children of earth, once again, it is my pleasure that I be given the opportunity to take hold of this physical instrument, that we may once again walk together in the garden of eternal life. Follow me my beloveds, follow me, let thy cares of the physical world fall away from your shoulders, and let us find, our presence in eternity. So, let us walk into this beautiful garden of eternal expression, and let us walk to the rock that we have sat on before, and let us take our place there.

Let us find, and look through the eyes of the spiritual eternal light, and let us see this garden in its true essence of expression. Let us see its beauty as we have never seen it before, and I, in my turn, shall walk in the light of my Father and give unto thee a few words of light, a few words of life, a few words of eternity. Let us not just take these as words, but let us know that they are true things, expressions of your everlasting presence of the eternal now.

Therefore, beloveds, today is the day. Today is the day that you change your thought expression out of that which is the density of your physical earth, and expression. For what makes that earth dense, but the expressions of your own thought patterns. So it is, that when one lifts these thought patterns, you walk not alone but in a closer proximity—you hold hands more closely with your creator, your divine and eternal Father, your Father, my Father. For let us realize today that we are one in all things, as we have never realized it before.

You, beloveds, of the physical earth, have found expression—many of you for many years, and yet, your expressions have not given forth to you that which is the abundant life. You have not found the true happiness yet. You have not found the true releasement of that which is suppressing you. Why is this?

There are some two hundred million souls of expression in that which you call your country, some two hundred million. Can you imagine this? Can you see two hundred million souls expressing in untold and devious ways? And yet, out of the two hundred million souls there are but very few—so few that it is almost useless to mention it, of those that have found complete releasement from the density of those expressions that you have put into your physical earth.

You are drawn to these things thoughtlessly, completely thoughtlessly, and you can take part in them, and you add to them. You create such density around your physical earth, that it is just black, and if it isn't black, it is grey and brown. Why do you do these things? Why do you not realize that you are adding?

One may walk off the path of light, and because he holds a high office— two hundred million peoples will add density to that which is taking place, without ever realizing you are making that density become a part of you, that it is killing you, that it is taking your body and literally ringing out the light in it. You do it without giving one thought that is creating out of it.

There are over two hundred million of you that are expressing on the physical earth today, in your own country alone, not counting any of the other countries, which some of them have five hundred million, such as China, such as India. Almost five hundred million, and yet, what have you experienced in your physical earth? Possibly here, in your little home you have not traveled many miles on your physical plane of earth. Possibly, if there are those of you that have traveled many miles, you have traveled and seen nothing, or experienced very little happiness, or joy, out of what you saw, or what you were doing. You experience more happiness on your return than you experience while you were doing it. This is not the way.

You must experience beauty while you are expressing. Then, that expression will be a many fold more beautiful in its return to you.

Why have you not experienced your world? No. There are many that have lived in a city and have gone very few miles out of the city. Even in your day, today, where there are all manners of travel. Yet you have very little experience about that country which you call your own, which is not yours—it belongs to the world and your universe. Nevertheless, you call it your own country. Selfishly, you call it this. Any time that you say, "My country is the most beautiful country in the world," what have you expressed? You have expressed nothing but selfishness. Not one particle of it is yours, and yet it is all yours and every country in the world is yours. You see how selfish mankind has become, and how few have realized in your physical world, and in your own country, that you call your own.

Very few have experienced the divine creative powers of your God expression. You have not looked at the garden at all. You have not experienced the garden, and yet, it is right with you. If you will just take the time to become aware, and become unselfish, and throw away the pattern of greed, then you will begin to realize and become aware of the greater abundance around you. You will not be isolated—for when you begin to experience these things unselfishly you draw to you those that would be unselfish and, therefore, then you share your experience with others.

But why not even open the unseen world? For this door is not locked. All you have to do is open it. All you must do is make the attempt to open it, and then you will have many expressions of awareness with you. You will go forth into your world—not just that which is around and about you, but, you will experience that world that is completely yours. It was given to you to experience, to enjoy, to find greater and ever greater expression in. But, you know in your divine creation that your God gave you all of this. Not just your country, but all countries of the world are yours—one just as greatly as the other.

You are going to experience them one way or another. Either through being able to draw the abundance of the physical world to you, or to be able to go about that world and expression and see it, and love it, and enjoy it, or you are going to be able to see it through the spirit, the spirit light, by taking yourself out of this physical temple that you are expressing in, and wandering your earth and seeing it in its true light, and in its true beauty. Yes, seeing it, even through the densest of man's creation.

Then, again let us go a little bit further. That which is Asia, that which is the western world of America and South America, but we have not expressed yet some more beautiful expressions, the North Poles and South Poles of your earth. You would say, "Why there is nothing beautiful about that. It is nothing but ice and snow." Beloveds, awaken, for paradise awaits you. Those poles are being yet, even today, released of these ice caps and snow. The lush beauty of that earth that is below, shall once again present itself upon your physical earth, and more so, now that you have explored the outer space of your world.

For soon, there comes a new pattern that shall be set out there, that shall help you release these conditions, and bring about gradually—this is going to take a little time, for man must experience gradually, because he is fearful. Because he is not only fearful, he is jealous of his fellowman. He is grasping. He wants it all himself. He doesn't want to share. He is selfish and greedy, but do you have to follow this act, dear ones? Of course you don't. Don't think that you'll be walking alone just because you are not following those that are going into ever and ever complete density. What is happening to them? You see it every day, and your youth is beginning to collapse. They are not truly aware.

But, those that are aware are living the awareness, they are expressing it in their every motion, their every thought, and their every deed. That light that they send forth is the true light expression of the Father expressing through them. They are the teachers, and you are going to find those of your youth today that are going to teach that truth without fear. They are trying to tell you, but, there are many of you that are not going to be told. So, what is going to take place because you are not going to be told? But in truth, you are not expressing *life*—you are just existing—existing in the pattern that the *money changers* of your physical earth left with you.

So, what are you continuously doing, beloveds? You are continuously trying to tell your brother what he should do, how he should express, why he should express this way. Then the least little thing that you call "happens"—that happens in your physical world, you find nothing but dense expression to give forth to it. Rather than to let that expression find its own path, it will find its own pattern because it is already expressing it—so let it go. You may say, "Well, if I did this they would hang me for doing it, but they let him get away with it." No one gets away with anything in God's creation. Whatever is negative is negative. Whatever is an expression of balance and beauty shall always be balance and beauty. It shall remain that way, so, you cannot allow yourself to overflow in the pattern of negativeness or positiveness.

You must follow the path that your Father gave to you, the balanced world of eternal life—love and expression. When you express in either way that is taking only one branch of your life into motion—you are throwing yourself completely off balance, and you are creating death for yourself. You are creating something that is going to happen. But as it happens, it happens in its true justification. Nothing just happens.

So, why then should you take time out of being creative and creating joy, pleasure, life and love? To look at someone and say, "He is this way. He is that…" You are only causing death to be your pattern. Remember this, before you ever put words into motion—for the minute you cast that word out you have cast it into motion. For thoughts are things, when they are expressed they are *dynamic*. For, whether they are created for the good pattern or the evil, your God experiences it all with you. If you create evil, God experiences it with you. Do you want your God to experience it? Create good, and God experiences it with you. Because all of his energies that flow in and through you can be used whatever way that your will wishes to use it. You see? He gave you that and He will not take it away from you, but if you will yourself to be in His divine will, then it is up to you.

You can then experience that which is the everlastingness of life, that which is the greater abundance of life, that which is the true expression that your Father willed for you. You can experience now—now, not tomorrow. For there is no future—there is the past through your mind pattern, but the everlasting now is yours. It is through this everlasting now, that you can completely make your world the garden of everlasting life expression.

So why not do it? It is not difficult. Stop. Enter within. Express those expressions that are bombarding your physical self continuously, not the patterns that are out of balance. These are the ones that you bring into yourself, but you constantly are given that which is the true pattern of life. You're constantly being guided, guarded and protected. But you will not listen to the *little voice* of eternal life that constantly speaks unto thee.

I would have never been able to fulfill the Father's light—to fulfill that expression of everlasting life, had I listened to the negations as you have listened to them, and then followed them through. I saw them, I was bombarded with them. I fell, yes, but I lifted myself once again, and I am no greater than thou art. For I am one in the Father, so too are you. Yet, you doubt it. You doubt this expression. The Father expresses in every fiber, cell, bone, and tissue, every atom of your physical body. Every thought pattern that you reach to, you can reach yet even higher and more beautifully. Take time to see and express your divine creative self in His name. Peace be with you. Peace.

I am your brother Jesus.

CHAPTER 10

Your Beloved Mary
Mother and Jesus

By Ashtar

(Author's note: At the time of this session I inadvertently failed to start the recorder until after a few moments; however, very little was lost.)

The Elder Brother was no different than you, nor different than I. Had he been different than you or I, he would have had very little to give to you. But through his life he struggled to rise above many conditions and these conditions have never been given to you. Why? Because they were written only after Jesus resurrected from that so-called death and these conditions were stolen or, let us say, taken from the archives of the great library in Egypt. So, of course, this part of Jesus' life was never given except through such instruments as we are capable of taking hold of. Of course, your great churches have known this for many centuries, but especially the church known as the Roman Church—these conditions were never to be given out because they could not have functioned in the way they had been functioning had that truth been given unto you.

Jesus was born the same as you. There was no difference in his birth. It was not a virgin birth beloveds. It was a birth exactly as your mothers have brought your children into the world. Yet it was a greater birth, in a sense, because Mary was such a wonderful mother and one so capable of great love.

But let me go back—and I see Mary as she was a young and a very beautiful maiden, a dancer by profession, dancing to make herself a living and to help her parents. Of course, she danced in a very high class dance hall and functioned in this higher vibration where those of the upper crust of that day were meeting and she met a young prince. This prince was, of course, from the House of David, and he and your beloved Mary mother fell in love. The young prince wanted to marry, but, of course, Mary was not of royal blood and this was not to be. Therefore, they came together hoping that if Mary were with child that they would be allowed to be married. Again, this was very sad, but a complete refusal.

Then, there was that Mary having conceived this child with a great depth of love for this young prince and he for her, for their love was absolutely boundless. But, nevertheless, it meant death for the prince were he to remain with this maiden. So, it was that Mary sent him upon his way with love and turned all of that love that she had for this wonderful young man to that child. Every thought in her days turned to the beautiful child and love that was within her womb.

So it was, beloveds, that Joseph came into her life, and in order that that which was being talked of would be changed about, he took and she agreed to become his wife. So it was, that they left then, that part of the world and headed towards where the child was born, but, every moment of her days, of her nights, her thoughts of love were complete in this child.

Therefore, that child was born different than most of you because of the complete love and understanding. And there was no bitterness in Mary for that which had taken place, for she knew she was going to have an exceptional child, because she knew that young man also had never ceased to love her. His love and her love were constant in the growth of this child within her womb. And, therefore, that child when it was born was exceptional. It was a child of love. It was a child that did not take long before he realized through his many incarnations of what he had to do. He had to rise above the conditions that were yet whispered about his birth and about his background, yet they knew of the beautiful background that he had. But, nevertheless, it was the churches of old that berated the conditions of his life, of his birth.

Then, came to the time of his early years, and his mother spent a great deal of her time with him teaching him of the great love. Teaching him, of course, not to listen to some of the conditions and remarks that were being made—and he had to rise above all of this in order to try to bring to mankind that which he knew he must. For he knew of his birth, he knew every moment of his being born. He knew all of this because he had lived such beautiful past incarnations; thirty-three in all of them, beloveds.

But what did Jesus do when he was in his early youth? Well, in his very early youth, he used to kill his playmates every once in awhile and that's something that man knows, of course. If you've studied the histories of Jesus in his early youth, whenever he was unhappy with one of his playmates he'd say, "You're dead" and that person would fall dead. And his mother, of course, had to come and tell him about it, and so on. So, he'd say, "you're alive again," and so that person came back again, that child that he was playing with. But he didn't do that very often, because his mother showed him that he was misusing the power of life.

Then, at the age of twelve years he actually came into a greater realization, and knowing that the conditions that were now with man had to be changed, that he had to work towards taking the money changers out of the churches. He had to work towards taking dogma out of religion. And, of course, he entered into the temple and he spoke with great wisdom to the rabbis and the priests, but they would have nothing to do with him.

Of course during his teenage years—I want to say to you his temptations were the same as every other man upon the physical plane of earth. But with the great love that he was conceived with and also the great love that he had for his Father, his heavenly Father, he knew that there were greater things and greater works to be done. He knew also that he had to show mankind there was no death.

Therefore, he left then, when he became fully aware of his capabilities through the actions of the spirit, through the natural law of God, that he was able to take himself, in his physical body, and transport himself wherever he willed. And, of course, he was looked down upon often, about this also, for they had their thoughts about these things, as many of you, in your world of today have. And, even though, they saw that he was capable of transporting himself in his physical body from place to place, they yet would not believe it. They yet would not accept it, and so it was then, that he left that part of his world and was gone for a number of years. Where was he then, beloveds? But traveling throughout your world, and every part of the world he traveled. And, of course, you know that he didn't have to take a ship to get there. Nor did he take a ship from one continent to the next, but he transported himself there in the physical body.

Now then, what nationality was he then? Beloveds, he was not of any one nationality, he was all nationalities. For he was universal, and he knew it, he did not accept anything that bound him in any way. He did not allow himself to be bound, and this is where the controversial condition arose in his life because he was so different. But, he would not allow himself to be bound by anything. So, it was that when he delivered himself to, let us say, your country, America, he was an Indian, for he took on the features and the stance of an Indian. It was through this body, then, that he taught the Indians how the great universal God is within.

As he went to different parts of your world, this was the way he did; he changed his features. He changed himself to take on that which was the beings of those parts of the world. The colors and the features and so on— this was the way he did and he taught. You may say, "Oh, no, this could not be." I say to you, you could go into your jungles, beloveds, even today, and you will find that they have those that are capable of painting—will have painted their Jesus in black, the same colors they are and so on and so forth. This was the way he did it and you will find that the black people of Africa have painted their Jesus black.

He went to all parts of your world to give the light and to that which he knew must be given and to teach man not of death but of life. He taught them all as he went into different countries and about that which was going to take place. He knew it. He didn't wait until he was thirty years of age— knowing that he was going to go to his death. He knew it. He knew when he was traveling throughout the world that this was going to take place. Because he knew he had to do it in order to show man what he had come to fulfill.

He didn't change one thing of the laws of man excepting that he came to fulfill that law, that it was fulfilled, that which was the death pattern of man. He came to show man, now, I have fulfilled it and now it is time for you to look towards life. Of course when he returned to the Holy Land at the age of thirty years he knew full well that now "I am going to give the fullness of all—for I know death has no hold over me."

So it was that he did teach in earnest then and, of course, you know what took place. The leaders of the world and the high priests and so on decided what manner of man is this, that should try to give the world such awareness? We cannot have this. We're out of business. We're out of business if that man stays and if people follow him. And they were not about to go out of business. Well, beloveds, the churches are out of business today. Well, I mean they are on their way out. But, they are not going to die, don't you believe it. But, they are going to teach the truth, for this truth will be before you in not too long a period of time.

These things that I am telling you, now, and the great writings that Jesus spent his forty days and forty nights after he arose from the dead with his disciples to write, and that the Pope pleaded with the one that took it out of the library, pleaded with him, "Do not let the world see this. Do not let the world see this." So, it was that it was taken, but it shall come to the foreground now. For it is understood in the higher places that man has become a little bit weary of being storied to.

Not only this, beloveds, but your children have become weary of it and you will say to me, "Well, how are our children weary of this?" Beloveds, they are born today with a greater understanding than you have. That is why they are weary and that is why they are doing what they are doing today. They are not doing it just to be destructive. Because they feel as though, that maybe if they can do this, that maybe they will be getting a little attention, that some of you might pay attention to what they are trying to tell you.

But when these parchments that this was written on and these many pages come forth, beloveds, you are going to see how blinded you have been. But, it isn't only because you have been blinded, but also the many, many ministers, priests and rabbis throughout your world are teaching because they think it is true, too—because they have been blinded throughout the years of their teaching. So, don't feel bad nor condemn those ministers. Don't condemn those priests. They know not what they are doing.

But those younger ones that are coming up know, and they are biding their time and then there will be the great change. But why wait? Why go on destroying yourselves, physically? Why go on doubting, when your world is yours and you know that you were created to all abundance? And if you believe in any God at all you know that a just and loving God would never have created his children to destruction. So, it is only through your own negations that you are going down the path to destruction. It is time to about face. For I am saying to you, we are close and only those of you that show the proper light shall be lifted and we want to lift as many as we possibly can, if the earth envelopes those of destruction.

So, beloveds, don't try to go forth in your world and say, "Well, I can't do it in one incarnation." Beloveds, every one of you have gone through many more incarnations than Jesus ever went through, so there's no excuse. Then, the other excuse was, "Well, Jesus was born already a pure high being." Listen, what Jesus was born with he earned and you can do the same thing. He did not lie to you, beloveds, when he said that, "You could do greater things." But you have made a liar out of him. For over two thousand years trying to alibi yourselves and say, "Well, if I had been born as great a being as he, I could do it too." But I am going to say to you, you were born as great a being, for you are the sons of God. He said it to you, "Ye are God's." He wasn't saying it to hear himself speak, was he, or to hear an echo? He was saying it to you and he wanted you to realize it and recognize it.

Now is the time, beloveds. Now is the time. Now, especially, that you have entered into the greater vibrations of your earth and every one of you are entering into great new cycles of understanding. Delve into those cycles and draw out the great light—and speak to your God Father and He will guide you through, and you will gain that which your brother Jesus did. You won't gain it living in the negations and fear. You'll only gain it in the knowing that I walk in that light and I fear nothing. All is well.

So I am going to leave this with you beloveds. Oh, there is a great deal to that pattern of Jesus and you are going to be surprised, and the things that he and his disciples wrote that never have been given to your world yet. But believe me it won't be long. So, I leave this with you beloveds and peace be with you, peace.

I am Ashtar.

CHAPTER 11

The Master Jesus Was a
Teacher of How to Live
and a Way of Life

By Salamar

P eace. Peace. Dearly beloveds, it is my pleasure at this time that I have
been called upon through the expression of the Father that I might
come forth and share with you that which, I'm sure, that each and
everyone of you are looking for; looking towards a better and more fruitful
life that you might find yourselves capable of reaching to that which is the
mastery of life and, of course, this is the purpose of man.

Although, man in the general expression in your physical world is not
aware of this because of the many conditions of confusion, and the limitations that have been expressed and given to you through the various backgrounds. But, nevertheless, this is the purpose, and this is what the master
Jesus has always been a teacher of—is one that gave forth *life*, the lessons
that were of value and would always be of value to each and every one of
you—that would set it into motion in your own lives.

But I find there is a great deal of difficulty in man accepting that you were created in the very image and in the likeness of the creator, due to your acceptance of the density of the physical body, and is of the force of the animal energy and, therefore, causing man to let go of his capabilities and the purpose that he was set into this expression of life to be in dominion of the Father's eternal creation.

As he entered into the force of the animal, then, he has found himself in a dual-expression, wanting to express more deeply into the force of the animal rather than expressing through the higher course and the force of life. Due to the Adamic Age commitment that, I sinned, therefore I died, has been a situation that man has accepted blindly. Only the few who have taken the course of life in their consciousness have been able to reach the mastery, such as in your physical world of billions of souls you find that there is relatively a very, very few that realize their capability of reaching the mastery.

But, again, as we speak of the mastery, or the mastery is spoken of in various courses of life, we find that man seems to think that it's a difficult thing to do, that it has to be holy, that it has to be under pious conditions and that is not true. You have to be free. You must be free to be able to take dominion of your own personal world. You cannot do so if you are bound by the limitations which we call the dogmas and doctrines of man in his various expressions.

So, the main thing for man to reach the mastery is to be as free as you possibly can and to be as happy as you possibly can, and to express that love, that freedom, to enjoy the world that you are in, and to maintain and sustain a pattern of thought that is not confined to limitation. You've got to, let us say, shed from your consciousness that which you have been through a number of times and reincarnated through many, many of these incarnations.

Yet, you have asked yourselves, "Why is it that we always have to come back? Why is it that I always have to come back to this realm of the physical, especially one that is rather, what you might call, advanced?" Even though he has gone into the death penalty he, let us say, has done a little bit more studying about life and has at least a faint idea as to what his purpose is. Even that person having to come back, comes back to this plane of earth, very, very reluctantly and usually has a memory of his birth or her birth. This, of course, makes it a little bit more disenchanting for coming back.

So we ask you that you are in this realm of the physical, you have been given life, but yet there is another thought that enters the expression of man. This also has been a condition that has been adopted and accepted by even those of us who were reaching for the mastery. We felt that, after all, yes, I am not supposed to let myself go into the death penalty, but the animal me—the animal. That which I call the "me," that which is the physical body should go into the death penalty. Therefore, once it ends up in the grave, then that which is the I AM of "me" goes into a "heavenly realm." This is, of course, is the great untruth, but yet, it is often being taught that way.

Then, as we reach into the death penalty we come to the conclusion that I have done something that I shouldn't have done or I would have entered into "heaven." So, I come back with that kind of consciousness to the physical world, and I have not done anything towards making my world a better place for me, nor for my fellowman, nor have I attempted in anyway to reach towards the mastery.

So, I've got to say to you, you've got to be mindful that everything, everything—*there isn't a thing* in the universe that the Father established that dies—nothing, nothing at all that the creator set into motion and turned it over to those of us—that is, at that time, to Adam to take dominion of and to enjoy everything. Everything that my Father established is absolute perfection and does not know death.

But, man has, in his third-dimensional world accepted death, and thinks that everything dies, the trees, the grass, everything that is in your physical world somehow must go through death. You don't realize—man does not seem to want to accept it. Even though, in a sense, man wants to accept it, but to put it to the essence of reality in your personal world, somehow, you fail yourself. Because you see the conditions of death all around and about you, and seeing all of this and feeling all of this, you accept it as reality.

Of course, as you eventually enter into the conscious progression in the physical, and you begin to realize that there has to be something more than just this repetitive expression—that this is not what the creator gave to you, but that you as co-creators accepted this and, therefore, moved in that consciousness. But, it is as simple to move out of it, as it is to accept it, and this is what we eventually began to do. But this is what the master Jesus, also, in his expression of life gave and taught, but it was never given to you through the various backgrounds of dogmas and doctrines.

So, you can make your world a very terrific, abundant, generous, happy, healthy, strong avenue of consciousness, and a world of beauty for yourselves by just becoming fully aware and conscious that my Father, the creator of the universe, gave me life—and life is what I intend to express and generate in my consciousness and share with my fellowman.

There are so few, in that realization, that have come to the conclusion that they are no longer wanting to accept that which is the expression of limitation that has been so profoundly accepted by all of the generations of man for many, many thousands of years—even prior to the establishment of Christianity.

Yet, we look to that which was prior to Christianity and the many that were very unhappy with the orthodoxies of the past and not just one religious background but a number of them. In India there was a profusion of religious backgrounds—in China also, the adoption of the Buddha of India, who eventually went over the mountains there to Tibet and China. Man seems to even think—because they have never studied the histories, they always have thought Buddha originated in China or in Japan, and this is not true. Buddha originated in India, the Buddhist religious backgrounds.

All of these things man should have looked into to find out what was back of it and to realize that these backgrounds were all by man, established. Therefore, when they were established by man they were given certain limitations which you call the dogmas and the doctrines. Every one of them had their own dogmas and doctrines and looked at each other with, let us say, an eye of thinking that, if you don't belong to mine, you are not going to reach that heavenly realm.

Then in 325 A.D., when Christianity was started—it was started because there were those that wanted to be in a position to dominate others. Therefore, they started that which they called Christianity in 325 A.D. So there then began a new generation of background and, of course, splitting into various what you call denominations—because one was unhappy about a certain part and another unhappy with another part, and so they created their own backgrounds.

So, beloveds, it is a rather sad thing that man let go of his freedom now, to allow someone on the level of consciousness that, actually, even was of a lesser consciousness then they were in. But yet, allowing themselves to be dominated by these situations and conditions—never stopping to realize that God, the creator of all that is, gave you dominion over it in the way of not dominating your brothers or your sisters, but in taking dominion over your own life. Setting your world back in the joy and the pleasure of being free, and enjoying, and loving, and filled with peace, and especially, filled with love for mankind under any given condition, yet not allowing yourself to look down at your fellowman because your fellowman is not, let us say, accepting what you are accepting, or thinking that person is evil, or not going to reach the higher ground because they do not believe as you believe.

The thing is, that each and every one of you as individuals, yet one in the divine order of life—you cannot in anyway, no matter what background you are following—you can deny it, but you will never, ever amount to any condition of balance until you are receptive to the knowledge that I am one in all of my Father's universe.

Take that which you call time, to question. This is what we are teaching, what we are asking of you. The master Jesus constantly asked of you to question the spirit. The master Jesus when he asked you to question the spirit, many of you looked at him—at that time you saw a man that wasn't bound by books that were telling him how to live. There was no bible at that time excepting one in the part of the world, in Israel. All his years, even as a child, he didn't go into the temples except once.

But, when he was in India he studied with the masters there for a time, then he left there and went into Tibet, studied there for a time. Then, he finally went down the mountainside into China, studied there for a time. And at the time that he reached the age of thirty, he all of a sudden, became aware now—he hadn't entered any temples, all he did was sit in groups such as you are doing right here tonight, excepting that they didn't sit on chairs, they sat on pillows down on the floor or sometimes it was in a cave. They would sit in this cave, on the ground, on pillows, and a master would give forth a lesson. There was never anything that was pious, holy in any way. It was just as God asked of man to be—happy, peaceful, loving, creative, and abundant in the self—never entertaining conditions of bitterness, or hatred, or fears, or doubts, or selfish motives and greed.

This was the main thing that we as masters attempted to ask of you, to question yourselves, if you were being selfish, greedy, fearful, doubtful, bitter or hateful, in any way—to let go of these things, replace them with love, inner peace, and creative abundance within the conscious understanding, moving into the consciousness of knowing that I can talk to my Father and my Father hears me. I can ask my Father, if I am not aware, or how to cope with a certain situation, I can turn to my Father and just say, "Father, look here I am. I know, Father, you have given me a whole universe to enjoy and to be peaceful, and loving, and to sing, and dance in. Whatever is necessary for me to do, as long as I don't hurt myself or my fellowman.

But right now, Father, I'm just a little bit confused. I am only asking, Father, not that you do it for me, but just show me the light Father, so that I can look into that consciousness, Father, so that I can see what I should be doing and how I should be able to cope with this condition or situation that I am facing, Father. I have asked you and I know you have heard me, therefore, I know that the answer is forthcoming." I am going to say right now, "Father, thank you, thank you."

Then, you go about your business doing that which you feel is necessary and knowing that what I am doing is something that is of value to me and of value to my fellowman. But, every time you do something you've got to be conscious that what I am doing has value. But, it has to have value that is loving, a way that is peaceful, a way that is not destructive for me— then I know I've got something now. As long as I know it is constructive to my well being, and then it has to be when I share it in like manner.

So, I simplify my world and this is the way we were taught, and eventually the day came that the Elder Brother just knew that death had no hold over him. That is when he decided to come back to the western world, but he was not very well received. They wanted proof that he was never going to die. That's the way the master said, "They wanted proof that I was never going to die." So the only way that they could get it was to decide to destroy him physically. So, that's what they did, and so he came back and showed them they hadn't destroyed him at all. When they laid him in that cave there, he put the wounds back together, but he did maintain a few of the outer wounds to show them that he was right then in his own temple.

They couldn't destroy him, but the temples didn't want it that way. No, they wanted to tell you he went to the cross willingly to rid you of your sins. He went to the cross for your sins, which, of course, doesn't make a bit of sense. It doesn't come together, at all, if one stops to think about it, that here is a man that is going to rid you of your sins— and why are you yet doing all the things that you are doing, and yet destroying yourselves?

Until we, of the mastery, delved deeply enough into ourselves to discover the past, then we took the cross out of our lives. By this, I mean I took those negations out of my life, the cross is the sum total of negations, death. Then you say, "Well, then Jesus was a negative person because he went through death." I say, no, definitely he was not, but he purposely did this—no one did it to him. You say, "Well, it was the Jews who did it to him." The Jews didn't do it to him. If anyone did it to him, at all, it was the Romans, not the Jews that put him on the cross. It was the Romans that put him on the cross, but they didn't do it *to* him. He wanted to show you and I, and all of mankind, that death was a condition that need not be. That we were not created in that sort of a thing. And he wanted to show you and I that we can rise above that. So, he, knowing that he had mastered life, he knew that death could have no hold over him. So he let himself be put on the cross and came back to show man.

In the histories—you know the histories are many as to who saw Jesus when he came out of the cave; out of the cave. They put him in a cave. It wasn't a tomb. It was a cave. Then it's said, when he came and presented himself to where his mother was and the few others, that they didn't know him. This is not true, and not only that, but, there were over five-hundred there that saw him when he came out of the cave. Then, there was said that he disappeared or went up into—well he didn't do no such a thing. Jesus walked with man for a long time after he had come out of that cave. And, he did an awful lot of writing, and he left a great deal of history of reality but they buried that. They would not let that be given to man.

Then, you have the story, again, today that's being told time and time again that Jesus is coming and he will be coming for the second time, and so on. You know, to me, I can't understand why man would let himself be led so thoroughly in a rut of thought such as that, because Jesus never has left the earth. He presents himself almost daily to people, like we do. We walk together often—it is very seldom upon this plane of expression that I go any length of time without seeing the Elder Brother. We call him Jesus. Five foot ten, well established man, doesn't look like the pictures you have. You made him look like he was—I don't know just how to express it, but you try to make him look like he was something out of an etheric force of light or something, that he had to reduce himself to present himself, and this is not true, that he was one of these persons that held his eyes skyward—that was going into a faint of some kind. This man was all man, and is all man, and hasn't gone anywhere. So how can he come back when he hasn't left?

You write histories, and every one of your histories that you have written is either, to do like they did in the dear, dead days, that are so far dead—or to wait for something to take place. And what are you doing? You are only the cause—you—each one of you that are living in that or existing in that frame of mind are the cause that are going to be the effects of, again, the downfall of your empires—and you're not far from it. And, unless there is a great change in the actions and the thoughts of man, you're going to go right down the same gutter as you did in the past. And there will only be the few that refused to go down there in that gutter, which will remain upon this plane of expression.

So where are the warring conditions coming from? The various religious backgrounds—you never saw a war yet that wasn't considered what you call a Religious War. God never established anything such as this. So, all of these things—if man stops to realize he is going to become free. He is going to let himself be a free, loving, creative, abundant, moral being, bound by nothing. Not even God has even attempted to bind you. When He gave you a universe—and He gave it to you freely and He said, "Here it is, take dominion over it." He didn't say, "Now look, I've given you dominion over this universe and I want you to do this. I want you to do that. I want you to belong to this. I want you to establish this and that and the other thing." He didn't say a thing. He wanted you to enjoy His creation. The only way that you're going to ever attempt to do this now, is to, first of all, know that I am that which is the child of the universe—I am God's child. I could not even begin to move or have my being were it not for the energy and the power of God flowing in and through every fiber, cell, bone and tissue, every atom of my temple. Now, knowing this, I fill my heart with love. I become at peace with myself. I am ready to forgive anything and all things that I've ever held in my life. I am ready to make myself completely what I am supposed to be—a free, loving, abundant, universal being.

The master said this to you, and he also, never ever said for you to pray to him. He never at anytime said, "Only through me would you ever get to the Father." Again, that doesn't even make sense. Why? What happened to all of those before he came? How could they have ever got to the Father? They didn't have him to go through. How could they ever get anywhere? You have got to take time to realize that the master Jesus was a teacher of how to *live* and a *way of life* is all he was attempting to give you, how to rise above the last enemy called death. Yet, you do not want to accept it. Because there are so few—look at the billions of souls on your earth today, look at how few reach the mastery. It's a sad thing because you're not being taught how to be free.

Even in the temples, every so often, I hear some preacher or minister, a priest, a rabbi say, "Seek ye first the kingdom of God within and all things will be revealed unto you." It's a superficial voice that is talking, but yet, beloveds, it's true—if you did it. But they don't even know why they are saying it. Actually, most of them don't even know why they are saying those words "Seek ye first." That's what we've always asked of man; "Seek ye first the kingdom of God within." And you will find that no matter what you are seeking—everything, everything, that you will ever want, will want to know, will be revealed unto you. You will have dominion over your own world and you will bring this temple into its own. You will come to the wonderful day that you will know that death no longer has any hold over you. Once you have decided you have expressed all that you need to express in this physical plane of your third-dimensional world then you will just quicken this temple and give it back to its own—and be ready to move on.

They said Jesus was blaspheming against God, and yet first, usually, when he opened up his message to man—to his brothers and sisters each day was, "Seek ye first the kingdom of God within and all things shall be revealed unto you." But you see, when it got into the temples they said that Jesus said, "Seek ye first the kingdom of God and all things shall be *added*." How can anything be *added* to that which is finished?

Everything that was given out of the master's mouth was changed and put in the *Book* that you call the Holy Bible—and is as holy as the evil that you have set forth in your own selves and made a devil out of it. Certainly we know the truth is in there, but why do we want to live by that which is distorted? Why do *you* want to live by that distortion? That Bible has been rewritten—just that one Bible over three hundred times, that you're going by, rewritten over three hundred times since King James wrote it and set it into motion.

Like the one that was written called the International Bible—that was supposed to be written simpler for you to understand. It was written so that you can understand what they in the temples want you to do, so you can understand more fully how their wanting to brainwash you, to help you to destroy yourself, to help you realize, and to think warring conditions are good, that they are necessary in order to bring peace. Have you ever seen warring conditions bring peace? They're going back to the Old Testament

JESUS SPEAKS

vibration—well, they've been living by it for generation upon generation. The New Testament is seldom given as a lesson. Usually you will find that the minister, priest or rabbi that is reading out of the Bible is going back— always back to the Old Testament that has destroyed empire after empire and will destroy these empires of today.

Beloveds, I am only trying to bring to you *life*—this is my purpose, because God is my Father, your Father. God is one in you and there is no separation in God and you and I. There is no separation, whatsoever, in the divine essence of reality in this universe. The sooner we get to realizing this the sooner you're going to live, not exist—you're going to live.

So, in order to truly evolve one cannot limit the self to this your third-dimensional world, because if you do, you find yourself backsliding, every so often into that which are the conditions of a second-dimensional world, or those that are just evolving out of that second-dimensional world into your dimension. Sometimes these influences then—you are caught up with them if you let yourself function too densely in this third dimensional world. It is quite easy to function in the various dimensions, because you are moving towards a fourth-dimensional world and sometimes you are taking on part of that dimension—at least, an awareness of it to some degree. But, then you let yourself fall into, let us say, a second dimensional avenue of expression and you become lost, or you feel there is a vacuum created there.

So, it is well that you realize what this dimension that you are expressing in is, and begin to know it more fully by allowing yourself to reach into that higher consciousness. So the consciousness has got to be pretty much kept on a high level to really and truly sustain and maintain the balance that you are hopeful of attaining.

Now, we also find that in your third-dimensional world there are those that are in a higher consciousness and are on the border of the fourth-dimension. We find that sometimes they are very apt to be receptive to a fifth-dimensional expression, because that fourth-dimensional energy and power sometimes, also, is flowing and edging onto a fifth-dimensional consciousness. If one is consciously highly evolved and in this avenue of expression, then you are going to find that there are those, then, that are definitely expressing here in your third-dimensional world on a very, very, highly evolved consciousness.

You might ask, "Does a person—a soul, in this third-dimensional world that is in that consciousness, that fourth-dimensional consciousness,

112

to some degree, is that person always capable of functioning completely in that fourth-dimensional consciousness?" From what we see I would have to say to you—no, they don't continuously function in that manner.

Now, you take your Elder Brother Jesus when he was teaching here in the physical expression. He was, of course, conscious now that he was already in the fourth-dimensional consciousness. He was fully expressing in that consciousness, yet he had to deal with a third-dimensional world that sometimes even bordered onto a second-dimensional expression.

So, sometimes it was very difficult for him to maintain and sustain that fourth-dimensional expression. That is the reason why the master Jesus, oftentimes, as he felt himself almost ready to *join,* let us say, once again the third-dimensional consciousness. He would move out and go into what he called the garden, and he would then commune with himself, with his higher consciousness. He would commune there and sometimes he would reprimand himself rather stringently. Understand? He would give himself quite a talking to.

And, of course, his disciples, most of them, were barely functional in the third-dimensional world. They thought that he was talking to God and asking God for all kinds of things. He wasn't doing that, he knew better than that. He already had it all and so he wasn't asking God for that, to give him any certain expression. He was just taking out on himself—the talking in communion with the higher consciousness of, himself, which, of course, is the God-self. Because, after all, he was in that divine consciousness there, that was reaching into the Christ awareness within himself—so, definitely, he would talk to the Father, at times, and ask the Father to *show him* what was to be done here in order to maintain and sustain the balance. He wouldn't ask the Father to do it for him—he would just ask the Father to show him. So it was, he could go back now to teaching again and feel the consciousness now, of the energy and the strength that was necessary for him to maintain his physical, mental consciousness in a stable awareness, so that he wouldn't allow himself to, again, fall back into that third-dimensional consciousness. But, this took place quite often throughout the three years of his teachings in the Holy Land.

So you're going to experience these things. You're going to experience these fluctuations from one consciousness to the other. You're going to find yourself feeling as though you were in a vacuum, at times, or you are going to feel as though God had forsaken you. In this vacuum you feel as though you can't reach out far enough to reestablish in yourself, the consciousness that you had so beautifully found expression in. Now, suddenly you feel yourself in this vacuum returning to a denser awareness, sometimes falling back into a second-dimensional consciousness to some degree. So, it is well that you recognize these things, so that you don't let yourself fluctuate too much from one dimension to the next—other than going into a higher one but not going back into a lower vibration.

Now, going into the higher one, of course, you will fluctuate back and forth from your third-dimension to the borders sometimes of the fourth-dimensional world. But if you do, you are going to find that you feel beautiful and you feel abundant and you feel as though you have the world right in your hand. You have the whole world right there, it just is so beautiful. Man too often says, "Well, you can't maintain that." But we say, "Why can't you maintain it? You got there, why can't you stay there?" It is because you are thinking in that limited world of the third-dimensional consciousness. Subconsciously you are saying, "I've got to be in a third-dimensional consciousness in order to function in this third-dimensional world," and this is not true.

We, the masters, are here because we are not allowing ourselves to be controlled by the limited third-dimensional expression of life. We have moved beyond it and, therefore, we stayed beyond it. Yet in that consciousness, we can maintain and sustain ourselves to such a degree that *we can* take on the density of the physical body. But we take on that body that we have cleansed and we have purified. Therefore, we don't feel the density that you of the third-dimensional world feel in your temple. We don't feel grounded in other words. You see?

You are on the very same level as we are. You are on the very same level as Jesus. But, you see, again there's a consciousness that has been flowing in your world that says, "No, that Jesus is a being that is almost untouchable. That Jesus is the son and the only son of that which is the living God." So you have subconsciously accepted this also and sometimes you're functioning there as though you would be *sinning* if you accepted the consciousness within yourself. Jesus was and is no more than you. You see? Jesus is no more the son of God than *you* are. No more the daughter of the living God than *you* are. You see?

Your world has gone so completely over the edge, as it were, that Jesus is now the creator—Jesus did this and Jesus is that. You could not do anything without Jesus, and so on and so forth. You see, if man would only stop, but he can't, because he is not thinking any longer. He's letting everything else do the thinking for him. He is allowing himself and is just functioning like a zombie in the physical world, because he is not doing anything consciously on his own. You don't realize that that consciousness, that computer out there, in your physical world was created by you. And what you have put into it comes back to you, and you're accepting it on that level, and you're going nowhere.

Better to recognize "Look, I'm the computer. I am the one that feeds that animal there, that piece of equipment. I am the one that is the controlling factor of it, and what I put there I can change whenever it is necessary for me to change it—and I'll change it. I am not letting it become the control of my being. I am only putting in that which is necessary at the moment—with the recognition that I have no limitation.

Therefore, I can put greater abundant information in it as I move into my greater dimension and consciousness of awareness." You see? You then are doing what is necessary to maintain and sustain a world around and about you that is no longer held back by a dimensional consciousness that is limited. So, once one recognizes this within themselves then you have a much greater consciousness of awareness working with you, because you are no longer hampered by those thoughts that were once expressing limitation.

So, you're freer to move into that world of reality that is so beautifully necessary in order to reach that higher ground. That takes you fully—not on the fringes any longer of the fourth-dimensional world but steeped right into it, moving now towards a greater and a much more beautiful dimension because you have these dimensions in the Father's house—here are many dimensions, many. You have written it in your Bible as mansions—alright, what's the difference, dimensions? Your dimension is your mansion. The dimension of consciousness that you are in—that is where you are.

The birth of one of the greatest masters that knew this and wanted to share it with us, and did do so—let us realize right now that when he was sharing this he knew that each and every one of us had it right here and now within us. Because he knew when he said, "Heaven is here and now within us." So, he wanted us all to know what he knew and had gathered through his thirty-three years of expression.

Beloveds, let us know this, let us feel this, let us let God be the very motivation of every essence of our temple. Let God glow, so when we celebrate Christmas this year and celebrate the birth—not only of our Elder Brother, but the birth within us of knowing that we have opened the gates of eternal life. That we, now, are walking on the path that he set into motion for us. Not only the path that he set in motion for us and the great masters before him set in motion for us, but, we are going to go beyond that which he set into motion. Because he asked us to do so, and every one of the masters have asked us to do so.

So we're going to walk with the masters this coming year. Beloveds let us walk, all, with the great masters. The earth is filled with a great many of them now. There are a great number of masters—know this because this coming year let's each one of you speak to some of them. Don't look at the way they are dressed. Don't think that they have to be in flowing gowns filled with emeralds and pearls and so on. No. Beloveds, remember the master came to the door three times before they let him in. He came as one that was poor and ragged and they turned him away. Not until he came in the way of beautiful garb that they let him in.

Let you know this year that we're going to meet face to face. Let us realize that you, this year—I am no longer going to move and have my being with closed eyes. I'm going to see, because I'm going to raise my evolution, my vibration, into the light, where I can see the masters, speak to the masters—knowing that I spoke to them. Yes, beloveds you may have spoken to some before and I know you have. But you looked at them and you didn't believe because they looked so poorly. You didn't listen to the word. You looked at the surface.

Alright, beloveds, I am going to take my leave from the instrument and I'm thankful to the almighty universal Father expression, life energy and power, and balance that called upon me to come through this evening. Peace be with you, peace.

I am master Salamar.

CHAPTER 12

I Walked With Many of You

By Jesus

(Author's note: Although this lesson is incomplete, it's included since it does have value and, after all, it is from Jesus. At the beginning of this session the tape recorder malfunctioned for a few moments.)

. . . shall be the voice of the unseen and the voice of the light, the voice of all energy and power, the voice of that which has been finished and fulfilled. Therefore, in this expression you shall find your capabilities awakened to such a great degree that whatever is necessary for each and every one to fulfill, and to find physical or mental and or spiritual expression, shall be ready to fulfill these things, and to find great expression in them at the moment of need.

I walked with many of you, and I spoke to you on many occasions, both in the multitudes, as well as, hand to hand, due to the fact that many of you had been deeply indoctrinated in the expressions of the money changers. You were rather incompetent, for the simple reason that when you were with me you listened very carefully and your hopes would rise. Then, immediately you were discharged from my presence you would then re-enter into the temples, and again, you were as absorbed in that which was given, more so than when you were with me. For the simple reason that you had been held in that sort of suppression from the time of your early years until the time of your coming forth out of the temples to listen to that which I had to give.

Some of you were respectful of the gifts that I was sharing with you. There were those of you that showed very little respect and were very doubtful. So it was, that which I had revealed unto you was only as compensating as your receptivity, and of course, that wasn't very much. But, as I have always known there is nothing lost in the universe and through the incarnations that have followed, you have progressed to a much greater degree, and are more fully able to be receptive to those things that I am to share with you, to a greater degree.

But, be mindful that whatever you are doing, that first of all, I do that which I do foremost, not for the Father—for it is often said that one has to do what they do for God, for the Father. The Father needs nothing. The Father doesn't need one thing. For you have been told when you went into the money changers' temples that you were to give of the sweat of your brow and the earnings that you had, and the fatted calf, and so on, to the temples.

But you were not told to give it to the temples—you were giving it directly to God and so God had the greatest of everything. But nothing was returned to you excepting that you were told if you did it and lived in such and such a manner—which was constantly given to you under their way of suppression, that you would have a beautiful place in their little heaven of your creation, and theirs.

There were many disappointments, for they found not the little heaven, and you never did find them, but you did recognize that those teachings that I gave unto you were not lost. For then, you did use them in the world of the unseen in your true preparation that you could come forth again to the world known as the physical, to once again prepare yourselves, now, to more fully assimilate the teachings that were shared with you through those few years that we spent together.

But, of course, again as you returned again to the world of the physical, much of this, again, was buried into your subconscious world due to the fact that the parents . . .

(Author's note: The tape recorder malfunctioned here for a moment but very little was lost.)

. . . and that many times, each and every one of you right here present had walked in the very exact footsteps that I walked, right here in this your own country, or crossed the paths that I walked when I left the Holy Land as a young man and traveled the world, and to seek out my way, up towards reaching the mastery.

Remember, beloveds, it isn't difficult to master yourselves. It is only a matter of letting go of those things that you have found destructive in your personal lives. And when I say that you have found destructive, I mean those things, beloveds, that have little or no value to you or to your fellowman. Most of all, you must find that respect of your own self and if you will have that respect for the self, you will find that it becomes very simple to share that respect with your fellowman.

But, also, you are going to find that in this manner of expression, that you will always be aware that you will not ever attempt to share anything with anyone lest they seek you out, to share it with them. You will never foist upon them a condition of: "You must accept what I say." You will lay it there to them in a manner of either accept it or reject it. It is up to you. You have asked—I share. Now you use it in whatever way you feel the most value for yourself and your fellowman. If you don't accept anything at all, that is up to you, but you asked. I shared and I respect your wishes. I respect you because I know you too have been given the same will, the same free-will, the same capabilities and capacities that I have. And it is up to you to use those capacities in a manner that you will to use them. But if they are of no value to you, of course, they can only be rejected. If they are of value to you and your fellowman then they must be most receptive.

Now, then, there is much taking place in this your outer galaxy, beloveds, a great, great deal. And, again, I spoke to you of these things when I was on your earth in the days of my teachings, in the land across the sea. But you see, your histories are but repeating themselves and very few have done greater things than I. Yet I told you that was a promise of the Father and it remains so.

You are going to be contacted. You say, "I don't remember of you speaking these things." Certainly, some of you must have some idea or inkling within the subconscious of your being that I spoke to you of these things. But these things were never brought into the temple. You see? They were suppressed. Nothing was allowed in the temples, nor is yet, allowed in your temples of today, if it is not suppressive. And, so these teachings were burned, or taken from the libraries of Egypt. All of these teachings that all the great masters have taught you—I taught you, beloveds, as well.

You are going to find that you are going to be contacted by those in space, and in a very short period of that which you call time. You may be taken into space. You may be taken into the instrument that they reach your earth with, that only voluntarily will you go there, and when you do, if your temple is aware enough, you may be laid upon a special table. Now, what they will do will not be taking control of you or taking control of your mind, but, they will ask you if you want to have your awareness more thoroughly fulfilled. That is, they will not do for you the things that are going to be presenting themselves to you in your physical world. But, they will make you aware of what you can do to avoid certain things, and to partake of others, that you will be so thoroughly aware, that you will be able to immediately partake of those things that are of value.

Now, then, as you are going to be approached by these beings which you will find shall not look as you appear; they shall be much different in their physical expression. But, also, they shall have the wisdom and the capabilities of helping you to open up the gateway of awareness which will strike a note within your temple, that shall make your temple tingle from the bottom of your feet to the top of your head. For you see they shall touch to every cell in your temple in a new expression—of a condition of a magnetic force that they are aware of. Also, they will open up the facet of awareness within your temple that you shall no longer be encumbered by the magnetic forces that your earth is involved with, and that you will be able, at will then, to levitate your temple, if it is necessary to do so.

There were times when I spoke unto you, that I showed you that I could release within myself the density. I could release that density of my temple, and quicken it, and in the eyes of your being I no longer existed there. Then, I would move and release my temple again to express the density that could then make my temple appear unto you, or reappear. This is what they are going to give to you—that you are only going to be given the awareness of it. Then it is going to be up to you, now, to use the forces of mind that you have to make it work for you. And if you don't do it, then you will not be able to, let us say, move about in the way that you would want to move about, under certain conditions that are going to be manifested in those days when the age is, and the fulfillment is in expression.

I taught you these things, beloveds, I taught you these things, but that is, I expressed them in every facet that they were going to take place in your earth. But, you see what took place, rather than you accepting these things, you returned to the temples. There were very few that accepted that which I shared with you. All of you returned to the temples and found yourselves in dogma and doctrine, and not in any of the realizations of what you could be, had you accepted those teachings and followed through.

(Author's Note: The taping of this session suddenly ends here due to a malfunction of the recorder.)

[By Jesus]

CHAPTER 13

Your Brother Jesus Said, "Greater Things Than I."

By Follower of Jesus

Peace. Peace. Peace. Beloveds, once again it is our pleasure, whenever we are called upon through the forces of life to greet to you, and hopefully to share with you those things that are valid; of course, as I was standing by and taking part in that which was being said—because you are truly free moral beings if you will to be that. Of course, have you asked yourself that question, "Am I a free moral being? Or am I bound by, not only the past within the expression of life since I have reincarnated in this the physical world, but am I yet bound by the dogmas and the doctrines of the past?"

And I would say to you, the dogmas and the doctrines of the past are no different than the dogmas and the doctrines of the present day, even though you may have had and entertained through many incarnations—the only ones that have ever reached the mastery of life are those that did and dared to move by themselves. That is, you cannot ever walk alone, no one walks alone. But yet, do I have to be supported by some dogma or doctrine that I am forced to support? If I am bound by these things, then there is no possibility of reaching that higher ground. There is no possibility of reaching the mastery of life, as long as I am limited. I cannot move beyond the dimension that I have elevated myself to. Of course, you are in that which is the third-dimension and you have come forth since the creation—you have reached out of the first-dimension. You have reached out of the second-dimension. You are in the third-dimension and are seemingly through many incarnations, in complete repetition of that which is your own limitation.

You cannot blame it unto the religious orders of your earth. You cannot blame this unto them. Your brother Jesus didn't blame it unto them, but what he did was to move into the freedom of his creation. He recognized that God is the very center of my being. The Father, the creator is the very center of the being of every man, woman, and child.

Therefore, then, in order that I move and have my being in accordance to the freewill that my Father gave me, and to recognize that in that freewill I was not suppressed in any manner, I was not limited in anyway; the Father didn't even tell me, in creation, that I was to die. You see? Death is and was and shall always be—I'm talking about the physical death because there is no spiritual death—the result of my own inconsistencies. Whether you want to call it sin, or whatever you want to call it, death can only result through repetitious conditions of imbalance—of being bitter against myself, hateful against my fellowman, fearful, doubtful, whatever—dishonest with myself, dishonest with my fellowman.

If you will read the first book of your Bible, and eliminate completely out of your mind, the story of Adam and Eve; take it out of there—it doesn't belong there, that again is for those that are not thinking. That is, again, created by those that were and are yet the leaders in your temples of the various religions of your world. But, now, delve into what man really is—and it's all there in the Bible, if you will use what God gave you.

You will find, then, the reason why we have spoken to you of the two worlds that are existing. The world of the Father's creation, which you and I, and all man were created in—that world that we were created in was the world that we recognized that we were established in the very image and in the very likeness of the Father—which, of course, God has neither shape nor form. God is the essence of all pure mind of all that is peaceful, loving and creative.

Then, the second world, the second creation was my creation when I decided to accept what man has said, "Fall from God," fall out of His expression of love, which was never true. Man didn't do this because he was bitter against God. Man invaded the physical temple or that which is the hu-man temple—the hu-temple which became human afterwards. God created only man. Now, man is known as human, and it's right in your first book of your Bible. It's all in there telling you of the second creation when you took this hu-body, and from there you became a living soul, and also it calls you a co-creator in the Father.

But who, out of your thousands of ministers throughout your world are going to tell you about this? Yet, the Bible is free for every man, woman and child to pick up. But if man would stop to think, he wouldn't even need that Bible, would he? If he would just stop to think that my Father created me in His image and in His likeness. The only place I can see God—in all things with love, and peaceful energy, and power. I can now look beyond that which is the density of my own creation, and see the reality of life, and feel the beauty of living.

As I breathe, I feel I breathe life. As I use my hands I am doing what I am doing with love, with peace, with all the power of God and His divine energy. So, I am reestablishing. I am doing just a little bit to reestablish the garden of life upon the earth, I am taking away the densities that through my selfishness and greed, doubts and fears, through the many incarnations. I am now cleaning it out, and I'm setting forth the power and energy of life, now.

So man, then, needs to listen to the reality within the self, because you're not going to hear it outside of you, excepting on a very limited vibration. But, when you enter within and you talk to the God of creation, the Father eternal that is within you—and let go of these false Gods that you have established; all of these gods that you have set forth in your world, that you say I can't get along without these gods, they are all a part of me, they have tentacles, they are binding me, holding me in their grip, and so in their grip I slowly but surely am deteriorating. I become eaten up as it were. My temple becomes controlled by the conditions that I am accepting blindly, because it has been told to me by all of these that are supposed to be so great and supposed to be so intelligent. But, remember, there is not a one of them that has used his own intelligence. He has listened to the ones that have spoken and accepted it blindly and then he passes it on to you.

I say to you accept nothing, I say to you don't accept what I am telling you until you look into yourself. You're not going to find it outside of yourself. You're going to have to find it in the balancing within your own being. You have God. This is your temple. This is where God is living, if you will allow God to live here. But if you will continue to put all these conditions of negation inside of you, how can God be alive in you?

No wonder you find those around you and about you trying to establish different Gods because they no longer seem to be able to contact what they think is the real God. So, they build-up all of these false contacts and reach out there until they get so ill that they can't even pray. They can't even talk to God anymore, they get so ill. They say, "Pray for me, I'm too ill to talk to God." How many times have you heard this? Who did it to you? You did it to yourselves.

Beloveds, I went through many incarnations, but yet, I wouldn't have had to if I would have used the teachings of the great masters. If I would have listened to them—because when they spoke they didn't try to indoctrinate me into anything. They did not attempt, at any time, to say they were completely and thoroughly right, because every one of them, including your brother Jesus said, "Greater things than I." What was Jesus saying? He was saying, "Look, don't be afraid to move into your universe, it is yours." Simplify. As long as you are honest with yourself and your fellowman, move and have your being. Do I have to be bound by something? Man is not happy until someone has got the thumb on him. He is not happy unless he feels he is bound somewhere. I say to you, beloveds, make your world simple. How often have we spoken this through this instrument?

So, commune with your God, and get acquainted with your God, because this is where the answer is. When I can commune with my God, I'm going to get answers. There are those—and we hear this every day, that say, "I talk to God and I never get any answers. I don't know, God seems to be so far away, I don't seem to be able to reach Him." So what is the thinking? They think God is out there and so they are reaching out. They can't see Him, but He's somewhere on that cloud or something out there, or maybe He built a special little mound out there where He can sit on. They don't stop to realize, that right here and now is the answer to life, right here and now within this temple that you have invaded, that has made you a co-creator in the divine presence of God. The moment you took it you became a living soul.

So now, then, it is up to you, because you did it on your own, God didn't force you to do it. God didn't say, "Take and invade this temple." He said nothing at all about this. He said it was yours, "Here's my creation, take dominion over it." He gave you complete dominion over it. He gave you your freewill to take dominion over it and you didn't even do that. I didn't, you didn't, none of us did that have invaded.

I am not saying that all of the souls that God created—all of those identities in God; no, there are those celestial beings that never did leave the Father and are in dominion of the conditions of the universe, not dominating you or I, but they are in dominion of that within their province and they are ready. As we turn within unto the Father to establish ourselves, to really ask the Father, "Look, you show me the reality of life." There will be that time that you shall reach so thoroughly into the Father that you'll hardly even have the time to ask, "Show me Father," that it will already be shown to you. You will see it in a vision. You will see it in a picture within your mind's eye, immediately. If you want an answer, it is here and now.

Heaven is here and now. God is here and now. Yet, no, I've got to go to Jesus, I've got to go to Saint Michael, I've got to go to Saint Thomas, I've got to go to the countless gods that I have established on my own. You have made Jesus the son of God. Jesus is never anymore the son of God than you are. Jesus is not anymore the son of God than all of the great masters prior to him were the sons of God. You are all the sons of God and he told you so. Jesus told you so, time and time again, and why do you try to leave this out?

You reach out to him singing songs of praise. Why don't you sing songs of praise to God, your creator if you're going to praise anyone? Jesus didn't ask you for these things, and neither did God ask you for praise. All He asked you is to use His gifts, to use them for the good of yourself and your fellowman, and you will not even accept that.

You have talked about Jesus, and you have said that he stood with a multitude, five thousand that he spoke to. Have you ever stopped to think that if he would have had five thousand out there that he was trying to talk to, the first one hundred or two would have heard him, the rest of them wouldn't have heard a thing. All of these things were exaggerations, and you have put them in the *Book* as absolute truths.

If there were five thousand out there that were listening to your brother, and I'm going to tell you it wasn't so, because I was there my own self, because I was a follower of Jesus and I was very close to him, as a brother, and so I know what took place. Those that were there, most of them—and

I'm not saying this lightly, most of them that were there were there to heckle him. They were not there to accept anything. They were coming out because they were sent out by the priests, and the rabbis, and by the army to be there to make noise, to disturb the peace, and so on, and so forth. Why can't man be honest with himself when he writes something? Because he wants to suppress his brother man. He wants to keep his brother man under suppression.

Beloveds, I ask of each one of you, be never under suppression. Your God is as great—because there's only one divine essence in the universe, and there is no one who can tell you better than your God within yourself. If you will learn to talk to this God, and know that when I talk to my Father, He hears me. He knows my needs and He'll show me. And recognize, when I speak to my Father I am not asking my Father to do a thing for me. He's already done it all, and He's handed it all to me, but I just haven't got a clear enough mind to recognize and to see it where it is of value to me and my fellowman. So, Father show me, so that I can move in and I'll do it.

So you're not speaking empty words. You're not crying to a god out there that can't hear you. You're not asking for something out of the Father, because the Father has already given it all—so all I'm asking is to be shown. I've also got to be wise enough to be thankful for whatever I get, or when I see an answer. But, also, why shouldn't I be thankful that I have enough mind left in me that I can enter within myself and speak to my Father? I am thankful, Father, for that beautiful mind that you have given me, and the mind of the universe that you have let me enter into—to speak and to come closer into you.

Let us begin to live, because this is life my beautiful children and He gave it to us. The greatest of gifts is life, but also understanding how to use that energy and power to benefit. How thankful am I for the greatness of my capability of energy and power to be of service unto my brother man as well as unto myself—because if I am being of service unto my brother man, I cannot be other than of service unto myself.

Now, there are those of you that say, "Well, yeah, but I'm doing this and I haven't got time for all of these sorts of things." Well, if you haven't got time, when are you going to get it? Every one of you are moving into various beauties of expression. Some of you are remotely aware of it, some of you are very much aware of it, and some of you will not even see it if it were to come right here and face you. You probably wouldn't even see it because of your density. It's time that you ask yourselves where am I in the expression of God's divine evolution? Where am I on this ladder of life?

When you enter here, beloveds, and talk to this divine energy and power of God within you, this is when you are going to begin to feel reality. You're going to begin to enjoy what you are doing and everything that you do. You're going to awaken in the morning with "Thank you, Father, for the beauty of a new day. Thank you, Father, because I know that today is a better day than yesterday and yesterday was beautiful." You're not going to say it and wonder if it's going to be better. You're not going to wonder at all, because you're going to know, because that is the evolution of the divine essence of the universe. That is the cycle of life, that cycle that knows God.

When I move into that cycle, I am thankful because I know my yesterday—I made that yesterday the day of days, it is terrific. Everything I did, I did with love. Everything I moved into I moved into with love. Everything that was there was filled with love, energy, and power, and peace, and quiet. Those other things were still there, but they didn't interfere. I didn't have time to let them interfere. I was too joyful in my being of service.

So I awaken this morning, "Oh, Father thank you for the light. I thank you, Father, for the blessings of the night. I thank you for the rest and the food. I thank you Father for the rest and the care because, Father, all of these things have established my world and made it something really beautiful." I look at this world and I find that this world—there is no place for anything but energy and power of peace, energy and power that is health in every facet. There is no imbalance now in that vibration. There is nothing but good. You see *good* means *God* and when I say there is nothing but good, I say there is nothing but God!

If there is something else that I am looking at in my physical world, and I say, "Wait a minute, that isn't God because it's all out of balance." No, I won't say it isn't God, but I will recognize it as what I have established or it wouldn't be in my eyes—the imbalances that I have established. So, now, I am cleansing them out as I move into the greater and greater vibrations of love, and peace, and thankfulness to all of life. The understanding within myself that my world is an unlimited world, and that I can actually know and realize within me that there are never going to be any needs in my life, because I'm walking in that balance. So how can there be anything ever needed? Whatever my needs are, I know that if I am not quite aware of how to bring them about, "Father, you show me. Show me and I'll do what is necessary in order to bring it about. Right now, I'm a little thick on it. I'm not quite aware—show me."

You will find that you will be able to move into any direction you will—no longer saying to yourself, "I can't do this, I'm not able to do that," because every time that you will be saying this—and you have said it thousands of times; I know, I said it millions of times in my past incarnations, "I can't." So, what was I doing? I was telling God He couldn't do these things. It was there, it needed to be done, and so to—to get out of it, all I did was say, "I can't." So, what was I doing? I was postponing my duty of balancing out my negations. So, I was waiting around now, not giving any thought to it. Pretty soon it came back in another cycle, now, with greater force than it did before, and I am in greater density than I was before—so, again I am denying my God. But I can clean it all up by saying, "Father, show me. You show me. I don't understand it. I know that I've caused it somewhere and all of the causations, maybe many, many, many small causations, little bitterness's, little hatreds, little doubts, little things that say, 'I can't.'"

Whenever I talk about the "I," what am I talking about? I am talking about the great I AM expression that is within my temple. I am denying that I AM power. I am denying the very life that is there, and so I am causing myself, slowly but surely, to enter into density that creates age, illness, doubt, fears, all of these illusions. They are all illusions, because they are not real. They are my creation. They are the second world. Are you going to live in that world, or are you going to clean it out and live in the world the Father gave you and I? You can do it, right here and now in this creation, and in this rebirth, just by letting go and reestablishing, and knowing no limitations in the Father.

You will find that whenever any of these conditions arise in your life it will be simple for you to move right in it, through it. Each time you move through it, any one of these, you will find that your sense of direction is keener. Your awareness moves into something more beautiful. Every one of you has that capability. Every man, woman and child—I don't care who they are upon this earth, this third-dimensional planet that is moving into the fourth-dimension. There will only be a few of you that will accept this and yet every one of you has that capability.

But you're going to let the animal in you, destroy you. You're not going to lift that animal out of its density, which it wants. It wants to be reestablished in the divine creation. Some of your animals if they could speak today they would tell you that many of man are lower in their vibrations than they are. Your temples are accepting everything that is lower and changing everything within their temples, but what is the difference? It wasn't valid to start out with. It was built on selfish hypocrisy. The whole thing is built right from the start on selfish hypocrisy.

So, if you will study your histories of your world, you can go back—actually, if some of you would go into the jungles of South Africa, into the Transvaal, you would find that there are those that know the history of the world that goes back twelve to fourteen thousand years. They will tell you what has happened in each one of the—and it's nothing but repetitious destruction; every two thousand five hundred years through those fourteen thousand years have been nothing but absolute destruction, and they are supposed to be primitive people. Nowhere on your earth is there truer history then in the Transvaal of South Africa. You could find five thousand years of history in Egypt, that's only a part of it. Go into that part of the world and you're going to get the absolute truths that have not been distorted because there was no reason for distortion there.

And right today, you are practically in the same condition that you were at the time of Jesus. When Jesus said, "Your empires are falling" and they did fall, and you're right now on the edge of it. There will be new religions again. Why? Because every time there has been the destruction—and slowly but surely, they rise once again and pretty soon someone wants the power. So, they establish something that says, "We'll do it this way." What do they say? Who do they say said it? God said this to them. God said to do it this way. God said to do it that way. So, man has said when something is wrong with me, "Well, I guess it's God's will." They think God has willed everything to them that is not valid. They say it is God's will. What kind of god and what kind of gods are you entertaining?

If you want to live, every opportunity is yours, but don't wait for your brother to live. The thing is you have to function in your own vibration. You have to build your own expression in God. You have to mount the stairway to evolution in your own beautiful way.

When I came through this last incarnation I refused to accept anything else but one God. This God never let me down, and I had more fun and enjoyed life more than any of you have, even at the best in this your present incarnation; I enjoyed life more fully, had more fun, did more things and expressed more fully and had more pleasure—laughed and sang and danced and did everything that was good. And, believe me, one day I found I was filled with light.

Although, some of my brothers and sisters didn't like what they saw—you know some people don't like the light because they don't like themselves. Some people don't like pleasure and joy in somebody else. I say, live and let live, but don't do anything to hurt yourself or your fellowman.

God is filled with laughter if you will let Him laugh with you. But if you don't want to, that's up to you. God experiences your experiences, because He gave you the freewill to experience it. If you are going to give God pleasure accept His gifts of joy and peace. Accept His gifts of love and understanding. It's when you're not accepting God's gifts—that's when God is not having pleasure. How is He going to be happy in seeing you destroy yourselves? He didn't create destruction, He created Life. He wants to see you live, and so if you are destroying yourself that is not giving God pleasure.

Let's, now, enter into the quiet. Let's go home with a clear, clean temple tonight. If it's only the first time we ever let our temple be cleaned, let us clean it tonight. Let us take out every facet of anything that binds us in anyway. For a change, let us let God smile upon us. Let us feel God's power and energy. You know when we say power and energy we are not speaking of the power that can destroy. God is not a power of destruction. God is a power that moves and has its being in us that creates, that says, "Oh, I'm so filled with love. I want everyone in the whole universe to have a part of it." That's the real power of God, that doesn't just permeate you for the moment. So, let us enjoy seeing every fiber, cell, bone and tissue, every atom of our temple purified, cleansed and moving into reality.

(Author's note: Meditation for nine minutes)

Now, I've got a few more words I'd like to say to you and then I'm going to take my leave here. But, remember what mastery means—mastery is doing what your Revelations has spoken of, "Rising above the last enemy called death." Now, the last enemy that man on this planet earth, this dimension—it wasn't in the second-dimension because you hadn't come up to that awareness. This third-dimensional planet is a planet of rising above death permanently; permanently, where death no longer has any part or parcel of your being, and you're returning to the elements that which you have invaded. You see? I am going to leave this with you and may God bless you.

[Follower of Jesus]

CHAPTER 14

Jesus Taught You and I These Things

By Kuthumi

Peace. Peace. Dearly beloveds, it is my pleasure to be called upon, that I might enter in and take hold of the instrument and greet to you. As each of you know and, I feel, understand as you may have, let us say, looked into the changes in your physical world—that the changes that are taking place—that sometimes you don't really fully realize what is behind the condition that is moving, and the reason for it or even the causation. But nevertheless, we understand, and I'm sure you know that all changes that are taking place are the results of causations, not just from the present day, but by causations that have been, let us say, set into motion through many, many generations of life. Of course, these changes do have to reach a certain peak, as it were, before the full results of these conditions manifest as a complete change, or as a complete renewal of the physical.

Of course, man has to realize, also, that he has built the tower, and we call it the Tower of Babel. Your Bible speaks of that, but they have given you so many reasons for these things, such as, they were going to build this tower to heaven and, of course, when they were going to reach into heaven with this tower,

God didn't want that, and so He changed their languages and everyone could not understand one another. So, they had to stop building it, which of course, doesn't make any sense at all, but yet, man believes it. Because you know that you can understand one another regardless of whether you can speak the other person's language. There's a way of making one's self understood. Then, besides that, where is heaven that they were going to build that tower into? You see?

So, this is not the thing. Man was building a world of self-destruction through his selfishness, his greeds, his fears, his doubts, and so on. This is the tower that man is building and has continuously done throughout the generations of life.

Therefore, every so often, there are those that build the towers in their own personal life that falls upon them. That which they have established and created in their own life has its repercussions. This is what they call the Tower of Babel falling on you; for your indiscretions, and being too indiscreet with everything that you do. So, you have the repercussions from these things.

Of course, there is that which ends out as the destruction of your empires, which is the great Towers of Babel that are being built, which eventually are going to fall upon mankind, as a whole. Those that are in the midst of this, and have established it, and have given it power, and built it on its weak legs, then are going to find that it will destroy them, and that's what we call the Tower of Babel.

There are answers for everything in the Bible, and there are answers that do make sense and balance. Understand? They tried to teach man those things that don't come together, at all, and leave man dangling somewhere where he is at a loss as to his purpose. So man doesn't know today—you could talk to millions of people, millions of your brothers and sisters, and very few actually know the reason they are expressing in this third-dimensional world and what the purpose is, even though they may have listened to the priests, the rabbis and all the various religious orders; not only the Christian but the pre-Christian religions, and they still don't know what it is that they are to fulfill. You see? They have no idea. So it is a sad thing, because eventually, that tower is going to fall, and it's going to destroy those that have not attempted to really understand their purpose in life, and the reason for their coming forth into that world that they call the physical—and what they are to do in this world of the physical.

The pre-Christian leaders—that is those that the pre-Christian religions were founded upon, not upon God, but upon these so-called sons of

God as they did with your brother Jesus. They have founded the greatest of churches on your physical earth, not on God but on the son of God, that is, supposedly the son of God, because they made him that once he was removed from the physical picture.

So they built upon this expression, and they don't really give man the true essence of what the teachings were that this man Jesus was teaching, or those who were put as leaders, or as the founders of the church of the pre-Christian religions who were teaching exactly the same expression as your Elder Brother Jesus, was about *this* third-dimensional world. They were not teaching the second-dimension or the first-dimensional world, they were teaching you what you had to rise above in order to fulfill the Law in this your third-dimensional world. So, that law is clearly told to you, and you know this if you have even read the Revelations.

Yet what have the priests, ministers, the rabbis in the temples taught you about this? When they read, "Rise above the last enemy called death—man is to rise above the last enemy called death." Here, they teach you about that place, in the sky, that you are supposedly building on by going into these temples. They're actually telling you to build your Tower of Babel again, to reach that place called "Heaven," somewhere out there that you can't see and don't know the results from reaching out there, instead of doing what the brother Jesus had told you, to find it here. Enter within, and see, and know yourself.

The greatest thing that the man Jesus asked of you was to know yourself. If you know you and if you love you—you know the self. Now, when we say, "Love the self," we are not saying for you to create of yourself, or set yourself up as a special god, or anything such as this. No. We ask of you to know yourself, to find yourself capable of doing for yourself those things that will have value for keeping and maintaining, and sustaining that, which is the church. Because this is where your brother Jesus built the church—he said, "Upon this rock I build my church," Peter the rock. You see? Upon the rock, not upon his life, but upon each one of our own personal lives, to maintain and sustain the temple, in order that I keep this temple in perfect order, then I have the perfect expression of the Father expressing in and through this temple. You see?

So, what this man was trying to give you and I, is how to function properly and simply in this world. To make my world a place that is not difficult to live in, and especially, one that I will not contribute one iota of

God's divine energy to anything that is destructive. If I see a condition that is of no value I am not going to speak of it in a derogatory way. That is, I'm not going to give it power. I am not going to add to it. I am not going to condemn it. I may speak of it, but not in condemnation, only speaking of it as a realization and understanding that it has no value.

Let us say, like Jesus spoke of those in the temple. He didn't speak with bitterness and hatred at those in the temple. He only spoke of these conditions that man would see what was being handed to them that was of no value and would destroy them, physically, in the physical world. So, he had to mention it, but not ever with any hatreds or bitterness. So, this is where man has got to become capable of doing these things, and keeping out of adding to it, or becoming a part of it.

You have followed that which says, "I am born to self-destruction." I am born to self destruction and so you have continuously built your little towers and lived in them until they toppled. And, you went into dust or the earth, and you were told that that's the way it's supposed to be. Even as you say, "I don't believe that this is the reason I am here for." But you're haunted with that same expression, and you let that expression continuously haunt you. You are afraid to let go of something that is destructive.

Why is it that man takes a grip on something and he holds tenaciously to it, and destroys himself with it, rather than letting it go and finding himself in harmony with the energy and powers of the universe, where he feels no longer the suppressions, he feels no longer the fears and the doubts that were once there? He no longer feels the conditions of selfishness or bitterness or hatreds. These things are no longer a part of your vibration.

I was listening to you talk before this session about saving your little god, the almighty dollar. And I said, "Now, what are they talking about that for?" The best way to save that "god"—when all they need to do is know, within themselves, is that, I'll never be in need. That's all you have to know. I'll always know how and what to do. No matter what takes place in that density of destruction, that man is bound to have it fall on him, it is there.

It is going to fall. There is no doubt, because you are putting all of these pressures and energies into it, and so it's going to destroy itself. It's going to destroy those so intimately involved in it. But those that know, no matter what takes place—it doesn't make any difference. I'll be alive, happy, functioning in the perfection of my Father. I'm going to move and have my being only there, and so I'm taking no part in these densities.

Certainly, you're going to use those little gods like the almighty dollar, but they are not going to be gods to you. You see? Use all of these things, but use them because they are a part of the gifts of the Father to man. They are gifts that are yours to use, but, not to worship and fear that there's no other way out of, or action to take, if this were to be out of your hands, that you know that you have the divine essence of the universe. You have that energy and power, and you will find that immediately, you will know what to do and how to do it. The door of awareness will open so clearly that you will just move into it, because it will be utter simplicity and it will take no forceful action of any kind. You just step right into the picture of reestablishing and renewing your world. It will be that simple. Do you want to believe it or don't you?

We know holiness and piousness was—just like the master Jesus looking at those in the temples, he says, "You're hypocrites." He didn't say it bitterly to them. He knew that they knew, that they were not teaching a way of life. Therefore, he told them, and let them know that he knew, that they knew—and so he called them hypocrites. He called them the money changers. They are still right in every one of your temples. I can't say everyone, because I know there are a few of them that are not money changers. But, these are so few and so scattered in your world that there are only small groups that gather, but at least they are not hypocrites. They are not money changers.

So, beloveds, we attempt to work in this way and we are happy to have that wonderful privilege. We thank the Father daily for that wonderful privilege to be able to come to our brothers and sisters in this your third-dimensional illusion to be able to, at least, hopefully help you to help yourselves. Because, until you know yourself, you're not going anywhere but down into hell—for that "grave" is "hell." That's where hell is, the grave.

So, too, beloveds, if you look through the eyes of reality, you're going to find that heaven is now. It's no place else but now. You can experience it right here in that temple that you are letting slowly but surely die, but you can change it. You can change it. You can make that temple what you will because you took it.

Then, you've experienced temple after temple, after temple, after temple, after temple, from one incarnation to the next. Beloveds, you have been through every religious order on your earth and all it's ever done for you is six feet in the ground. That's what it's done for you. Isn't it time that you should recognize the fact that God didn't establish these little kinds of dogmas and doctrines that prevent you from thinking for yourself and keep you living in fear? Those that stand there in the pulpit and tell you, "God is love" and then on the next turn say, "Fear God." How can you love God and fear God at the same time? How can you think a God that gave you an entire universe, that you should be afraid or fearful of this beautiful, loving, creative, abundant source of eternity? Words cannot express the joy and the pleasure, beloveds, of those of us who have reached the mastery knowing that nothing is beyond our reach.

Certainly, we don't attempt to draw all that is in the Father's universe to us. No. We only know that when it is needed it's there and we'll accept when it is in our cycles of moving in and through the various energy powers of life in the entirety of the beauty of God's universe. Something is needed—it's now. We know that there is no need to struggle, or fight, or fear, or doubt. None of it, do we ever accept the thought of holding onto it, and being afraid and fearful that someone else is going to come and take it away from us. We use it and when we are through, we release it, because we know that no matter what, there is no shortage of anything in God's creation. No shortage. But, in yours, oh yes. Certainly you created money, and if you don't have money you don't have food. If you don't have money, you don't have a roof over your head. If you don't have this and you don't have that, you're going to starve to death.

I am going to say to you, again, you must release yourself from these doubts, and fears, and bitterness, and hatreds that are establishments of your limited world and caused by your dogmas and doctrines. Once you release those things, you're going to find a complete renewal of your way of thinking. You're going to find, now, that you are able to see clearly what is necessary for you to do.

Therefore, you will find that all of your needs have always been taken care of, because they have always been right here and now in the universe. The only reason that you think they are not is because of your limitations and fears and doubts that you are looking, "I've got to have—oh, I want this. I want that." And most of the time what you are wanting, or thinking you need, is because you are selfish and greedy. Actually, you don't even need it, but you want it, because my neighbor has it, and I want to keep up with Mr. Jones. So, in doing that, keeping up with Mr. Jones, I get myself in debt, and I get myself in a turmoil and a frenzy. So, I am slowly but surely destroying myself, because I am wanting everything that I look at, and see, and don't need. But I want it—don't need it, but I want it. So, beloveds, once you get in the world of conscious reality—it's wonderful because you are free now.

Now, beloveds that man Jesus was a great teacher, and he should be given every ounce of credit for his wonderful capability of showing man how to *live*. He never at one time ever taught man to die. But, he taught you how to live, and there wasn't a greater teacher—well, Mohammed was, yes, a great teacher, and so too was Buddha.

> Participants: "Now that we're talking about Jesus, can I ask a question? In the last, I think, two to three years before he reached the mastery another master teacher said he was close with someone."

Well, he was close to everyone, actually. There wasn't anyone that the master Jesus didn't love, even those that spat on him, he loved.

> Participants: "Right, but I was told that two or three years before he reached the mastery he was very close to a woman. Was it Mary Magdalene and was he married to her?"

This is not for me—no, Jesus was not married. They seem to think that Jesus was one that was a sanctified being. Well, he was a man, and a beautiful soul, and one that did nothing to hurt himself or his fellowman. But that didn't stop him from having a woman close to him, because he wasn't hurting that woman, nor was he hurting anyone else. There were those that looked at him and thought that he was doing things that were evil, in the temples. The money changers looked at him and thought he was evil, because he had a very close woman—not only to one woman, there were several of them in his life. When he was in India he had a very close female there. That didn't stop him from reaching the mastery. He was teaching you how to be free, and yet, without hurting yourself or your fellowman.

That man was a beautiful soul. Yet you hear in your temples that this man was a holier than thou pious hypocrite, himself. That man was a man that loved to tell stories. He loved to laugh, and he loved to do everything that was of value to himself and his fellowman. He was never one to be confined to this holier than thou hypocrisy. A great man, wonderful, I knew him very well. I remember sitting in circles with him in the evening. And you know sometimes he told so many jokes to us that the evening went by without even a lesson being taught. But yet, there was a lesson, the lesson of being able to laugh, and to love, and to express peace, and a joy—a fruitful evening that we would spend, a few of us in the group.

Yet, there were those that were closest to him, or supposedly according to the Bible that didn't learn a thing. It's sad, and yet, your Bible is supposed to be written by them. It's sad to think of these things. Every one of them died a very miserable death. Did you know that? Beheaded and all. John was the only one that mastered.

> Participants: "That was John the Beloved, not John the Baptist, right?"

Yes.

> Participants: "John the Baptist was beheaded, right?"

This, again, beloveds, is definitely not true.

Who was the only one that was not Jewish of the disciples? Luke. He was the only one that wasn't Jewish. But, of course, that doesn't mean anything.

You know what? You go back—the first bible came out in 1611. That was a long time after Jesus, and you know man will stand there in the pulpit and say every word in there is absolute truth, right directly from God.

But, what I was going to say here was, if you go back just two or three hundred years and take your Bible of that time, and then take your Bible of today and compare the two and it's going to be quite different. But you see, they have to keep up with the times you know.

> Participants: "Was that first bible in the Greek language?"

No, in Aramaic, then Latin, also, then Greek and each time it was translated in a different language, they—well, they didn't lose anything, because it wasn't there anyway. But, it is said that they lost something—that is, they lost the meaning that was in the previous book. Understand?

So now, beloveds, we are hopeful of the conditions of levitation. We are going to work with this. The reason for this levitation is because there will eventually be a need for it. Along with levitation we are hopeful of, also, through the one mind communication, also to bring about your capability of quickening the self. Because through this manner of communication you are automatically quickening yourself, you're quickening your temple of awareness. You're opening up the avenues of life within your temple.

Believe me, you're going to also find that in this communication you are also communicating very strongly and creatively with your own self, and generating perfect health and harmony in your temple. You are going to find that, in a period of time, you're going to be able to command your temple to shaping-up the way you want it to. In other words you are going to be able to rebuild your temple without having to go through a mother again. Understand? You will be able to regenerate it, renew it and at the same time I'd like to have my temple built in such and such a way, so I am renewing it, changing it a little bit. You see? You're going to find that these things are absolutely simple.

Jesus taught you and I these things, and before I entered into the vibrations of the mastery I was doing many of these things. I was able to do all of the things that your brother Jesus did. Like walk on the water, which, of course, was not walking actually on the water. I was levitating. Understand? Going over the water, that's all Jesus did, he levitated. The same thing that he did when he went to the cross. He didn't die. You see? All he did was lift his spirit out, like you have heard of those that move out of that body while the doctors and nurses are working on them down here. Why did they move out of that body? Because, there was so much pain in it that they just moved out of it, but they didn't cut the cord. They didn't die because they were not wanting to die. All they wanted to do was to get out of that painful body, so they moved out here and that's all Jesus did.

He stayed that way until they moved him into the cave, and then, at the same time as he hovered over his body, he also—not only to stop the pain of all of the stab wounds, and so on, and so forth, but also to stop the flow of blood that was coming out of his temple. He also started a healing process. You see? He wasn't a stupid man, you know. He was very capable.

Then, of course, they thought he was dead, and he wanted them to think that. So they took him down, they put him in the cave, and therefore, then, he used his healing powers to quicken that body, and to renew it, and so on. Then, through the mind he rolled that stone. Those angels didn't do it for him. All he had to do was just use his mind. He knew what he was doing. That's why he was teaching simplicity, he wasn't trying to create magic things that were beyond your capability of thinking out. You see? But man was so indoctrinated in the temples that they made a bloody mess out of it, out of Jesus going to the cross. He didn't even have to go. All he did it for was to Fulfill the Law." He had fulfilled it, and he went into this to Fulfill the Law.

Of course, when Judas went to him—Judas didn't betray Jesus we know that. You know it. I'm sure. Because the soldiers knew all the time where Jesus was, everyone knew where Jesus was all the time. So no one had to betray Jesus. But Judas ran away right after they left the upper room because he was afraid. Judas was Jesus' cousin, and he ran away to join the forces of the Romans. Then, he felt sorry about it, and so when the Romans came after Jesus, Judas walked out and went over to Jesus, and all he did was whisper in Jesus' ear, "I am sorry, please forgive me," turned around and walked back again to the Romans. He was not able to forgive himself for having done what he did, and so he went and hung himself.

So there it is—it's simple. Jesus didn't do anything to baffle man. Everything this man did was utter simplicity. You are going to do those things and more, and they shall also be done completely with utter simplicity, because when you do it—God created this universe with thought.

So you see, beloveds, the very simplicity of living was what our Elder Brother was bringing to you and I. But he brought it to you so simple, so clear, that it was confusing. Because you have been taught in the temples—not only in the many past incarnations, but ever since so called religion has been a part of the physical world.

You have been taught the hard way, the difficult way. You have been taught that there was nothing gained in your world unless you suffered. No heavenly expression could be of any value until you suffered. Until you earned everything that you earned with the very sweat of your brow. All of these things were not true because it was given to you by the money changers that were in the temples that wanted to keep you under suppression. And so far they have been very successful.

So remember, beloveds, you have one divine and eternal God, and this God divine creator created each and every one of us in His image and in His likeness. He gave us all that there is—to see us through anything that we ever will need in this divine galaxy. So then I question, who am I? If I thoroughly question who am I, then I must come to the conclusion that I am a son of God. I am to come to the conclusion that I must believe then what my Elder Brother Jesus told me, for he said, "I am one in you, you are one in me. I am one in the Father, the Father is one in me." Alright then, where is the logic that I should have to turn to my brother Jesus and say that he is the only begotten son of God?

I find that I would be belittling my brother by bringing this in, for my brother earned everything that he mastered. My brother became a master, not born one. He went through all of this that you, that I—no matter whether we have mastered or whether we haven't, have the same opportunity to reach the highest expression in the universe.

It's time that you recognize that I am created in Gods image and likeness—and then if I begin to see what I am, I am going to have a little bit more consideration for the church of God. For this is the only one there is, this which you call your physical body is the only temple that God can express in and through. Remind yourselves of this quite often that you might have a little bit more respect for yourself, and you might have a little more respect for your brother. You might have a little bit more love for one another and through it all, what happens? My temple becomes more perfect and healthy, and I haven't had to crawl on my hands and knees. I haven't had to walk into the temples and cry to false gods.

Also, I can turn within and know that upon this rock I build my church. You see, this is what your Elder Brother Jesus, as he put his hand upon the brow of Peter, "Upon this rock, upon mankind, upon *all* man, that I build my temple." He was not speaking of himself building the temple—he was speaking of the Father, now. For he said, "I am one in the Father, the Father is one in me. Upon this rock I build my church." I, you, each one of us then, let's all be the true church.

Let us not be bound by all hypocrisy, by conditions of indoctrination and dogmas that are destructive and destroying all mankind, and creating confusion between all the various religions of the world—to the extent that they now then expand into warring conditions. Why are they expanding into warring conditions? Because the greatest churches—there are seven of them that own all that there is on your earth, actually. As far as anything that is physically capable of being owned, they own it all. I don't care whether it's your automobile factories, your ammunition factories, your nuclear factories, your aircraft factories, they have the biggest percentage of the stocks, and so they are in control.

So they can command you to your religious world in confusion, and then stand through the selfishness and the greed's to have you commit yourselves to warring destruction. Then you stand a Protestant here, a Catholic here, a Baptist here, and holier than thou in their hypocrisy. Pass the ammunition to destroy my other brother over there. So they say, "Praise the Lord and pass the ammunition," all for what? The prophesy is being fulfilled again because we dare not to live. We dare not to know that I am the temple of God.

My God in me is a free, loving, beautiful God that loves all mankind. I have no illusions of destroying my fellowman. I have no illusions of anything but love. I have no illusions other than to know I am at peace with myself and all mankind. Listen each one of you, listen to that divine God within and you're going to walk tall. You're going to walk in perfect health. You're not to have half a God—you're going to have a God that *did give you life*, that God that gave it to you and will continue to fulfill you in every facet of expression, and help you polish every facet upon that diamond of eternal life—let you live, that you live in it.

Remember, the prophesies of old have been fulfilled all too many times. They have been fulfilled with great destruction to your earth, to the great empires upon your earth. Let's you no longer live by those prophesies. Let's you live by what Jesus said, "Live by life." And, if there are those that still want to live by the age old prophesies that have been given by the prophets of old, and they still want to live by that, then they must die by that. So let them, if they wish, if that is their will. Let them do so, but do you have to join them?

If you will know the teachings of Jesus and the teachings that Jesus taught through the Father—and as all of those of us that have mastered life have taught—for it is very simple by just uniting yourself with your divine inner self, your God-self. Simplify your own world, and filling it with peace from within the self, with love that can expand throughout the entire

144

universe. Simplify your world and you will find that it's beautiful. You will find that you will experience every wealth that there is. First, by knowing eternal life, unlimited health, and unlimited expansion of awareness, that can fulfill you in anything and everything that you will ever need.

Well, beloveds, it has been wonderful and I am thankful to the Father for the wonderful privilege it is for me to come and spend a wonderful time with you. I'm thankful, also, for this wonderful instrument who has been a wonderful standby for those of us who have come through him. So, I am going to say thank you and God bless each and every one of you. Stand tall wherever you walk, take no backseat, stand tall, and be counted in Gods universe.

Peace be with you.

I am one known as master Kuthumi.

(Author's note: Below is an excerpt from another lesson pertaining to Jesus and Judas just after the Last Supper.)

(13-916)

"Then you say that Judas betrayed Jesus. And it is written that Judas betrayed Jesus and he never did any such a thing. You say that Judas came up to Jesus and planted a kiss upon his cheek. He never planted a kiss upon Jesus' cheek. When Judas, Jesus and the Apostles—the other eleven Apostles met in the upper room, which they call the Last Supper, just before Jesus went to meet the soldiers that were coming and when the supper was over and Jesus and the Apostles sang a few songs that they knew, and then he said, "I must go now for they come to the gate." And he went to the Gates of Galilee and Judas, in fear, ran away and joined the Roman soldiers.

You see, beloveds, the Roman soldiers knew where Jesus was all the time. They didn't have to have Judas try to point him out. They knew they had him there. They held court and they had everything. They knew where the man was at all times. Why did they have to have a man called Judas to go and point Jesus out? You see how man doesn't stop to think?

You see how you accept everything without giving thought? And there it is written, and they laugh at you. Those in the high places of your religious world are laughing at you. They say, "How stupid can you be?" You don't stop to think. They knew where he was at every moment.

So, then, why did Judas walk over to Jesus? It wasn't because he was going there to betray him. It was because he had run away and was ashamed of himself, and was sorry for having turned his back upon his cousin, because they were cousins, and so he went over to Jesus and whispered in his ear and said, "I am sorry." Turned around—he wasn't so sorry that he didn't turn right around and go back with the Roman soldiers.

But it preyed upon his mind and he asked forgiveness of Jesus, "I am sorry, please forgive me." Then turned around—but he couldn't forgive himself, and it preyed upon his mind, so then he went and committed suicide. That is the simplicity of the story. (Orion)

CHAPTER 15

The Pyramids and False Gods

By Jesus

Peace. Peace. Peace. My dearly beloveds, once again it is my pleasure, having been called upon through the energy powers of the universe, that I might come forth through this instrument, and share with you some of the experiences that may be of value to you, that I had at the time of the building of the pyramids.

I know that there are many of you that wonder as to how those pyramids were built, and they were not built in just one way, but there was much power in the hearts of man in that day. They knew the powers of the universal God because they were living the *life*. They were living in a manner that was of love, of peace, of sharing, and of receiving. Therefore, in the building of the pyramids they were able to transport tons and tons of rock over many of the mountains and deserts; that they could place these rocks then, in their perfect cut, in the building of the great pyramids.

But, this was not all that there was to this, for these pyramids had a purpose. They had actually many purposes. They were not built as tombs for the kings and queens of that day. They were built in a manner to be of service, to regenerate, to renew, and to preserve—to renew the temple, to preserve the temple, also, for the preservation of various foods that they had in that day that needed special attention—that is, could not be put in there in a manner that it could become dried out, but, that it should retain its perfect expression as it was, either taken out of the ground or from the trees or from whatever it came from—from the animals, and so on.

But, then there came the day—before I go beyond this, I would like to say to you, that you do not yet know all about your pyramids, because even those hieroglyphs that are in those pyramids have been lost, that is lost to the mind of man. They are yet there. They are as clearly defined as they were when they were put there, but man does not understand; for he lost the meaning of that which he had identified himself with at that time. The reason for these things was because they *became* involved in false gods. They took, now, the god of man, rather than the God of their identity.

Therefore, it caused a great deal of disturbance in that part of the world in that day. For you see, your pyramids were lost to man for hundreds of years due to the blowing of the sands and burying the pyramids deep, deep into the sands, and they were not discovered for centuries.

But, let us take a look at those pyramids, and let us know that under the Great Pyramid there is another pyramid. Now this other pyramid is in reverse. You see, that one is setting in this way, the other one is directly underneath it. This is to be uncovered one day when it is time for it to be done, and you are going to find many answers to many, many of the problems that you are facing on this your earth today.

Many of you were unhappy, and especially those in the countries of the Mediterranean were very unhappy when they built that large dam called the Aswan Dam, because of the fact that they were burying many, many relics. I call them the false gods that caused the destruction in that part of your world. Not the statues themselves caused it—of course not, but, they were the false gods that were created, and put up there for man to worship rather than to knowing the God within the self. Therefore, it caused a great deal of conflict and confusion. There were many, many, that were buried in the sands when the winds covered those pyramids, for in their density they listened not to the inner voice that spoke to them.

There were only but a few of us that left that part of the world. Some of them went into the Holy Land. Others went into the country of Tangiers and Morocco. That is where I went. That is where my family was, at that time.

They went because we were given that awareness that these things were going to take place and we did not run away. No, we took our time for we knew that we had been given a notice that we must leave that part of the world, and we left. You may ask why, was it then, that I didn't master life at that time; because I was too fully indoctrinated with the religions of that day, yet, not so fully dogmatic that I couldn't listen to and hear what God had to say.

How many of you are going to listen to God, for he speaks to you each day? Or are you going to live by your false gods? How many of you dare say unto yourselves "I am one in my Father. My Father is one in me?" How many of you are living and enjoying living? Or are you saying to yourself, "Well, I've lived long enough and I'm tired of life. I'll be glad to get on the other side." Have you not realized that there are those of you that are speaking those words, and are saying, "I am tired of life and I'll be happy when I get to the other side," that might come back again to this earth in a lesser vibration than you are today, in a lesser awareness than you have today, just because you are denying the Father?

When you are seeking the physical death, or hell, which is the grave, you are seeking the conditions that are opposite to that which the Father created you to do. Your Father gave you life, and you are living by the dogmas of the past. You are living in the exact dogmas that were created during the time of those pyramids. You are living in the dogma that came out of the temples of *my* day. You are living by the *Book,* and in living by the *Book* you are denying yourself the joy and the pleasure of communion with your God *within* you. You are denying yourself the pleasure, the glory, and the beauty of the Father within you, because you are looking out there, and out there are the false gods. You have to have a god in the flesh. You cannot have a God that created you. You choose not to abide by the Father, the God that gave you eternal life.

Beloveds, even in the day of the pyramids, we lived many, many years. I lived almost one hundred and seventy-five years. You should be able to do a great deal more than that because you're always talking of your progress, your scientific progress. Where is it? Your medical progress and you barely can reach seventy years, and even at that time you would have probably been asking for death—for ten years prior to it, denying the very God that gave you life. I didn't teach you that. I taught you only, that in communication with the Father could there be eternal life. I spoke unto you and said often that you would seek the Father from within, that you could then, share His love in your every action, word, and deed.

Anyone that is seeking death is selfish and greedy, did you know that? It's selfishness. Why is it selfishness? Because you find yourself without purpose, you have no purpose. I cannot do this. I am not able to do that. You are telling your God within you that He is old and worn out. You are telling your God that He is *dead* within you. Did I teach you this? No, I didn't. But you see, I didn't teach by the *Book*. If I had taught you by the *Book* I would have taught you that. But you see, never did I carry a book, nor should any of you carry a book, because you are denying yourself the beauty of reaching within and greeting to your God.

If you would awaken each day and seek, first, the Father within, knowing that you walk this day in His eternal light, and this day is the most powerful, most beautiful, most creative day of your life. I walk not alone, for I walk with Thee. You will find that day, with more purpose to it than you have ever known, at any time, in your life. You will find that your temple will respond to any power of healing that you can give to it.

But you don't want to accept these things. Why is it that I spent my time, and the great masters before me, and since—and those that are greeting to masters such as this instrument, that greets and gives himself over—that we might come forth and share these things with you? You might say, "Well, we have never seen him with a book." He doesn't need it, does he? That's because he works and he talks with the master's everyday; he talks to us; not that he comes at any time, to seek us out. You see, that is the one reason why we greet to him; is because he talks to God, and he talks to God almost constantly in his work, whatever he is doing. He loves to be doing, because he can be in communion constantly with the Father. There is no separation. He hears the beauty of His voice. The voice of eternity. The voice that has no beginning. The voice that never ends.

That voice, if you will hear it—listen to it from within the self, you will find you need nothing else. You will find your temple will respond to your every need, and you won't be saying to yourself, "Oh, I'm too tired. I can't do this. I'm too tired." You see, when you are in communion with God you are never tired. You are never without energy and power. You always had that energy and that power. It never is released from you. The only way it can be released from you is by denying God, by denying the Father. By closing the door to the Father, "I am tired. I am worn out. I hate this. I dislike this." Then, of course, you are closing the door to those beautiful energies, to the greater powers, to the greater love of the Father.

So, the response is the condition of tiredness, illness, lack of energy and so on.

This is what took place at the time of the building of the great pyramids. When they prevented God and became caught up with the false Gods of their creation, they lost all of their powers. They were no longer capable of doing the work that they had been doing, and they lost the meaning to life completely.

Beloveds, how many incarnations do you want to go through? Or do you want to stay and *fulfill* while you are in this present temple? Then, if you are looking forward to this, then you will not deny your God. You will not be going by the *Book*. You will be going by the inner self—that self that God created you with. You see the *Book* came in the beginning from that inner self. Then, with selfishness and greed it became distorted with that which was the outer self.

But if you will turn within the self, you will never get a distorted picture of life. You will find life is joyful, it's happy, and it's filled with eternal energy and power. That you could stand before the multitudes, as I stood before them, and said, "I am one in my Father, and my Father is one in me." Until you stand before your Father and know you are one in the Father and the Father is one in you, you shall never attain mastery.

For it isn't just going into the death of the physical temple that is the part that I am concerned about—the part that I am, most, concerned about is that when you let yourself go into the death of the physical temple, it's possible that you may come back with lesser awareness that you have now. That you may come back and make many choices that will be of no value to you. You see, you can fall back as well as progress.

But believe me, beloveds, in God you always progress. In the Father there are no limitations for he gave you no limitations. He didn't create you to look upon your fellowman and see something that takes place—and you look at that and you say, "It's a miracle." No, beloveds, He created no miracles. He gave each and everyone of you the same awareness. But who is the one that uses it? Until you use that awareness, until you become acquainted with your God within you, my beloved children, you shall never know the greater dimensions of life, and believe me they are wonderful.

For once you enter into this greater dimension, you are yet always capable of communication with the physical. But yet, you can go into other dimensions of expression, and you can communicate and help many, many, and the beautiful part of it is that there is no lack in any manner. You are in this last dimension that there is lack, and the only lack that there is in this dimension is you. Not God, but you. When you recognize this God you will never recognize lack of any kind.

This is your school, the greatest of your schools of learning. This is the garden through which you must rediscover your God and the garden of life, it is here and now. Until you rediscover it, you shall be going back and forth and saying, "I'm tired of living, I'll be happy to get on the other side," and when you get on the other side you'll do the same thing as you have done here. You'll say, "I guess I better get back into a physical body, so that I can reach something of a greater nature."

But, until you recognize your oneness in the Father—that spark of eternal life within yourself, that spark that is the Christ life within you, that is the Christ God creator, almighty, within you, and, until you expand and become Christed within yourself, in your awareness, you shall be going back and forth from the grave to the physical, from the physical to the grave.

My dearly beloveds, listen closely when your God speaks constantly to you. And, His love never changes. His power and his energy is always beautiful and is constant. It is absolutely constant. I would love to look at each one of you here, present tonight, and go walking through the days that are ahead with each one of you. And I wonder how often I would hear you say, "I am so tired. I hate this. I wish I was doing something else," rather than looking at what you are doing with pleasure and joy, and saying, "Father, how thankful I am that thou art with me here, with all of Thy energy and Thy power, that I could do this which I am doing." I can do it with love and with peace in my heart. I can do it without wearing myself out by saying, "I am tired," by closing the door upon the Father.

I am going to follow some of you in these days that are ahead. I am going to be close to you because there's a great deal that's going to take place here on this your earth. And those of you that are tired won't have to be tired long. That those of you that will recognize the Christ light within yourselves, that God within, that divine energy of God within you, will stand, where thousands fall. I told that over two thousand years ago to those that I spoke to in the Holy Land. They believed me not. Let go of your false Gods and begin to speak to the God of life. Your God. My God. Our God, the one and only creator of this universe. Peace be with you.

I am your brother Jesus.

CHAPTER 16

The Gifts of Life That Are Yours for the Asking

By Garth

Peace. Peace. Peace. Dearly beloveds, once again it is my pleasure, having been called upon to come forth and greet to you this evening.

Of course, we understand there is a great deal of confusion in your physical world, and we understand that the confusion is because man has failed himself. It isn't because God has failed you, nor is it because the forces of light are further away from you. It is only because man himself has denied himself the privilege of the gifts of life that are yours for the asking. If you will only realize and recognize it and accept these gifts, but then again, you must recognize how these gifts must be asked for. That is, they are yours.

But, why do you want them? What are you going to use these gifts for? Are they for the good of yourself. Are they for the good of your fellowman? What is the reason? There has to be a solid reason for the acceptance of the gift. Because, if it is not a solid reason, if it is of no value, then if the gift is yours, it becomes something that can be rather self-destructive rather than something constructive.

But tonight, rather than delving on this let us first cleanse the temple. Then, let us—and if you will let me, delve on various things, hopefully, bringing into your personal world that assurance that you don't have to hunt for God, that you will not find God by reaching out here, but you will know that God is the very essence of your being. He is the very thought of the essence of your being. He is as close as your hands and your feet. He is as close as your very breath and were it not so, you would not function. When I say to you, beloveds, that heaven is here and now, you might not believe me, but I'm only having to tell you the truth that *heaven is here and now*. You see? But, you have to accept that heaven or else it isn't. It's only to the degree of your acceptance of the here and now, is what you are going to find of value to you. And if you are not accepting any of it, then, you are going to find yourself rather in confusion and out of balance.

So, tonight, let us accept the beautiful energies and powers that are ours to accept. Let us let the energy and the power of God, let us feel the prana of life enter within our temple—feel this beautiful prana, and the manna of life entering within our temple. Let us feel ourselves being purified, cleansed—not holier than thou hypocrisy. I am talking about a cleansing, a wholesome cleansing in the temple—living, enjoying what God gave you. He gave you and I—He gave us that privilege as long as what we are enjoying is without hurting me, without hurting my fellowman, without distorting my world around me, it's wonderful. You see?

Let's feel that energy and that power. Let's empty, also, some of these conditions accumulated within that are of no value to us. Let us cleanse them out of our minds, our subconscious world. We don't need it. What we need is something that has value, that I can use, that I can unlock the door of the very real me. That I can see within, that me, the I AM expression of life. Now, I'm beginning to live. So, let us realize this and let us follow through.

(Author's note: Meditation for eight minutes)

There was a good deal of energy and power, and the very beautiful vibrations and colors. I am sure that there was a good deal of healing vibration here, because the lavender and purple and blue were there and also quite a good deal of powder like—just like flaky gold and silver penetrating all through the whole room here. It was just absolutely beautiful.

Now, let us take three nice deep breaths. Because I notice that when you entered into the meditation I see this energy and power flowing in and through each one—and man seems to breathe more in the lower part, the woman a little higher in the breast part, but not clear up into the top of the lungs here, due to the fact that you're drawing in this energy and power, and sometimes there's a little bit of a blockage here, and we like to clear it out. So, let take three nice deep breaths and now we know that it's clear.

Alright, thank you.

Now, I would like to touch on various things here. Because of the fact that we have touched to many things here in the past, yet everything that we have touched to; we have attempted in every way to clarify these things and to simplify your world, to make you realize that your world doesn't need to be other than utter simplicity. So, we would like you to recognize this, and attempt in everything that you do to recognize there is always that simple way. The very simple way is your direction out of the Father.

And, of course, if one will really recognize that I don't go to any god other than the Father. I'll go to the same God that my Elder Brother Jesus went to. Understand? He said for me to go—enter within, seek ye first the kingdom of God within and all things shall be revealed. So, he was telling you and I to do that.

Of course, this is not so in the varied temples. They say, "No. You can't go to God. You have to go through Jesus." But Jesus said, "Seek ye first the kingdom of God." You see? Jesus went nowhere else except to the Father and this was his example to us, to follow him. But, he didn't say, "You have to go through me." But, they put it down so they could draw you to the side. Because, you see, without confusion they felt that their temples would suffer. I mean, after all, God is broke. So when you go to the temples they say, "Let's give as much as you can to God." You see? But Jesus didn't ask you to give anything, did he? So, make your world a simple world. Do unto others as you would have them do unto you. You see? Establish the basics of life, and when you've got these basics you're going to find that everything else, as you go along must be added. It cannot help but be added, because this is the natural law.

Now, you have been told in various temples that you must go through Jesus. Others have said, through other churches upon the physical plane of expression, "Jesus went to hell" and, of course, after going to hell "he arose," and so on. This is true, in a sense, because "hell" means "grave" and so when he was taken off the cross they put him in the cave which they call "hell." You see? I am going to try to bring this to you. Let's see, he descended into hell, and the third day he rose again from the dead, and ascended into heaven, and sitteth at the right hand of God, the Father almighty. Then they say about him, "Now, he is sitting at the right hand of God, and from there he going to come back, and he is going to pass judgment on you." You see?

Now, all of his teachings he never, ever said he was ever going to pass judgment on you. He asked you and I never to pass judgment, didn't he? He said, "Do not pass judgment on anyone, lest you be judged." Now they have put in there and said he was going to come back now and judge you and I. This has absolutely no value because he has asked you and I—and his teachings throughout was of love and never passing judgment on anyone, lest you be judged. So, he is not going to judge you. You are your judge. He also said, "You are your own judge, you have been given freewill to express in your world." So, whatever you do through your freewill, you're passing a judgment over the self. If it's something beautiful, worthwhile, you have judged yourself for something of greater value of awareness and expression in your physical earth.

Now, then, of course it tells you in the Bible, if your hand gives you trouble, spite it, you'll take it off. You know man would be in one worse condition than he is today, wouldn't he? If he was to take off his hands and his feet and, well, pretty soon he would have to take his head off. Because through his head comes most all of the conditions of negation that had caused, let's say, these conditions in the hands and the feet within the temple. So what does this mean then? It was not written that way, originally, but I'm going to tell you what it means. It means that if I've been doing things with my hands that I shouldn't be doing, that are causing pain for myself or others, change that whole situation. Change it that this will no longer be painful. You see?

But because man has taken so many things in the Bible literally, it has created great confusions and wars. Because you can't heal anything by destruction. You can only heal it by changing the causation of that destruction. Whatever condition arises that is threatening your peace of mind—anything that is happening in your world that is threatening your well being, then must be *changed* by the individual to cleanse that condition. But, oftentimes, we do things in the physical expression of life, and rather than saying, "I'm sorry," I say, "Well, I'm just too proud for that." So, the aggravation continues, and it grows, unless the other person that has, let us say, been aggravated is of a peaceful, loving mind and might say, "I forgive you."

So, these are the things that are causations of imbalance and cause, often, little aches and pains. Conditions that can become very serious in time because after one adds many things to one's self, eventually, the temple cannot stand it any longer. The soul or the identity vibrations of God seem like their trying to move out. There's an imbalance there and you feel uncomfortable.

Now remember, beloveds, God gave you your freewill. So, let us go now to Lazarus and others that Jesus raised out of the grave. Why did Jesus raise Lazarus and others out of the grave? Why did Lazarus allow himself to be raised out of the grave? Because, Jesus couldn't have raised him other than Lazarus would have given him permission. Because, you see, he had his freewill. You have your freewill, no matter if you're on this side of life or on the other side—or wherever you are, because you had freewill ever before you entered the physical temple, because you had identity God. So give a little thought to this, because it means an awful lot.

So, Jesus when he raised Lazarus—even though his kin blamed him and were saying to Jesus, "Look, if you would have been here this would have never happened." But, it would have happened unless Lazarus would have agreed to perfect health again. But if he had turned about and said, "Oh, I don't want anymore of this, let me go," Jesus would have not interfered, even though he loved him too. But, he loved all mankind. So now, Jesus raised Lazarus and others from the dead, but they were raised and they gave permission to be raised. Now, let us leave this a little bit to the side here.

Now, let's take a look at what is taking place here in your physical world. If one has done many good turns and has been, at least, decent in their lives—though not knowing that death is an illness. Death cannot be other than a sickness. In other words, death cannot be anything but condi-tions of imbalance in your world. Accumulations, maybe little things, but remember you can put only a feather on a camels back—but you can pile enough of them that the camel will break his back and they're all feathers.

So, eventually through all your misgivings, your little hatreds, your little fears, your little doubts, unforgivness, you finally break the camels back and you enter into the spirit side of life, while never doing anything to really that hurt your fellowman to any great degree. The biggest hurts were you, to yourself. You see what I mean?

Then, let us go back to Lazarus now. He was said to be a very good man—that is his own people said it. I don't know what happened outside there, but his own people said he was good. Jesus was said to have loved him very dearly. But Jesus would have loved anyone no matter whether they were, let us say, deep sinners, or whether they were minor sinners. Jesus loved all mankind because he was looking beyond the physical being.

But why did Lazarus consent to be brought back? That is, why, if everyone is so happy on the other side? Why didn't he say, "Well, wait a minute, I don't want to come back to this rat race. No. I'm too well off over here." The evidence must be brought into balance here and the evidence speaks for itself. And, those that were lifted, they were not as comfortable there as they could be. So, they felt they better allow Jesus to take them back.

Another reason why I am bringing this to you is because Jesus said, "You are creators." He said, "Ye are Gods," and that everything that you do, you are creating something, whether it has value, or whether it hasn't. Alright, being that I am a creator, I am a God—then what am I creating? What is my reason for creating? Jesus spoke of these things, but, they were thrown away. They were discarded because those in the temples felt that if man knew all of these things the money changers wouldn't be living off the fat of the land. So, what am I creating? God has finished the creation. It is said in the Bible that the Father has finished the creation. It is all finished. It is done. It is very good, nothing to be added or taken away. So what am I or you to create? How can I be a creator to something that is finished? But you are not trying to create what God created. What you are trying to undo are the conditions that you have created, in your imbalances.

So, in undoing them you are creating. Or each step that you are taking, you are coming back into, and suddenly you become aware of God's creation. You step right into reality again because that which you are seeing is unreality. It is unreal. It is that which you have established. But then again one might say, "Well, that's difficult to do." But I want to say to you it is not difficult, because you can take a ball of string and you let it roll out, and then you find yourself with lots of knots in it—that is, it's tangled. But, yet, if you will take time to spread it out a little bit, you'll find that you can, down here, and take one string and get rid of a lot of the tangle, all over here. Can't you?

Well, that's the way life is beloveds. That you, in doing those things that are of value to me and to my fellowman, and now I am undoing these selfish, greedy conditions that I built-up around me; useless things that I have set into motion, I am suddenly finding myself more and more aware and awakened. The reason why I tell you this is because you may not notice—it may seemingly be a little slow in presenting a more beautiful balance expression around you.

But, I say to you, make your world as simple as you possibly can, and you're going to open every one of your chakras. They are going to flair out. They are going to light your temple. I am not saying this lightly to you. They are going to open that temple. They are going to lighten that temple, and believe me beloveds, you are going to begin to know things, to see things so clearly that seemed to be so difficult for you to see in the past, because you were struggling in the dark, but now suddenly things are becoming clearer to me. My world is a much simpler and happier and a more joyous place to express in.

Watch and see, not only that—I don't care what your ills are—I don't care what density is in your temple today. I am not speaking lightly to you now—I say to you, I don't care what is in your temple that is not in balance, if you will just step beautifully in that direction of simplifying your world and knowing that, in my God I walk today. In my God I recognize this today, and today all things must be of value to me and my fellowman. I'll guarantee you, at night, your going to feel something just a little bit more of an improvement in your world. You will have penetrated, and you will have pulled the right string that takes many of these little knots out of your personal life.

You'll find the reason why you feel better is because these little conditions that you have built-up throughout your temple—they may not be serious things at the time, they may be just little aches, a little stiffness here, a little muscle strain, a little this and that. But they're conditions of weakness that you have established in your temple or even brought a little of it back with you when you built your temple in your mothers womb. It doesn't make any difference—all of it can be cleared.

The God within you, in everyone; that God is not limited. That God is only limited to the degree that you are going to limit that God, that divine creator, that God that is the very essence of all things. Don't let any forces other than the divine energy forces of a God, unlimited, be the essence of your energy and power that can motivate you into the highest of vibrations in the universe.

Your brother Jesus has told you, I have told you, every master influence before Jesus told you. It makes no difference who that master was they all spoke the same language. Why did your brother Jesus walk out of the temples? Why would he have nothing more to do with them? Because they were taking these beautiful masters and doing the same thing with them as you are now, today, in your temples, with your money changers, to our Elder Brother Jesus. You are going to Jesus rather than to the Father, when he asked you to go to the Father. You are praying to Jesus. You are praying to Mary. You are praying to Joseph, to Saint Paul, Peter, anything and everything but God.

When all of us, everyone and Jesus—that brother that went further than any of us went—he didn't have to do what he did. Did he have to go to the cross? Of course he didn't have to go. He wasn't forced to and nobody forced him. They couldn't have taken him to the cross if he hadn't have wanted to. Why did he go there? Oh, sure you're saying he went there for my sins—to wash my sins away in his blood. Oh, no, don't you ever believe it. He didn't do that, he taught you and I, and all mankind—as the masters before him in the pre-Christian religions taught the same thing, exactly. Look, stand up for God and with God you live, otherwise you die.

So, they wouldn't believe him, even his disciples when he stood there with them, and they were right at his side. When the magistrate threatened him right then and there, and he said, "Look, you can destroy this temple, but I will have brought it back, *within* three days." This is the reason why he let them—to show them there is no death and to show you and I and all of us that we don't have to go through that hell hole of death. You see? Because "hell" means the "grave," that's the meaning of the word hell—grave.

We don't have to go into that condition, because, if we will cleanse and keep cleansing and purifying this temple, and enjoying and doing the proper things in life, I say to you we'll cleanse this whole thing. And where is heaven? We will find it here and now. You see? Your Bible tells you this and yet you don't want to buy it. Why?

So beloveds make your world a place of joy and happiness. These are the things I want to share with you, because I want to see you going on into the greater things right here on our doorstep.

Oh yes, we would like to have the whole gamut of all mankind—but we know that Jesus couldn't do it, and he did everything that he possibly could. He entered into the temples and they were denser in there; many of the priests, ministers and rabbis were much denser in the temples than the average man on the street and it's right this way today. Actually, it seems a little denser today now than it was then.

It is not a pleasant thing—and the reason why we speak to you this way is that when you see and feel these things, don't let it get deep inside of you. Understand? You feel a sadness in there and you feel like I want to shake something into that person. But don't, just send some love out. Send something good. Send a wonderful vibration. Oh, Father let your vibrations penetrate through, Father, because that person needs it. You see? Take that gnawing away from yourself as quickly as you can. After a time, then, you will find that you will do this more and more naturally.

Because, we are not looking for dead people, understand? We are looking for people that are alive and you can't live with the dead. You know Jesus said, "Let the dead, bury their dead." This is so true, but you stand up in the average temple and if you were to speak like I am speaking through this instrument tonight, well, probably he would be on the outside looking in now, because they would probably kind of guide him out, which they did with your brother Jesus. You see?

Make your own world something that you can enjoy, something that you can be happy about, because sadness is a lack of understanding of reality. So, build your world around something that has value for yourself and your fellowman. Let's begin to awaken. Let's begin to live, now. Beloveds, lets live. Let's make our world a place that we can enjoy, and find peace, and contentment within ourselves. When we have that peace and contentment within the self, it's contagious.

There are others that are going to look at you in wonderment and say, "How can you be so happy? Why is it that I am so unhappy and you are so happy?" Well, I wouldn't volunteer to tell them. I would only say to them, "Well, you're asking, do you really want to know?" If they don't really want to know, forget it. But, be the example. But, if they really want to know, then don't try to give them the whole thing at one time. Just give them a little taste of it, just enough for them to want to come back and try some more. These are all things that are pertinent to joy and to happiness. Believe me, you can't have joy, you can't have happiness with a broken down temple. But when you go that route, your temple has to respond to those things that are valid. It's just the universal law.

You, my beloveds, were not planted here. You, my beloveds, did come from another planet—yes, but we had to raise ourselves, didn't we? We are on a third-dimensional planet. I'm sure all of you know this. Alright, you came from a second-dimensional planet. You came from a first-dimensional planet. You had to advance in your awareness from one expression of life to a higher one and to a higher one. Alright, let's not stop because I'm going to tell you something—that once you have raised yourself out of this one, the universe is yours. I'm not saying it lightly, because this is the promise out of the Father. He said, "I give you dominion over my creation." You see?

We have separated the Father. We have separated the Son, and we have separated the Spirit. Body, mind and spirit, bring it all together now. You have this universe. It is yours, beloveds, and I am not saying this lightly. I wouldn't be talking to you this way if I didn't know.

Those of you that have made Jesus your God are recognizing that Jesus is somewhere beyond reach almost, too. He is almost as far out of reach today as God is to most of the religious orders of your earth. Well, I am going to tell you something; that Jesus never left this earth. He's here and now. This instrument has talked to Jesus many times, as he has talked with me and he has talked with us. But the instrument has never asked at any time for any of us to come to him. Never does he ask. This is the way it should be. You of the physical expression should never ask any master, teacher or guiding influence of any kind to come to you. Talk to God. The Father knows your needs and He'll take care of the situation.

So, the time comes that you are aware enough and your centers are open enough, you will see Jesus. He'll come to you. You won't have to ask for him. He will come, and so will I, and so will any of the masters. So, don't say my master is such and such. This master is such and such. I have an Indian that such and such. Then somebody else says, "Oh, no you don't, that's my Indian or that's my master." Forget it. Because this is not true, and this is what you're so called Spiritualism is teaching. So, it's as dense or denser, even, in many ways than your other religions. You call that Spiritualism. You call that religion. I call it confusion. You see?

Don't put anything before God, because God knows all of your needs, and He has already given you everything. But all you have to do when you contact is to be thankful for all of the wonderful things you already have— but I am asking to be shown here Father. So, we then come to you out of the Father because this is what we chose to do. It is our own choice that

162

we come here to help you, that's all. God didn't force us. We have made this our choice. This is our pleasure and our joy to be able to be of service. Because who would be happier than to see every one of you in the beautiful vibrations of mastery of life—into a greater dimension of awareness that you no longer need to go through death? This is what were happy about; when we can help you to realize that death is a very, very complete and thorough dense disease. That's what it is. It's as much a disease as any condition, because everything that you call disease upon your earth is caused by you, everything.

Oh, I know some of you are not going to accept this. I'm not forcing anything upon you. But, I'm telling you what we know, because we came out of that condition, and those conditions, and came into that which is no longer a diseased world and allowing ourselves to have diseased minds—because a mind that is not functioning properly is a diseased mind.

So these are things that you've got to work with and you've got to take command of yourself. You've got to be the one that is taking dominion over the situation. And when you take dominion, "Father, look, you and I are one. We're working together. We are not separated. No more of this, I walk in Thy light." Then I don't have to crawl, I don't have to cry.

Michael says, "Make a happy noise unto the Father," but what do you hear in most of the temples? There's a lot of noise going on, "Oh, do this for me and do that for me." All selfish noise. Let's make a noise alright, but let's make a good noise, a joyful one and a thankful noise unto the Father. Then, let's take most of our hymnals and let us make a big bon fire. That's about all they're good for. Why? I'll tell you why. They're all singing praises to Jesus and God is forgotten. Why can't you write some hymns now and songs of light, that praise God?

Certainly you can praise the Elder Brother Jesus, but you're making him God per se' in there. If you can praise him for his teachings and all of the good things he did, wonderful. How often do you see a hymn that praises God in all His glory? And thanking God for the life that you have, the health that you have? These are things you should begin to recognize and realize. Some of you are capable of doing these things. Let's get with it and make our world a beautiful place to live in.

You know something, I am here with you. I am no where else. I am right here with you. Now let's open our eyes that we will all see each other, because there is no separation. Only higher vibrations. Only quickening—that's what I would rather call it, only quickening. Let us work together beloveds and let's quicken your temples, and we'll all be able to function as one in this beautiful universe, alright?

Beloveds, we are brothers and sisters. We are the sons and daughters of the Almighty. Let us realize this that we may walk taller and more beautiful and more creative, and let us walk with respect for my temple. This temple is Gods divine gift to me, and I am going to use it the way it should be used. And believe me you'll enjoy it now, and that temple will treat you right. It will treat you as good and more beautifully, possibly, then you treat it.

I am going to leave you with these thoughts, my beloveds, and may peace be the hallmark of all of your lives in the future. Peace be with you.

I am known as Garth.

CHAPTER 17

I Come Not to Change the Law But to Fulfill It

By Akim

Peace. Peace. Peace. Dearly beloved, brothers and sisters, it is my pleasure, again, to come forth and share with you those things that can be of absolute priceless value in your personal world. We know that as we have constantly been in contact with this, the realm of the physical—even though we have moved into an avenue of expression, that we longer need to come forth into your physical world through a mother and father, we are yet not losing the contact of that which is your avenue of expression, nor are we withdrawn from any part of that which is the Father's creation.

Because, as you know, and as we have taught through the many generations of teaching, out of the spirit side of life, to those of you who are seeking, or hopefully seeking a better way of life, we found that which has brought us to that point, in the eternities, is that which knows no condition of limitation. The moment we began to release ourselves from those conditions of limitation that man, in the physical, as well as on a few other planet systems are bound by; due to that which man has accepted as a world of reality, rather than a world that you have set into motion, and have found that the limitations that you have accepted, in the many incarnations, are returning and are haunting you.

Yet, you do not realize that these things are not necessary, to be a part of your life. But also, you do not seem to want to make changes. You don't seem to want to bring into your world that which is the balance. And, oftentimes, as we speak of these truths you resent us for it, as you resented the master Jesus for his teachings—asking of you not only to listen to what he had to say, but to go beyond his teachings.

Yet, man has refused to do so, excepting the few. When we say few, it is because, if we were to take those that do in, let us say, one year of that which you call time in your physical world, put them in the midst of you those who have reached that which we call the mastery, or have risen in their awareness above the last enemy called death, you would not be able to find them. Because you have billions of souls upon your earth, and so if you would take even, exaggerating a great deal, five hundred thousand, or let us say a half a million, you would never be able to find them—spread out through the billions of souls.

There would only be a few in your dense world that could even begin to contact them, and, of course, it is up to anyone to be able to contact the masters. For any time that you are ready to make the contact, you are going to find that that contact can be made. But you've got to be ready, and you cannot be trying to want to remain in the confusion of your densities, and hope to reach out, and become aware of the masters that are expressing, awaiting for those that are truly seeking.

There is a great deal that is being prepared, prepared by those of us who have reached beyond that purely physical world, but yet, is not going to be open to everyone, because, we have told you, time and again, those who have eyes to see will see. Those that have ears to hear will hear. Yet man has limited himself to the thought that he has to be in a certain expression of life in order to be able to reach into that which is of the greater vibrations, or the higher vibrations, or the greater expression of life.

It is only going to be to those of you that when you say, "I want this," and will release yourself to the knowledge that as I want it, and why I want it, and for what purpose I want it, and then will relax to it. You cannot help but reach into it, because you have set the stage. And, until you set the stage you cannot walk upon it. You cannot find your way there. You have got to set your stage of life.

But, beloveds, there is beauty beyond that which is expressing in your physical world here. There is beauty on your earth that you walk by every day and don't see it. Why? Because you're so involved in your dense physical world that you cannot see beauty that is there, I mean the beauty of reality. You cannot feel the exhilaration of life. And if we attempt to tell you the reasons for this, then you become dismayed. You become miffed at us as though we were trying to belittle you. We are only laying it out here the way it should be laid out there, and it's up to you to be either receptive to it or reject it.

As you have continually rejected that which *is* the countless gifts of the eternal creation, we cannot seem to reach you. To let you know that what you are experiencing from one moment to the next, is what you have already set into motion. If you don't like it, it is up to you to renew your mind immediately and change the picture of life for yourselves.

But we ask of you to be honest with yourselves. How many in your physical world, or those that you are in communion with each day, and so on, are honest with themselves? How often do you get miffed at those that are dishonest? Yet how often have you looked at yourself and found out that you have spoken many, many times and all that came out was lip service?

You might say, "Oh well, the little things that I do don't hurt anyone." Oh, yes they do. Anytime you create a condition that will cause your brother man to become a little bit incensed, a part of that is yours, regardless. Because you created it, you're not going to have it all because, after all, your brother should say, "Well, I shouldn't allow myself to become dismayed or embarrassed or miffed at these conditions. I should just let it roll off my shoulders."

But the very thing is when you say, "I am going to do this, or at a certain time I am going to do that." It is best to say it if you know. But, if you are just saying it just to be giving lip service, you are creating for yourselves a little bit more density. You are not being honest, and that dishonesty is a thing that is very, very destructive. This is where your physical world is today.

How many can you depend upon? How often have you wanted to do something and say, "Well, no, I can't depend on him," or "I can't depend on her." They say things and they can't follow through. How often have you found yourself in that category? Quite often I'm sure, and you seem to think that you're getting away with these things. How can you create a higher expression and a greater vibration of life when you are not being honest with yourselves, let alone your fellowman? This is only one part of the day that man does these things to himself. How can I expect the best out of my life if I am doing this?

Now, also, the master Jesus attempted—oh, how often that he attempted to drill this into man, to make man understand that he is the prime source of energy and power out of the Father. Out of this prime source and energy, out of the Father, he is the one that should be in dominion and control of your own personal life. How many of you are in control of your lives? You can't be, if you are not honest to start out with. You cannot be, if you're not keeping your temple in perfect energy and in perfect power. Yet, you have every privilege to keep that temple in absolute perfect power and energy and health.

The master Jesus said it so often, "Physician heal thyself." How often have we and the master Jesus said to you, "death is a disease?" He was reprimanded many times for having said that death is a disease. But you wouldn't believe when he said, "death is a disease." You wouldn't accept it to any degree. In fact, most that stood there wouldn't even consider questioning within themselves how much value his words had.

So, man has stumbled through many incarnations. And, he will stumble through many more without recognizing that the experiences that I have, that I am experiencing today, are not my brother's creation but my own, my very own creation. I am the one that has set into motion that which is cycling back into my awareness, and if I have accepted some of the densities from my brother, it's adding to it. If I have caused my brother conditions of imbalance, if I have set my patterns of life by attempting to disrupt my brother's expression of life, that too is mine. So, what I set into motion is that which I experience.

Well, beloveds, I told you that we have many things to share, but who is going to take, and partake of what part of this which is manifesting in your world? Are you going to be ready to be receptive to or to reject? Again, it is only you that can do it. Your brother cannot do it for you. Your brother can be of service to you, but if you reject his service then that's as far as you go. We are your brothers and sisters. You are brothers and sisters. There is no separation. Yet, you insist upon it. We are not here to control you. If we were attempting to control you, we would be where you are in the physical world. It is when we no longer attempted to control our brother man, was when we no longer attempted to force upon man our way of thinking—that we began to rise above that which you call, "The Last Enemy."

Oh, we gave the lessons. We were not selfish. We taught, but we didn't say that you had to accept. But we have to be honest with you, if you are not going to be honest with yourselves and with your brothers and sisters, how can you be aware and have your eyes open when it is going to be necessary? Yes, when the master Jesus said, "Many are called but few are chosen," but it isn't that way. All of you are called. But, how many of you are going to listen to what we have to say, and accept it, and move into that expression of awareness? That's what it means. It doesn't mean that God is going to call many and then only choose a few. You have the freewill, and don't forget it, is not going to be taken away from you.

There is no holding or binding at all, and this is what the Father gave you and I. He gave you life, and He gave you the privilege of destroying it or keeping it. He gave you everything in the universe to create with, because He told you that you are co-creators in Him and you are His sons and daughters. But man has moved out of that, he does not want to believe that he is God's son or daughter. He wants to believe that God, after He was finished with His creation, that He created another son. After He had finished His creation—completed it all, and afterwards He creates a very special son.

Rather than you recognize—here is a man that came forth with the odds against him in many, many ways, because you don't want to believe how he was born and created and so on and so forth, and how he came back to the physical plane expression. No. You had to make up new stories about him. You want truth, and yet, this is what you have done.

But this man had everything working against him, that is, if he would have let it work against him as he grew up. But he didn't, because he decided in this his incarnation, at that time, that he was not going to be in the revolution of his world. He was going to be in the evolution of his world, in the divine evolution in that which is Gods divine expression.

So he made each day—and this is another thing that Jesus tried to share with you, and he said, "Look, don't try to live tomorrow. Don't try to live yesterday. Live now. Now. Today is the day to live." It wasn't until I started expressing in this manner that I could, each day, release myself to reality. But I had to live it today, and those obstructions that came in, I no longer looked at them as obstructions. But I looked at them as part of my creation that wasn't balanced. And, it was coming back to face me, not to haunt me. It was coming back for me to use my Gods divine expression and to take dominion over that condition—to put it into balance, in other words.

I was not bitter. I saw what was approaching me, and I said, "Well, alright Father, I look at this. I see it, and I know that it is either from the present vibrations, or it is from the past." But it doesn't make any difference whether it was something I set into motion now or whether it came from the past. It makes no difference. It was a lesson that I hadn't learned. So, I looked at it, and of course, if it is from the past usually it comes in with a little bit more of a density because it has had time to gather a little bit of that extra density with it. Of course, I, in my each day vibrations did add a little more to it, and so, when it came back it was a heavier condition than it would have been had I taken care of it in its first appearance or hadn't even created it to start out with. So, I look at it. I am not sure how I'm going to handle the situation, but I realize today is my day. Today I am living and today I walk with life.

When I say I walk with life, I am walking with my creator. I am now momentarily, probably in complete identity of my oneness in my Father, and that's enough. I don't fall on my hands and knees. I don't cry, but I certainly am not quite aware of how to handle that situation. I'm not going to try to run away from it, or try to think up something else, that I can push it outside, so that it can come back later—even a little bit more painful than it has this time. No. I am looking at it and I'm not aware of just how to handle the situation. Alright Father, I know I am the one that did this, but believe me I am not quite aware of how to handle the situation, but, I don't want to leave it go the way it is. I want this to be balanced out. I want it where it is good for me and my fellowman. I want it all completely cleared up.

You stop long enough to do this. Go into a little bit of a meditation. Feel yourself in the mood of joy and pleasure. Feel yourself in the mood of love that you can pour into this situation. You are going to find that it works, and all of the dense laws of your world will not have any part in this and it will not disturb you. I say to you, if you will work in this way you are going to find that everyday becomes just a wee bit more fruitful, just enough to make you feel more a part of reality.

We have given you, at various times, the knowledge that you are either taking dominion of your own creation or you are allowing the flow, that which is outside of you, to be the dominating factor in your life. So, if you allow that condition out here to be the dominating factor of your life, that's what you are going to experience and that's where the limitations are, because they are the effects of your own causation—how simple it is.

But why do you not want to accept these things? Why is it so difficult for you to accept reality, and yet the limitations seem to become simple for you to function in. Or, it is absolutely not constructive, because it is here to here, and that's where the limitations come in. Why cannot you open up the centers of your being to recognize that you have a universe unlimited, and this universe is yours to accept or reject?

I am not attempting, nor do I believe that any of the masters, including your Elder Brother Jesus ever attempted to tell you that you had to accept it all. Because if he had told you this he would have been absolutely wrong—because even the Father having given you the entire creation and the freewill to accept or to reject—He never attempted to say, you've got to do it this way, and this way, and this way, and this way. But, He said, "If you use that which I have shared with you and given unto you in the freewill of being of service to yourself and your fellowman, you have life." This again, was the master Jesus teachings. He never, at any time, attempted to teach you how to die, nor did he attempt to teach you how to live in fear of God so that you would find a beautiful spot somewhere in this universe.

Why do you insist that that which is out here is the answer—when the being of your being, the breath of your breath, the energy of your energy is the answer? Why do you go from one day from the next finding yourselves limited with a tired physical body? Yet you have not asked yourself: "Why is it I have this tired physical body? Why is it that I am lacking energy?" Because, you are listening to what is going on out here, and you, then, allow that what you are listening to out here dominate your thinking. Then, it becomes a condition of disenchantment with that which you are finding yourself doing or feeling that you must or have to do.

So you close off the energy of life, and so your temple doesn't receive, any longer, that which is the necessity to make your temple energetic—make your temple filled with light and love and inner peace with awareness and the greater understanding. So you end up worn out, tired, never stopping to think for a moment that you are *slowly but surely* committing suicide.

This was our teachings, constantly. The master Jesus was constant in his teachings that you create, you are creators, and you are co-creators in the

Father. Use that energy and that power for the benefit of yourself and the good of your brother man, and you can find only joy and pleasure, energy and power that is needed. I can command out of myself, that withiness of me, in a manner of life, and love, and inner peace—awareness of how to be in absolute dominion over my own world, making my world the world that I want to live in.

You will find that world, if it is an honest thought pattern and expression within yourself, is going to be a world that is absolutely unlimited. There will be the world of inner peace. It will be the world of love and sharing with your fellowman, the world that knows no condition of any selfish, or fearful, or doubtful, or bitter expression. You see? That world of these distortions is the world that you are existing in. The world that is real knows not those conditions. That world of reality is not a magic world. It is not a world that can't be approached. It is the natural world, the world that you were created in. It is the world that you first identified with—the living, loving, peaceful God of eternity.

The Father gave you His permission to command or take dominion over your creation, but man has not accepted—but has accepted in his selfishness and his greed, his fears and so on, to try to take dominion over his fellowman. Beloveds, it will never be successful. It will always end out in self-destruction, because it doesn't belong in the law of the universe, the law of balance.

The master Jesus said, "I come not to change the law, but to fulfill it." And, when he attempted to show you how to fulfill it, he was condemned by those that did not want to change their ways. He said, "Of myself I do nothing, but out of the Father all things are possible." He was not speaking of himself but unto all mankind. He said unto you "Physician, heal thy self," but you have centered that pattern as something that has to do only with physical distorted conditions of aches, and pains, and so on, and so forth.

Beloveds, if you are the physician and you will recognize that is what you are—that you are the physician that can heal all that is necessary to be healed in your world—in *your* world, not your brother's world but your own, then you can heal all expression. Everything that needs to be balanced then that's the part that is necessary for the physician in you to act upon. If you are unhappy then you must change the pattern. Why am I unhappy? If I am bitter, *why* am I bitter? If I am hateful, *why* am I hateful? All of these

172

are a part of man's illness and his selfishness. Why am I Selfish? Why am I so greedy? Why? Ask yourself. This is getting into yourself and finding the balance here. When you do, you're going to find that you begin to live, because you cannot enter within, in this manner, truly searching the soul self, right here in this temple and being honest, without getting some very terrific and bountiful results.

Let us become quiet now and let us call upon that power of the universe. Call upon it. It is yours—it's now. But, let it now not be stopped out here somewhere, or clogging the very identity of yourself. But let it flow. There is no limit to the power and energy of the universe. But, let that flow be such as to let yourself become aware, aware of what I am. Knowing that as I let this beauty and energy flow through me, I begin to come to life, I begin to feel alive. I begin to feel an energy that seemed to be dormant within me. So, let us let this power flow.

(Author's note: Meditation for eight minutes)

Thank you, beloveds. Now we have been asked, at times, why did Jesus cause those around him to curse him? Why did Jesus cause someone to try to stab him? Why did Jesus try to change the conditions of density in the physical world and bring about that which was his own death? As I have spoken unto you, everything, is cause and effect, and that this man named Jesus didn't attempt to try to make anyone do anything they didn't want to do. But he attempted to try to give you and I those things that would enhance our own personal lives if we wanted to use them. He was not in condemnation of his brothers and sisters because he knew they were already in their own condemnation. What he was trying to do, was awaken them to the law of life.

But, also, he knew while he was in that mix of these souls that were reluctant to accept and became bitter, and spat upon him or attempted to knife him and so on, that they couldn't do anything to hurt him. He knew this and he knew that in the midst of this, that he would again be an example to them, where they would attempt to destroy, and find that their attempts were of no value, that they might begin to think. And, some did, but most of them didn't, even with the proof right there with those that were close to him.

But, one of his disciples moved into life, the others ones, all of them, suffered greatly, because they did not accept everything or did not accept the way that the master was teaching. They were very fearful of those in the temples of being destroyed. So all of this together, they became completely out of balance and suffered death in many different ways, except one, and that was John.

So you have come—as those that gathered around the master Jesus wherever he was, to find himself teaching, to give forth the lessons that he knew were of value, if man would accept them. There were a number of them that did—that were not ever put in the *Book* because they were very quiet about what they were doing. They went about their business very quietly. They did not interfere with their fellowman. They did not allow themselves bitterness or hatred because of what the others were doing—that they knew was of no value to them. No, because they had gone through that and they had traveled those paths, and so they didn't any longer want those paths. So, they reached to the higher ground and then they stepped upon the rock of life. They became what they knew God willed them in the beginning.

Then there were those that were there around him, and around me, and around others that were teaching a way of life that said, "Oh, well, who cares I'll have another chance, I'll come back again." And they were right, but they found that there was a great deal of difficulty attached to it. Not only going into the unseen side of life through many physical hurts and creating many sad hearts, but also in the spirit side it was not that simple, only because of their density and their unwillingness to begin to look within themselves to find out why their laziness—to begin to really and cope with reality—finding themselves in a great density; to hurry their coming back into the physical realm, and doing so without preparation, without foresight as to why they were wanting to hurry back into physical life.

Therefore, coming back in with a greater density than they left with, and not recognizing the purpose of their identity in life, so their lives remained the same as long as they did not make any attempt at knowing what they are and what their purpose is.

So it is, that man moves on and on. And then he listens to those that would say to them, "Have more and more children. Have more and more of them"—never stopping to realize that they're just creating a condition of cloning of themselves through the splitting of the atoms, more and more, not able to give to that which they cloned any basics as to how to cope with their lives, never stopping to realize God in His creation created an unbroken, undistorted—that which is absolutely the perfect atom of life, and gave that atom identity and dominion. Then that atom decided to take on and experience the physical body.

Beloveds, a true master even one that has just barely reached the awareness of rising above the last enemy called death, just barely entering into another dimension, would not be unhappy of the one that would find joy and pleasure, one that would speak to his brother man, no matter where or what he represented, as the master Jesus did, but was condemned by even his own Apostles for having spoken to certain peoples that they looked down upon. But yet, he taught them—not once of these things but many times, and yet they condemned him, his own disciples. Jesus spoke to all because he knew his oneness in all expression.

So, beloveds, be aware of this and find the true expression of life. Find it because it's now. We ask you to, whatever you are doing, that you do it not with selfish motives, greed's—doing it with fear. But do it with honesty, being honest with myself. I do it because I love to do it. I definitely love to have the returns of that which I am putting into motion. But, I'm not doing it just to grasp, but that which I receive out of it gives me a greater opportunity of being of service or of sharing.

In my sharing I am also more conscious of attempting to maintain a balance in my life. Therefore, I welcome the gifts that are brought to me. I share, but I also am as good a receiver, so this is the expression of balance. And, I'm not making my world a place that is difficult to exist in, but I am making my world a place that is wonderful to live in. You will find that these things have repercussions and always will have repercussions. But, the repercussions can be beautiful, or they can be drastic depending upon my attitude towards either life or existence.

There is a difference between life and existence—a great, great difference. I can only have existence in that which you call life, as long as I hold onto the limitations that I have been consciously accepting throughout my many incarnations. If I maintain and sustain the same consciousness that I attained in my past incarnation, I am going nowhere, excepting right back again to where I was before, having to build another temple and come back again.

But if I function in the knowledge that I was created in life—and I have to have a basic understanding that I've got to have something solid to stand on. If I don't have something solid, then I'm eventually going to allow myself to slowly but surely and gradually, once again, find myself walking in the quicksand's of time. Slowly sinking towards the grave—that's what the master Jesus meant when he said, "Either you dig your grave with a teaspoon or with a shovel." He said this quite often and you can read it in the old testaments of the old bibles that were established many years before this, your so called Bible. That's what we call it, a so called Bible. Because it has so many distortions in it that we cannot actually call it the Bible, yet you do. You accept it as the "Word," but when you will become conscious of this one thing—that within me, within this that I call *me*, this temple, there is not one question that I can ask myself, not one question that I don't have the answer to.

But, if I'm only asking that which is the lower self, then I'm going to find myself coming up short. But, if I ask that which is my higher self, my identity in the absolute universe—I am going to get the answer, because it is here, it is now.

So I actually don't need the written word that has been rewritten many, many times, plus, not only changed due to the fact that the language in the years since that Bible was printed, have changed—these words have changed. They don't have the same meaning today that they had then. In fact, in your physical world today, right today, those of you that haven't been too close to the youth of your present day, let us say those that are now in school prior to going to college and have not been very close to them, and get in the midst to them, suddenly you will find that you'd think some of them are speaking a foreign language. Because that which they are speaking is entirely different. The wording is entirely different.

So you can imagine in 1611 when that Bible was first changed from one of the original old bibles, and that the wording in there has been very, very disturbed and changed. Plus, the students that sat around the table and rewrote that Bible argued among themselves as to the meaning out of an old bible, "Now what does this mean?" They argued among each other, and I can see them even unto this day, that they argued among each other as to what a verse meant.

So, when they couldn't come to an agreement, what did they do? They couldn't come to an agreement and so they would call King James, and King James would look at it and say, "That's what it means." So, blindly they accepted it and put it in there. It may not have meant that, but King James said that's what it was, and that's what it was.

So, yet, you will hear those that will say that every word in the Bible is absolute truth. I'm going to say this, if you want to do anything that you want to do, and feel a little guilty about it, read your King James version, and you can translate it anyway you want. So you can go right ahead and do exactly what you want, and it would take the guilt out of you. But I'll tell you one thing, it won't be as it should be.

That's why we say to you, that you've got to become conscious that you, as individuals, attempting to restore and renew your lives, and to build a future that is not going to be cut down by the negetiveness of your fellowman, look into your own self. Build your future on something that is worthwhile, build it on the rock. Build it on that rock of life, not in the quicksands of the past. To build it on that rock of life you must identify with your true self, that you will then take care of this which is the temple through which you do express a world worthwhile living in.

When I came back I did attempt to build a temple more aware and with more love, and choose a mother and father to guide me out of that childhood to recognize more fully that I was and yet am a co-creator in my Father. And what I put into life—that is what I was going to get out of it. Eventually, I became aware that the simplicity of life, the simplicity of doing, was the only way to establish that which would open up the door of eternal life or mastery.

This is the world that once you have reached mastery in it, you are never, ever, through any other dimension going to have to reckon with death again. This third-dimensional expression is the most—I could say most difficult or the most complete that you are going to evolve in to, bringing yourself into the being, fully aware of your co-creative powers in the universe.

You will find that, eventually, you're moving out of that consciousness of limitation that is so destructive and so definitely limited, to that which is the joy and the pleasure of knowing abundance, without having to struggle for it. You'll stop to think a little while before you take certain actions, because if you are struggling and fighting for everything that you need, it is because you are selfish, because you are greedy, or you're allowing greed and selfishness that is surrounding you to control you and so on.

If you are going to reach the mastery you have got to know that it is only through peace, and joy, and love, and pleasure that I function. It is only in the knowledge that my Father is love and that love is mine, that peace, that joy, that pleasure. All of the good things are mine, now, and forever. That is all I'm going to accept from this day on. So, each day I live that kind of life—I live it. I put it into action and I put it into motion. Even if I make a mistake, I pick myself up and I put myself back on my feet again. The master Jesus, he fell several times during his years in the East, but he picked himself back up and he went right ahead. So, if you fall, pick yourself up, wipe the dust off you, but don't be bitter and hateful for having done it. Be thankful that you are able to understand yourself enough to be able to take yourself and renew your world around you.

Well, beloveds, I am going to take my leave now from the instrument. Let's give some thought to your own beautiful world. Believe me, if you give some thought to it and enter into this beautiful garden of life, even if you only just peek in, it's wonderful. Peace be with you. Peace.

I am master Akim.

CHAPTER 18

I Only Walked With Him for Three Years and That Was Our Brother Jesus

By Apostle John

Peace. Peace. Peace. Dearly beloveds, it is my privilege and pleasure this evening that I take hold of the instrument that I might come forth and share with you those things that can be of pertinent value to each and every one of you. We know that we are attempting, at this time, to help you to open up the centers of awareness within your temple. We are hopeful that you are going to instill within the soul of your being, that which will have priceless value for you under any condition or circumstance.

I know it is often said that, "One does not know what may take place in your personal world, under any given condition." And, of course, in the limitations that you have found expression in, we must agree with you. But yet, we cannot agree with you one hundred percent, because *we* know that when we were expressing in your world of the physical, that is, in the physical soul, that there was a time when we knew what was going to transpire. In fact, we were abundantly ahead of all expression in your physical world.

So, therefore, we knew that which was transpiring. We also knew the results of that which was transpiring and to the degree that it was being accepted by man. We knew approximately when, according to the time expression that you are functioning in, in the physical world that it was going to take place. So, we were called not only masters but prophets as well.

But, what I am about to say to you is this; that each one of you have the same capability and capacity to know what is going to transpire under any given condition, but only to the degree that you know the self. If you don't know yourself, then how can you, through the density that you have accumulated within the sub-conscious mind, which is this, your temple, deviate one condition from another? You cannot separate them. You cannot find the answer because there is too great a density of negations and stoppages within the temple.

When you put into the cells of your physical body, which is the soul expression of your being, that which is the negations through the various sources known as doubts, fears, bitterness' and hatreds and so on, you create a density, to such a degree, that it seems insurmountable. It becomes such an expression within your being that you feel as though sometimes that God has forsaken you—that God is beyond your reach. Have you not felt this way? It is because you have allowed yourself to absorb so much of the conditions of imbalance that your cells are filled with these conditions and this rubble—that you cannot seem to be able to reach to the reality and awareness as to how to cope with that which is presenting itself to you.

It is just like a person—and there are quite a number of them on your physical earth that are running to their doctors every day, and once a week, twice a month and so on to get shots—to get this, to get that. They don't know what they are doing to themselves. And seemingly, the more they go to their physicians the less they are capable of functioning properly. Why is it? It is because they are over medicated. You have heard of these things. The bloodstream becomes like a gravy and lumpy within the veins, and eventually, that person has got only one way to go and that's to die. Either that or let go of all medication and suffer their way back to health. If it has gone so far that they are incapable of using the energy powers of the

universe to cleanse themselves, they are through, because that over medication destroys the blood and that's the life of your temple. So you see it's the
same way with putting all of this rubble into your cells of your body and
using only a very minute part of the brain matter. So, it is well that one
begins to recognize these things.

Isn't it rather time for man, now, to begin to awaken to the living, and
loving, and peaceful, and eternal God? Of course, if you want to join the
other forces and keep on mingling with them and accepting that, if I create more atomic bombs, if I create more missiles, if I create all this, this
is going to protect me. That's what you think, my beloved brothers and
sisters. There's going to be fireworks such as you have never seen. And it's
not going to come from just one side of the world. It's going to come from
everyone that has these things. And, by the time it's over with, it's going
to have destroyed everyone that has been thinking that they are going to
protect themselves by trying to be first to destroy their brothers and sisters.

Your Bible clearly tells you about this if you listen and look into it.
But, again, you don't have to have any part of it. You can be right in the
midst of it and this is what the master said, "You can be in the midst of it
and never be touched." This we know is true, but you can't function in that
kind of an expression by serving your many gods. There is one God to serve
and that God doesn't say you have to serve me.

This God that gave you life didn't say, "You have to serve me." He said,
"Accept my gifts, my gifts of life." That's all He asked of you, to accept His
gifts, to accept them freely and abundantly, to share with your fellowman,
and to be as good a receiver. How can you be wrong when you share, and give,
and find peace in your heart. And you love your fellowman, no matter *who* it
is and what they have done? You see? This is living my beloveds. But how
are you going to learn how to live? By entering within and knowing yourself.

So, let us tonight, right now, take the time to *quietly enter within.* Open
up our hearts and our minds to the super consciousness of the living, loving, peaceful God and His divine powers and His energies, all pure good.
Let us, just for a moment, take a look within ourselves, and let us see the
cells of our temple, and let us tonight empty those cells of any thoughts
of limitation. I'm putting into those cells, life, that it may be distributed
through all of the atoms of my body. I feel this power, love, entering in my
temple opening up all the centers of my being. I feel this love opening the
door to greater awareness.

Now, let us take a few moments to allow this to enter in, and flow through the entire temple, opening up the centers of my being, and entering into the most beautiful cells of knowledge and light, unlimited light in my cells, unlimited youthful expression of awareness. That I might move, Father, in the proper direction, to be of service to myself and my fellowman—that I will be aware, Father, that I am one in Thee.

(Author's note: Meditation for eight minutes)

Thank you, beloveds. Now, I am going to take another look here into the auras. I see some of you doing very well, I mean in your releasing of the self. But others are seemingly, you're fighting. I don't know what you're fighting, but you're fighting. You're struggling. You're not letting go, and you're fighting different thoughts—seemingly struggling. As I look at these pictures, as they function in the aura vibration, the picture shows me that some of you want a change, but are not yet feeling that you can let go of that which you have been bound to. Not that you were forcibly bound to it because you accepted that binding. You have accepted it, and therefore, it has become the very nature of your being in your cells. And, it often times causes you to be rather tight, it causes you to feel—you just don't know how, or even in the thought vibration are saying, in a sense, "Well, I want to, but I can't." And as long as you maintain that thought pattern it is going to remain there.

It is strange how you can become so bound within the self. You can be bitter against yourself and say, "I can't forgive myself" or you will say, "I know those around me and I hate them. I wouldn't forgive them for anything." But, you don't know what you're doing. You're killing yourself. You're absolutely committing slow suicide. Maybe underneath all of this is the fact that you are rather suicidal, afraid possibly to go and take a pill or something to kill yourself. So, you choose to destroy yourself in other ways by being hateful and being bitter, being destructive rather than constructive, being selfish rather than sharing, and so on—just because you don't like yourself.

The thing is you've got to learn to love the self. Why? If you don't love the self, you know that you are out of reach of your own life—the life force, the life energy, the life power. You're out of touch with it. That's what makes you feel as though God has forsaken you. You won't become quiet, because the little voice that is constant within you, the voice of eternity speaks constantly and I don't want to hear it. I'm afraid of what I'm going to hear, I'd rather take what's out here. So, that's where you are. But if you want to enjoy every abundance in your world and in your universe then let us begin to release.

Let us again attempt to function in this way—to open our hearts and our minds to life, the abundance, the super abundance, the unlimited abundance. That we can make not only ourselves happy, but the creative powers of life will also be pleased. That which is the God self will be pleased because we are accepting the gifts, the gifts of life.

You see, you've been taught that you've got to pray on your hands and knees, or bow to God. You don't have to do all of these things. All you must do is maintain and sustain your knowledge that you are functioning in that beautiful power of life that the Father gave unto you. And by accepting it, by accepting all of the gifts, or all that I need—not wanting things that I don't need, but the things that I need to be able to be abundant in myself, to share with my fellowman, that's all I want. As I need them I use them. I am opening the door to it all. Now, you're pleasing the God that gave you these things, and not only that, but, you are reestablishing yourself on the rock of life. Rather than on the quicksand of what you call time in your physical world.

Wouldn't it be wonderful if I could hear the billions of souls upon your earth, suddenly turning within and saying, "Father, we thank you for all of the gifts, the gifts of being brothers and sisters. The gifts of knowing that I am one in your divine nature, that you are one in mine, that I look at my brothers and sisters and I find that we are all that same beauty."

It starts with me, and when it starts with me, I eventually find that wherever I move I find beautiful brothers and sisters. And that which is not of that light nature doesn't seem to come into the effects of my temple any longer. I know they are yet there, but somehow they don't reach in anymore. I can hear my brothers and sisters saying, "I hate those people there, I hope someone destroys them." But yet, you know none of it is affecting me because you still know every one of those are my brothers and sisters. All you have is love. All you have is inner peace. All you have is the understanding, one day they too are going to fulfill—to know that which is so beautiful. And, I hope that they will turn to me someday and seek me out, so I can help them.

So let us know right now that there isn't a soul on earth, no matter how great that you may say they are, or think, or have thought they are—because they are a king, or queen, or a president, or some millionaire, that they haven't got one thing on me, because they are all equal. For God created us equal, no division, and no blood better than the other. I am the identity of my Father. I am the voice that speaks unto my brothers and sisters. What I have is all abundance that cannot be disturbed or destroyed, because it is for me to use and to share. And, that which is shared with me is also brought into my expression in the manner of thankfulness that I have it to use and to enjoy.

So, let us now, right now, release ourselves to the open door of God's divine creation. And, through that which is the brain cells, let us feel ourselves opening the cells in our temple that have been closed for so long, because we've only used a small part, that we are going to put the energy and the power of Thy love into motion that knows no limitation.

With a thought, I can move out into the galaxy, which is just only a minute part of the creation. Yet, it might seem out of reach to man that feels bound to the earth. But when you let yourself move into it, you find that it is as close as your very breath. Now, release ourselves to the movement of this that we can make a cycle, as it flows in through the brain down into the cells of the temple, to move back out again and cycle back. Watch and see how wonderful and how free you're going to feel and how beautiful your temple begins to feel as you release yourself to this beautiful energy.

(Author's note: Meditation for seven minutes)

I find that there were some very good expressions here, and some experiences, but I find that, again, there is a little bit of—I would say fear, fear of what? It seems as though you have a fear somehow of the unknown. I would like to be able to go to each one of you and erase that, because when you walk in the knowledge of the Father; you are my guiding light, my influence, the answer to all expression. Why should I be afraid?

Of course, the answer comes to me that man is fearful, because he has been told to fear, he has been told to doubt, he has been suppressed in those vibrations. So it seems as though man doesn't want to release himself from this.

It is such a glorious experience to move into the identity of what is the garden of eternity. You can always walk into that garden, at any time, at any chosen moment that you wish. And, you can absorb as much of the beauty of it as you want to absorb, yet without any of it being forced upon you. You are the one that is going to take as much as you feel that is necessary, in order to feel able to sustain and maintain the self in the avenue of a joy and of pleasure of living, as well as, being able to meet any condition that is expressing in the density of the physical, without any qualms whatsoever.

One seems to wonder, also, as to what it takes to become what is known in your physical world as a master. When we take and put it all together we find that all we can say to you is that it takes utter simplicity to reach mastery. The more you simplify your identity in the physical world, the greater is your capacity of becoming a central being in the identity of the creation. I am sure we have spoken to you and asked of you to not to try to live tomorrow nor to attempt to live yesterday, but there is the ever present now.

If I put everything of beauty in my brain—the brain that God has given me, and I draw into that brain the knowledge that only good can come to me, and only pleasure, and peace, and love, is my identity with the creation, then all I can do today is balance out everything. So, that which identifies itself with me, this day, can only be that which I have accepted, whether it was now or in the past as a condition of reality. And as I see it, now, it doesn't come together, so I have that knowledge, today is my day. So, today is the day that I bring all this into a beautiful joy, a happiness, peacefulness and a love. I put nothing there to extend that condition of imbalance and give it continuity. I give it peace, I give it love, I give it absolute balance.

So, today has got to be then, the best day of my life, and I know that in my identity with this day that I have set into motion that which gives me the capability of constant abundance. But not only that, it gives me awareness of how to identify myself with the unlimitedness of being able to accept the countless gifts of the universe. Therefore, I am ready to move, and take, and enjoy, and give, and know that the whole picture remains a balanced picture, but constantly changing or *evolving*. Therefore, that's what makes life a pleasure and a joy.

If it just remains the same old thing from one day to the next—I get up tomorrow morning, I have to drink five cups of coffee before I can stir. I have to do this because I am filled with anguish, and I hate to face my day because yesterday was such a mess. And I think I am going to run right into the same thing today. So, if I identify with that sort of an expression, definitely you're not going to be disappointed. You're not going to be at all disappointed.

But, if you turn it around you're not going to be disappointed, but you're not going to be killing yourself either. You are going to be finding that, suddenly, you are finding yourself aware of things that you never were aware of before, because you have been functioning in a manner of opening up these centers, because you are releasing that which has been binding you and tying you down. And, you're taking the gravy blood out of you and putting the essence of life in there instead, that's all.

I identified with seven different beautiful brothers and sisters before I took my leave from the physical temple, before I gave this soul body back to that which I had taken it from—gave it back to the elements of life, again. I identified myself that very day with seven of my beautiful brothers and sisters. Then, they couldn't find me. They wondered where I had gone to. In fact, I really didn't know myself, actually, at that moment what—I knew that I was ready, but I was yet contemplating whether I had finished everything that I had wanted to, to move into a greater dimension.

I can only thank one great soul that I traveled with, and I only walked with him for three years, and that was our brother Jesus, not the son of God, anymore than you are the son of God, just another man that found his identity in the Father and moved into it. But, a greater soul never left us any greater priceless gifts as to how to live in this dimension, and yet, it has been so thoroughly distorted that man doesn't know how to identify with them.

Beloved brothers and sisters I left with these seven souls, the day that I took my leave from the physical—to each one of them I left some of the wonderful, beautiful writings of the teachings that my brother Jesus had left, and not one part is in your Bible as I gave it. It was so thoroughly distorted that there is a saying in your physical that it would take a Philadelphia lawyer to ferret it out, and I doubt he could do it.

When is man going to stop and know the answer to life is here and now? Know how great you are? How wonderful are you? How beautifully made are you? It's time to ask yourself this, so that you can renew your whole expression if you are dissatisfied with it—there's no one else that can do it for you. Your priests, your rabbis, your ministers can't do it for you. But you can reach within and the answer is, if you don't doubt.

We are going to share with you everything that we possibly can, but you are the answer. We can give you the path. We can share with you a map of life, but if you don't want to travel on it there is nothing we can do about it. You are the answer. We are going to question you soon. We are going to go into a meditation and maybe several of them. Then, we are going to ask of you what you have been able to feel, to see in your meditations, how receptive you are, and how much at peace you are with yourself.

We want to see and hear from you these things, just to see what you are doing in the manner of opening up the centers of awareness. This is what we want you to do, to be thoroughly aware that you are living—not existing. We don't want you to exist. We want you to live. We want you to learn how to release yourself to the very absolute capability of taking out any ache or pain in your body, knowing the reason it was there in the first place, and how to release the cause, and how to command the pain or the ache out of those cells.

We don't want any of you to have your cells running away from themselves and destroying you. We want you to be in command of those cells. We can't do it for you, but were going to bring you the light and share with you that capability that you can absorb and use it—that energy and power that you already have. It's just a matter of knowing that I am the master of my ship. I command my future. I am the one that is opening the door to reality.

How close are you to the Milky Way? Have you found yourself in the midst of this Milky Way? Have you seen when you got into it how abundantly beautiful it is? How many suns there are? How many moons there are and how wonderfully lighted up all of the beautiful stars are and all of the beautiful planet systems are in that galaxy, the Milky Way? Let us take a few moments and see what we can reach to.

(Author's note: Meditation for nine minutes)

Turn within and look at the countless cells. Open the door to these countless cells and look into the billions of atoms, and you are going to see the worlds. You are going to see the stars, the moons. Not only that, you are going to begin to take a little peek at the beauty of your own cells.

Now, beloveds, thank you. You did much better, but, I'm going to ask of you as I did in the past, to attempt to enter into meditations during the week. But I ask of you, be very thorough with your meditations. Don't just blindly enter into a meditation, but seek first the kingdom of God's expression. Never enter into a meditation just to be entering into meditation, but the guidance of the eternity of the living, loving, peaceful, creative identity of God within the self—I enter into this meditation, reveal Thy self unto me.

What is the God self? The God Self is everything that He created. He put everything into His beautiful creation; all that is of absolute balance including you, that real identity within this temple. So, I ask my Father "Reveal Thy creation, that which thou hast shared with me, and I have so blindly turned away. Reveal Thy self unto me that I might then, in this revelation, be of value to myself and to all mankind." You're taking out of the self any condition that could be limited. You're ready now to be receptive to something, and expecting something marvelous to take place—something marvelous, a door opening of awareness to move in the self. You are going to have experiences.

Be in command. Be the master of your destiny. You were given that privilege to be the master. The Father said, "I give you command." So, let us steer our ship, not to just one port, but to the ports of eternity. And, we're going to enjoy every stop that we make, knowing that that isn't where we're going to remain, but we are going to experience even greater expressions.

Oh, my beautiful brothers and sisters when I walked with the master Jesus, at first, it was difficult for me to absorb the things that he shared because they were entirely so controversial, that is, to that which I had accepted, and anything that man does not want to accept, that is controversial. But yet, when one questions these things, then he finds that it is not obstructing the view of life, but it is actually opening the door. That it is not denying the power of life and the creative energy powers of the universe. It is not obstructing any of it. It is not denying any of it. Then, you know I am walking without fear.

And in three years with my brother I then moved into the great avenues of life. I did not suffer. I had no conditions of ill health. My days were absolutely abundant. There was nothing that I could have wished for. There was not a time that I spoke to the Father that I didn't have an answer.

Yet, at first, when I heard the master speak I thought it was magic. I thought that the master was a magician. I was putting him on a pedestal by himself, and finally, I looked at the master as he spoke, and I saw he was my brother.

So, my beloveds, I take my leave. I am sorry that the rest of my brothers that followed and walked with the master didn't do and accept his teachings. They had very distorted lives. Then again, they shall find their way. So, my beloved brothers and sisters, I take my leave from this instrument, and I say peace be with you.

I am your brother John.

CHAPTER 19

The Avenue of Life is So Abundant and So Beautiful and So Delightful to Experience

By Disciple Paul

Peace. Peace. Dearly beloveds of the physical world, it is my pleasure this evening that I have been called upon, that I might come forth and greet unto thee. As I reach in and take hold of the instrument, I once again reiterate the thoughts that are so evident in the annals of eternity, and that is, that which you are expressing in is but that shell of your own expression. It is a shell that seems often rather difficult to penetrate, but yet, I say unto you it is only as difficult as you accept it to be. And, of course, one can never penetrate that shell of density lest one has accepted the consciousness of reality.

You have made your earth a condition that has become a nightmare, rather than an expression of that which was, and is yet evident, to the eyes that are opened unto reality. Of course, I say the eyes that are opened unto that which is reality, but, these eyes do not open without your opening them. The avenue of life is so abundant, so beautiful and so delightful to experience, even though you touch only to the hem of the gown of eternity—there is a new joy and a new pleasure in life.

There is no longer, at least, the feeling of existence, or the feeling of being doubtful as to reality, and that which you are experiencing due to your acceptance of the limitations of your physical earth. Should I say the limitations of your physical earth, or should I say your limitations? Because, in reality, the earth is not physical. It is the perfect rotation and the perfect cycle of the Fathers gift unto you. Along with countless other planets, or worlds that are yet yours to find and explore.

I know, beloveds, we have spoken unto you in various avenues of energy of expression about how to cope with, and what to do, in order to change the expressions of limitation in each one of your lives. We know that some of you accept this, but, with reservation. And, only to that degree are you going to experience that which is the expression of true life, rather than what you call life existence.

Those that live in your physical world to, let us say, what you call a semblance of a great age, all have experienced at least the fringe of the world of the divine creation. Yet, with their backgrounds and their acceptance of the fears and doubts and conditions of your physical earth, even though they have loosed these to some degree—and have not allowed the deep penetration of these conditions to become a part of their lives, they have yet allowed themselves to every so often experience a relapse, as it were, into the consciousness of limitation.

Therefore, their death did come to them, but you will usually find that if you will look into the lives of those that have, let us say, lived for what you call a lengthy life, somewhere in the nineties and in the one hundred period, you will find that usually they will retire from life, as it were, very calmly. Usually without really any suffering in their release from the avenue of density that they have been existing in.

It is sad, for we have often looked into the consciousness of these beautiful souls. And, of course, we have looked into their surroundings, especially, after they have left the physical and reached into the consciousness of what you call death. We have looked into these pictures and we have often wondered why, why have they not shared some of that fringe of awareness that they had and were living in, to some degree, with their fellowman? And, then, we find the reason for it was that it would not have been accepted. Therefore, they kept it to themselves.

But, we also found that this is not the way it should have been done, because, if you don't share something that is deeply a part of your consciousness you begin to lose it, as it were. That is, you don't advance it any further than the first time, or the few times that you have reached into that consciousness, and you don't extend it any further. But, in giving it energy, by sharing it, you extend it further and further.

So, that is why every so often you will find in your physical earth those that are moving into a greater length of life, say, in their hundred and fifteens, twenty, twenty-five, thirty years, hundred and thirty. You see? You will find this in various parts of your country and world because where these persons are existing, or living to a greater degree, at least, they are much of the same thought pattern. Therefore, they share a little of this, but yet even as they share it, they share with a reservation that someday they must give their temple up. They're still holding to that fallacy that they cannot quite make themselves cope with the reality that God is life, and that this temple that you have, you were not created in. But again, I want to speak of this because it is valuable. It is valuable to those of you that are attempting to reach out more fully to the world of consciousness and reality.

Now, you say God created this animal you, the lower you. Your lower self which is the animal self, and the higher consciousness is the God self. But yet, you have given this temple the God consciousness to, at least, some degree. Now then, what happens when the body becomes deteriorated and it suffers illness and goes into the earth? What happens then? That animal is dead. This is only the elements. The physical conscious elements of man expression, in it are dead. But the cells and the atoms never die because that's Gods creation. God's creation cannot be destroyed. You see?

Therefore, your consciousness reestablishes the cells. And when you feel ready, then you take these cells with the same consciousness that these cells once had. You can change them in the spirit side as you begin to reestablish them in another body that is growing in the choice of your mother's womb. You see?

But usually you just take and you put all of these same cells—the cells that have been given the proper consciousness and the ones of the lessons yet unlearned which you call karma. You put these all back in, and you try to establish it in such a way with the consciousness of the mother, the father that you have chosen, and the consciousness that is within the cells to bring about a greater capability of reaching out to a much more energetic future in your reestablished body.

You, with your identity God that does not die nor does not change, yet you are faced with the karmic lessons yet unlearned that are in the consciousness of these cells of the animal expression. These are the ones that you must cope with through the higher consciousness in order to bring about your fulfillment of making this temple do what you want it to do, in order to bring it into that higher consciousness, where it will no longer be necessary.

But the animal lives in that greater evolvement, because all through the generations of man, the temple that you are expressing in will only evolve through you, now. Because you have taken that temple, you have taken that consciousness. You have to then fulfill that which the master Jesus spoke of, and we all have spoken of as Fulfilling the Law. You see? So it is that man is going to continue to come back and forth, back and forth until he has reached the point of awareness that he can now truly take dominion of his world that was turned over to him out of the Father.

Now then, man has done so many things to himself, and yet he has the consciousness of believing this. He has created for himself a world that is definitely of a three-dimensional expression. That's why we call your earth a third-dimensional world because you have made yourself a physical, mental and spiritual being. You have split yourself up in three. You see? Some of you call it Father, Son and Holy Ghost. You see? So you have moved into a consciousness that is of a three-dimensional expression, and so it is, that you have got to overcome this.

When I walked with the Elder Brother Jesus there wasn't a day that he spoke that he didn't tell you and I, that you and I were one, not three. You see? He didn't tell you that you were three different individuals, or three different expressions of life. There's only one consciousness in God and that's complete. And this is you, you are one.

You've got to bring this temple into that consciousness so that this temple then can move into its own expression, once again, that you once took it out of by letting it die, by accepting the consciousness that it had to, at least, experience death once. Your Bible tells you that. Your Bible says that man had to experience death once, but look how often man has been doing it. And he didn't have to do it the first time, but in the density that he accepted it, he seemed to become, let us say, rather lost as to how to cope with the situations that he confronted himself with. Especially after entering into the physical temple, that density seemed to overcome him. Therefore, made it difficult for man to realize that he didn't have to stay with this, he could move right back out of that consciousness if he wished to do so.

I don't know how to express it any different other than, let us say, you go into a glass house where they're mirrored. Or you've had those things in your physical world where you get yourself all lost in there. This is what man has done to himself. He has allowed himself to face a mirror that was not the way out of his dilemma that he had established for himself.

Now then, again there are other ways that you have also established yourself in a three-dimensional world. You have established yourself as a living soul. If you are not coping with life properly either you go into another dimension which is known as *hell* or another dimension which is known as *heaven*, again, a three-dimensional expression. Man has split himself in so many different avenues of thought that he has a difficult time bringing himself into that consciousness that these are not existing at all. They don't exist at all, only in your mind. And, of course, as you have accepted them they are as real as your third-dimensional world is—which is alive, existing and dying.

But the real world doesn't know death. The world that the Father created has not accepted death because there is no such a thing. All that the Father created lives, and not only does it live, but it evolves. It moves into greater and greater dimensions that are in your consciousness. It will because you are co-creators in that avenue of divine expression. Therefore, it is up to you to build your consciousness into that greater acceptance of the Fathers world of reality. All of this is out of the Fathers mind, it is all a complete beautiful expression, and yours is the same if you will accept it that way and grow into it.

So, man has created for himself that which is good, that which is evil, and that which is the final destruction from the evil. He has created and established in his mind all of these things, and so oftentimes you have, and are experiencing for your own self-destruction, or for your own good what you accept is good. Then, it has to be of value to you. If it is good and it has no limited expression there within it that is selfish, or greedy, or fearful or doubtful, then it is good.

If there are bitterness' and hatreds that are held onto then this quickens that energy power of self-destruction. Man does not realize how much of that destruction that you are putting into that temple and how marvelously made that temple is to withstand—for even the amount of years that you do, let us say, exist in your physical world. With all of that that you have done to yourselves, how marvelous it is that your temple is able to withstand these things to such a great extent.

You need not go, say, a hundred years back and you would find that it was very seldom you ever would see a person that reached a great age. It was almost a miracle to see someone that would reach a great age, usually forty-five was the age that you were ready to give the ghost up as you spoke of these things in those days. So, some of mankind has done a little something towards being able to cope with the conditions of your physical world to a greater degree.

Even though there seems to be in the physical world a great deal of turmoil, there is also the capability in many of being able to change that thought, and making it a forgiving thought for themselves, as well as for their fellowman. Because what I do to me, I do to my fellowman. Understand? You can't do anything, not one thing can you do to yourself without doing it also to your fellowman because there is only one in the universe.

So what I do unto myself, I do unto my fellowman. What I have done can be of value to my fellowman, or it can be destructive to my fellowman. It is all in the way that fellowman accepts what I have done.

So, it is that whole picture is cycles, running in all directions. But, when you have the eyes to see, you see these things and they are not only just cycles, but they are in countless and varied colors. So, if you have the eyes to see in these cycles, you would be able to very quickly change your world to a much more fruitful expression and a greater age in living.

Now, let us go back again to those persons that have reached, let us say, one hundred, a hundred and five, somewhere in that avenue, past the nineties. There are times that that person has been able to see the colors around them, what you call the aura, have been able to look into it and see the colors, and connected that color with their thoughts. As they saw the aura and their thoughts—and changing their thoughts, they saw the aura changing.

And even though they didn't know what the colors all meant they knew that when they were bright there was a difference in their energy. There was a wonderful difference in their being able to enjoy things more fully. But when the colors were dense around them they also felt that density within their temple.

Now, these things were not spoken of lest someone would say there was something a little bit deranged here. So, they kept these things to themselves which, again, was not the thing for them to do. But that's because they didn't know better, and didn't know the answers to these things, and were fearful of what someone might think of them if they tried to share it with them. Even if someone would have asked them they would have denied the fact they were capable of seeing these colors around them. But they could have, if they shared these things, extended yet even more fully and more abundantly their lives.

Now, you have met maybe someone in your physical world that was up in years such as ninety, ninety-five years of age and maybe you have talked to them and they have said, "Why I feel as young as when I was in my thirties," And they actually acted in that same degree of activity around them, but with reservation again, because their thoughts were, "When is it going to happen? When is God coming to get me?" And of course being taught that God comes after you, then that was their way of thinking and a very specific reason why their death was very calm, because they knew God was coming to get them, because they didn't know what that temple was and how they invaded that temple.

But, they couldn't put that consciousness together of these things, because they had constantly been living in a triune world, a three-dimensional world—a world of the Father, the Son and the Spirit. And yet, they were able to commune enough with their true higher consciousness, their real selves, to extend their lives and maintain and sustain a body that was healthy and capable of expression of energy. Many times you will find that person that is in that group of a hundred to a hundred and ten, as I've seen them—and I do see them in your physical world to a hundred and thirty six, but I find that many of these, even at that age, are yet doing more physically then some that you might call youthful at seventy and eighty years of age, because their consciousness is a higher awareness.

Right now, I am looking at two beautiful souls, right now, in Columbia South America, there and they're climbing trees. They're getting fruit off of trees. You see? One is a hundred and twenty-six and the other one is a hundred and thirty, but their consciousness is in that direction. Also, I see on the hilltop in Japan, here, the most youthful one is past a hundred years old, that's the youngest one. Then, I'm looking in Russia here now, again, I'm seeing—and yet, how little is ever spoken about this.

How often do you hear of these things in your physical earth? Once in a great while someone will say these things are taking place. Probably, most of the time you don't want to believe it, and probably wouldn't believe it, if you saw it.

These are the things that man has to thaw out of the self. You've got to thaw out those limited expressions, those conditions that create the densities that eventually cause the cells to collapse. So how can I do it? The simplest way that we can share with you is what kind of thoughts am I entertaining? Is it good for me and good for my fellowman? Does it have value? Am I learning something and accepting something greater out of my Father's house? Or am I remaining and taking just what is handed to me from one day to the next?

It's very simple and the consciousness that you've got to be in is knowing what I do, what I think, is it good for me and my fellowman. Has it value? That's the main thing. I like to say, "Does it have value for me and my fellowman?" That's the best way. What am I doing? Am I doing something that is of value to me and my fellowman? Am I daring enough to move into a greater avenue of thought? As long as I know, that that avenue of thought is of value to me and my fellowman, without fear of what my brothers and sisters are going to think, because I am in that avenue of thought. Or am I going to accept it and hopefully look around it, to share it a little bit here and there? "Look, I've discovered this. Isn't it wonderful? Look what it does for me. I am just so happy and I'm sure it's going to be of value to you if you use it," and so on.

Regardless of what my brothers and sisters think, it is only the one that dares to do something, that eventually, that which he or she has dared to extend beyond the self, that has been looked at and said to be controversial, it becomes now, something of value. Because, everything that you have ever done in your physical earth at some time, it took someone that dared to move into it and others that said it was controversial. Even if it was of value, it was still controversial.

So you see everything is very simple, but it has to be given and used in the consciousness of simplicity. Yet, it establishes you on a higher dimension of awareness which takes you into a greater and new cycle of life expression. These are the things that man has to begin to use, so that they don't deteriorate or destroy you physically.

When the temple begins to experience that which is destructive then your body becomes denser and denser. Therefore, the capability of thinking becomes rather scattered to the extent that your direction is confusing, because you have, now, accepted the limited direction, therefore, causing the temple to further and further, slowly but surely, become lesser capable of expression than it once was capable of.

You are the cause and effects of your future. You are the greater identity or the lesser, only as you express it in your own personal lives. These are the answers and they are simple, very simple. What am I doing to myself? Is that which I am involved in of any value to myself or my fellowman? What am I accepting out of my physical world? Am I accepting that which is limited to the eventuality of my self-destruction? Or am I opening my heart and my mind to the greater expression of life? Am I knowing something that is the true expression of the real me? Do I know the living and eternal God? Do I know that the breath that I breathe is the breath of eternity and that it never runs out? The only time it will run out for me is when I stop using it. Or, the only time that it will stop will be when I have allowed myself to accept that day of limitation in my own personal life.

It is up to you and I, beloveds, to keep the fires of eternity moving—moving in such a direction that these fires do not destroy anything, but bring blessing of life unto all mankind. These fires that extinguish the limitations in my world, they consume them. They no longer exist in my world. But, out of that consuming fire comes the glory of the torch of eternity, the torch of life, the torch of all beautiful expression that releases itself in me. In all the myriad colors I can, now, look into the cycles of life and identify myself in and through them, and know the path that I am choosing has value for me and for my fellowman.

Let us stop, now, and enter into the beauty of life. Let us feel ourselves opening up our centers to the cycle of eternity. And, let us begin to look at the self more often in the mirror of our own reflection, rather than taking our fellowman and using him as the mirror of my reflection. Let me see my real self—let me see the beauty of life. Let me look into the mirror and see the colors that are there. Let me change my thoughts and let me see how the colors change. Yes, we can all do these things because they are equally ours. No one has one iota more than the other. What are you going to accept? Yes, your aura will give you the story; will tell you the story of your life and then you can tell the story of your future by just changing my thoughts. (Author's note: Meditation for eight minutes)

Peace. Peace. Peace. I am one known as Paul.

CHAPTER 20

I Find Here That You Did Get Acquainted With Jesus

By Kuthumi

(Author's note: This chapter refers to my past life where I met Jesus. It is just one of the many past incarnations that the master teachers have presented to me.)

Peace. Peace. My dearly beloved brother it is my pleasure at this time that I take hold of the instrument, that I might come forth and share with you those things that may be of value to you. I'm going to do a little different this morning than I usually do. As I'm looking into the pattern of your aura and the colors that are manifesting there, I find that I'm going to enter into the Akashic, or the past, and give you a preliminary view of that which is the expression that you have expressed in, in past incarnations.

I'm looking, here, as I look into the past, I come into the country of Italy here with you, that is during the Empire, the Roman Empire. I find that I see, that you were born at that time and you had joined the forces of the roman soldiers. And I find here, that you were a very, very capable young man and when you had joined the forces, I find that you were but around at the age of sixteen years. You had already claimed to some very wonderful swordsmanship, due to the help of your father, who had been quite a swordsman in and through his life.

I find as you entered into the forces of the roman soldiers that you were rather quick with the sword and also very quick tempered. With the knowledge that you had with your swordsmanship you wanted to claim even greater capabilities than that which you already had. So, it was that your early years were attempting to proclaim yourself one of the best, or even, the best swordsman, and I find that your claim was justified, as far as being able to claim this swordsmanship.

But there came a time later on in your life that you began to see more fully that these things were not of any real advantage. It was well if it was necessary, but you found that you had proclaimed yourself a wonderful swordsman, and others had proclaimed you such. But yet, it seemed as though the heroism of it seemed to begin wear off and you were not at all enthralled with this any longer. And I find at the age of twenty-two you married. You married a very wealthy girl. That is, her family was very wealthy, and your family was not a very wealthy family, but they were able to take care of all situations and conditions. And, you found that your background was very good, as far as the home environment had been concerned, with your brothers and sisters, as well, as with your father and mother.

Then, I find that after your marriage, you found that the background, or the situation that you were in as one of the leading swordsman in the army was not all that you wanted. Not only that, but, after your second child arrived into the physical world, I find that you were no longer wanting to remain in that service. But yet, you felt as though you were not ready for the civilian world, because you had no background in this manner.

So, it was you asked your wife to sustain you during your release from the army, to enter into some sort of business background for, let us say, some schooling. But, I find that the schooling in that day, was actually doing the work. It was not going into a class and finding out how to manipulate and to do these certain things. You had to have the background of having done what you were hopeful of attaining in order to become what is known as a master at your trade.

So, you took up that which was building, the building trade. But, you didn't want to just be a builder. You wanted to be the one that was the—like your present day, the contractor. The one that sought out those that were seeking a home, or some sort of building, and to plan the situation that was necessary with them. You became very capable. At the end of a period of five years you were actually known as a master in your trade.

But, your background was such as one that wanted to be the best in everything that you did, as you were a swordsman and known as the best. And, your father had taught you these things too, if you're going to do something, do it with the fullness of your energies, and your capabilities, and be the best. So, it was that in this work that you attempted to do. You wanted to out do your fellowman, which you eventually were capable of doing.

So it was, that you became very, very capable in the work that you did and not only were you capable, but never seemingly in lack of some sort of building and work of various kinds to do. Always there was a challenge there for you. But, this became also something that you had gotten and reach, seemingly the zenith of.

So, you wanted some more challenge. You wanted some greater challenge, and so, you took up that which is the arts. So it was, that you went into this, and you wanted to become the best at this as well, and so it was, that you worked very hard at this art. It took a number of years, but eventually you got to where you were capable of creating art in various ways. Not just upon the canvas, but art that was necessary in the building trade. So, it was, that you applied all of these things, and that which you put on the canvas you wanted to put in the various buildings that were—such as temples, and so on, that you were building.

You became a very capable artist in many ways, because your sculpturing was magnificent, and very beautiful. So it was, you became a very wealthy man, but yet, by the same token, it was not wealth that you were seeking. You just were seeking to be the best in whatever you did, and the wealth took place automatically with you—and you could have proclaimed a great deal more wealth than you did. But, as I say, it wasn't wealth that you were looking for.

But, you had a magnificent home. You had your five children. Your three girls and your two boys were also brought up in the same way as you were. That is, you were—especially with the two boys, and you gave them that initiative to become very capable in everything that they did, to do the best that they knew how, and you never attempted to tell them they weren't doing good. Always they were doing very nicely, but you felt they were capable of doing even better. So it was, they were never disenchanted with the way you taught them, as your father had taught you. He always proclaimed that what you did was very, very nice, but always he knew that you were capable of doing even better.

So it was, that these two boys and also you, were not hesitant with your three girls in letting them know, also, that whatever they did they should do with their heart, and choose that which they were happiest with, not to choose something because of the returns, the monetary returns, but to choose something that they would be happy in doing, and that the returns in the monetary way would take care of itself.

So, you worked very, very effectively with your children and, of course, you had a happy marriage and you traveled now in your later years. You began to travel in various parts of the world, but most of the time your travels—not only because of wanting to see these different parts of the world, but you were going also to broaden your look at the arts of the various parts of the Mediterranean world. You found many things in your travels, and you were not critical of the others that did art work, but you could see the flaws that were there in some of the art. Some of it, you thought was absolutely magnificent, that there couldn't be any sort of improvement on, as far as your capability of seeing it with your physical eyes.

But, it was always a pleasure and a joy for you to go into all of these various places to see what was being done by other artists and, of course, you had become so well known, that everyone, wherever you went, seemed to put out the red carpet for you. Especially in the palaces, you were welcome as though you were one of the family of these various kingdoms, in the Mediterranean world.

J. A. Wright: "Can you give me the age?"

This was during the . . .

J. A. Wright: "Before Christ?"

A short period before Jesus came back from India. Because you had gone into this other art work, or at the time that you were in your retirement age, actually, of your arts by your travels, this is about the time that Jesus returned from India.

And so, I find here that you did get acquainted with Jesus.

J. A. Wright: "I was aquatinted with his teachings or him personally?"

Him personally and his teachings, because while you were traveling, and it seems as though I am seeing you in the country of England and you traveled through there and were very interested in the arts in that part of the world when the master returned from India. It was while you were in England that you began to hear of the various things that this man was talking about, and how controversial this man was, and how different his teachings were to those that were in the temples. You see? Because this man was teaching only how man should be *living*, not preparing himself, as they were teaching you in the temples to go to some false heaven and to die, and how to live under your own suppression. This was the thing that the master was very opposed to.

So, you, eventually hearing this—and hearing how the people were very opposed to him. You see? Because they were so thoroughly indoctrinated in the suppressions of the temples of that day, and that was not only in the country of the birth of Jesus, that was all over, you know? Everywhere, they were all opposed to this man, and the country that you were born in, Italy they were very opposed to him, because they were trying to form their own religious backgrounds. You see? Which was later known as Christianity.

So it was that you said very little, because you were in a position then, understand? That you were so well known and if you would have taken sides with the master Jesus, you would have been criticized very severely. You see? So, you had to very careful. You kept very quiet, but you knew that you had to go into that part of the world and hear this man speak, because in your years, your youth, you didn't do things the same as everybody else. And, you were considered to some degree different, and even your parents sometimes would criticize you for some of the things you did. But you told them, "Look, what I do, I do it and it doesn't hurt me. It doesn't destroy anything." And they had to agree with you that it didn't. That it was, it didn't hurt a thing. In fact, they began to realize that some of the things that you were doing were valuable.

But one of the things you told your father one day that made him stop to think was, with respect you turned to your father and said, "Father, is there anything in this world that wasn't controversial at sometime, then became after a time a part of that which man did no longer criticize?" And it was that, your father had to admit that this was true.

So I bring this to you, this message of that incarnation, because you did go from England to the place known as the *Holy Land* now. You did join some of the peoples that were there to hear what the master Jesus had to say and you saw and felt the pulse of the people that were there. Because throughout your years of having done work of various kinds, with various people, in various parts of your country, and the world, you found that it was best for you to listen to them, but to say very little. Because you saw and felt the density that was in many of these people, that is the density only due to the fact that they had been so thoroughly indoctrinated in their conditions of dogmas. Understand? The master was opposing these dogmas and doctrines and, therefore, was the pulse of the people there, and there was a great deal of confusion at times. But you remained very quiet and very silent.

But you did have to meet and talk to this man, privately. That is when he moved away from the multitudes or the ones that were there to listen to him and when he got finished speaking, eventually you did get closer to him, where you could speak to him and get more information from him. And you did this on several occasions, but mostly when it was more private. Because as you were well known it was very necessary for you to maintain the balance there in your personal life and the master knew this also.

So, it was that there were times that were arranged for you to go into a private room with him and the few that he knew, including those that were known as his disciples, and you would sit and talk. There was a great deal of wisdom that was shared there with you, and I say to you my beloved brother, *nothing is lost in the universe* and you're going to find that this incarnation is going to be of value to you.

So it was, that you lived a very long and a very good life. Although I'm not saying to you that you didn't get angry at times and didn't threaten a few people at times that were opposed to some of the things that you said, because you knew that it was of value. But the master told you at times, "Now look, don't let these things bother you." Because the master stayed calm, he didn't let these things become ingrained in him. Had he done so, he would of never have been a master.

So it was, that you let these things become rather, well, you became bitter at some of the people. So it was that—yet I say to you, many things that you did, and especially in this work too of attempting to put out whatever you knew was of value to the people to help them to help themselves more fully. Again, you were functioning in a manner of like you did in your building, in your art work, trying to be the best in your seeking the greater awareness. But those conditions out here, you let get to you every so often, and you broke out, and this is the only thing that prevented you from mastering life.

So it was that this life was a very good and a very long life. You lived to one-hundred and three years in that incarnation. The way you started out, if you hadn't been as good a swordsman as you were, you probably wouldn't have made it to a very long period of age. You probably would have died at the age of probably twenty or twenty-five, something like that. But you were a very efficient—and the beautiful part of it was that you began to realize that there was no future in that. You see?

So, there had to be other outlets and you accepted these things. With the help of your wonderful wife you did very beautifully, and your children, of course, also were well instructed, and they too went through a very beautiful world of their own in their various parts of the world. One of your daughters married one of the princes in that part of your world.

[By Kuthumi]

Chapter 21

Be Not Conformed to the World But Be Ye Transformed By the Renewal of the Mind

By Jesus

Peace. Peace. Peace. Be not conformed to the world, but be ye transformed by the renewal of the mind. There is a great deal to these words and I feel that it is time now that one becomes more fully aware that there needs to be a transformation. For man has too often said, "I cannot change these things, they are here, and I must abide by them." What is the reason that man has allowed himself to become conformed rather than transformed?

God is the same today, yesterday and tomorrow. Then if this is so, then why is it that you may say, "There is nothing I can do about these things." Has God become a myth to you? Have you asked yourself this, "How real is

God?" Or has God become something that you cannot reach to? Has God become distant? If so, then what has taken place and what is the reason for God being at a distance?

My beloveds, God is as close today to each and every one of you as in the beginning of time. But, you have let the element called *time* and *distance* frustrate you, and the more you become frustrated the greater is the distance and the lesser seems to be the time.

Is it not now time that you begin to look within the self, and as you look within, that you might endeavor to be honest with yourself, that you might then transform that which is your outer world, that you might look through that which you call the physical eyes and now look at your world and see God in motion? How can you see God in motion? You cannot see God in motion if you are concerned about yourselves.

If all of your motives are that you are attempting to keep, let us say, a wolf from the door, if you awaken in the morn disgruntled at having to face another day and making plans for that day to make your world conform to your physical needs. You are going to find that these days are going to be difficult ones. They are going to be days that you are going to wish at every moment that it was over with.

But, when you begin to realize that God of the inner self, that which is your identity; with all that you feel, see, touch, smell, and all of the twenty-two expressions of light (physical senses), that you are to experience in this your third-dimensional incarnation, you will find as you will look then beyond the self, you will begin to feel God in motion. But, the greatest way to feel the divine nature of your being is to transform the mind. Establish within that mind the knowledge that those things that you are finding so important, are not that important, but, that you know that this day you walk not alone, for the Father and I are one.

As I take my leave of this my little home today, I am going to look at God, and I am going to find and see God in all things that I meet up with today. I am going to leave my home today, and if I am going to work and I find that there is someone there that my mind wishes to say to me "Oh, I wish I didn't have to face that person today," that now, I have changed this, I have transformed my mind, for I walk now with the Father. And so as you enter into your day's work and you see this person, the first thing you say—for inside of you, you will see in that person different now than you have ever seen them before. So, you say to that person "My but you look nice today." You say something beautiful to that person. You look at their clothing, and you say something nice about their clothing or the way they are looking.

But, you'll say something that helps that person to also begin to transform within himself or herself. You will find that your day is a much more beautiful day. You will not be looking at the clock every few minutes and wanting that clock to hurry upon its way. No. You will be thinking quite differently now. You will say, "Don't hurry clock, I am not working with time nor am I working with space today. I am working with eternity. I work with my Father."

I stopped to speak to a little lady of ill repute at the well one day. There were those that were very unhappy for my having stopped just to speak to her. But, for you see, beloveds, I was not seeing a lady of ill repute. I was looking at God. I was looking at the Father. I saw my Father and I saw my Father within her and, of course, I asked my Father quietly that I might greet to my little sister in a way that would be of importance to her. My disciples were casting their little rocks at me, but I paid no attention to them. For I had to speak to my sister, and I was given out of my Father's light, the words that were necessary in order that my sister and I would meet on the same level of awareness.

Needless to say—although it is not written in the *Good Book* that my little sister was transformed. She was no longer conforming to the world that was around her. She went about and started a new life. It was not a simple thing to do, for you see my beloveds, she did not run away. She didn't go to some other little town that she might not be known, and therefore, making it simple for her to transform her world. No. She stayed right there where everyone knew her, and in her transformation—although oftentimes, there were barbs thrown at her, she blessed them and even stopped at times to say to them "This is not the real you that speaketh unto me, my brother. I know the real you. The real you is God," and then she would go upon her way.

Eventually she became a person that everyone in the little community looked up to. She didn't say, "I can't do it. I'm not able to. The only way I can beat the rap would be to run and go into some other place." No, no. She stayed right where she was, and she went to work, and she did things for her fellowman, and many a healing came through her ministry.

Tonight, I too beloveds, would like to share with each one of you a little of the transformation of your minds, that you will no longer look to tomorrow, other than you will look forward to it with eagerness, knowing I do no longer just exist, for I found my Father. I live, for my Father lives in me. So, lets you, at this moment know that there is nothing in your world, not one thing or one person or one deed in your world that you have conformed to. If it is of no value to you then it cannot be transformed. But first, you must start with forgiving, forgiving of the self—that you might awaken yourself to the identity of your *oneness* in the Father.

Once you have done this, beloveds, you are now ready to forgive, to forgive the self, to forgive your brother man. Thereby, you have awakened within you the light of awareness that is the transformation of the temple into the light that, now, you are ready to be receptive unto the beauties of the energy and the power of the universe. You have no longer any obstructions and you know no limitation in the Father, for you have now taken that limitation from yourself.

You have allowed yourself to be receptive unto His divine and eternal nature. You have felt His presence and you have felt the power of healing that is entering into your temple, going all the way through, lighting up every fiber, every cell, bone and tissue of your temple as the sludge of your negations goes out of the bottom of your feet with love, beloveds, with love; into the outer darkness that they may be conformed unto the divine nature of the Father, cleansed and purified once again. Don't limit that energy, for He gave you the capability and the capacity of receptivity. He gave you the freewill either to conform or transform.

Then, beloveds, let's each and every one know tonight that we have been transformed and that we are walking now in the strength of His divine nature that we no longer have fear. We no longer doubt. But we know, I sleep this night, oh Father, in the cradle of the universe. I awaken in a transformation of Thy love that I shall walk this day knowing that thou art always with me. That all I need do, Father, if there is any slight obstruction "Show me Father. I'll walk." Therefore, beloveds, let's you and I know no obstructions can remain when I have said, "Father show me. I have taken the steps and I have been transformed." Peace be with you.

I am your brother Jesus.

APPENDIX

(11-796)

Peace. Peace. Peace. My dearly beloveds, once again it is our pleasure, whenever we are called upon, that we might come and share with you those things that we know through our own expression in the light, that has brought us into that which we call the fulfilment of the age, and also, the fulfillment of that which is the dimension that all mankind is seeking, but yet are not aware of that which they are seeking.

Therefore, it is with great difficulty that man is moving on the expression of the physical plane, because man has not attempted to live by the heritage that he has. But, he has attempted to live by that which man has written for him, has guided him with and has said, "This is the way." So the way, of course, has always been given in such a manner that man knows that there is no future, excepting that which a few years of expression upon the physical plane, and then the results become that which is called death.

And then, of course, man again assumes that he must return and fulfill certain conditions of karma that he has built-up in that past incarnation. And again, he moves in his limitations, to that which he has allowed himself, to become totally guided by the realm of his physical world, and no longer is aware—truly aware of his free will, because he finds himself constantly beset by conditions of limitation. These limitations, of course, are foisted upon him by those who would hold them in suppression, in order to gain for themselves more of that which is the physical wealth and the physical expressions, that this wealth can buy for them.

So it is, that it has been something of a continuity of repetitious histories. And so, we are hopeful that those of you that we have worked with and are going to work with throughout the years that are to come, that we shall work with you to the degree of hopefully bringing into your own world that which you know is not limited. That you will find then, that you can walk with God, that you can walk with all eternity, that you can experience all that which is eternity, not by going through the death. You have done it time and again, but, by moving into the greater dimensions of God's divine expression and awareness.

(Author's note: Meditation for eight minutes)

We have a world. We have a universe, you and I. And, we have this universe to manifest and have our total being in it. And, in order that we can move and have our total being in this universe we cannot assume or even think of being able to reach into this unlimited expression of God if we entertain the least condition of limitation within our beings.

Now, I know that you and I have been told, oftentimes, that Jesus taught a certain way. The explanation of that which he taught was absolute limitation. And we know, you and I today know, and if we don't, we should know that no time in the years of teaching, at no time did your Elder Brother ever put any—even a thought of limitation upon anything that he gave forth. And yet, I know it is written in the Bible, and that there are certain conditions of limitations that have been set forth there, such as—let us take one which is the greatest of all limitations, that they have said Jesus has said, and put upon man, and that was, "Without going through him, if we fail to go through him, we have no chance of reaching the heavenly realm." Now Jesus never did give any such thing to man, and yet it is written in your Bible, and, it is being taught to you, and you have accepted it. Your children have been taught these things and have accepted it.

Now, when man was given his freewill and he was given this freewill to take dominion over the entire creation. Then how can man allow himself to even think that one man could come to the physical expression of earth, and now say that man could not reach the Father excepting through him? So, it is well that man give thought to these things, because if man doesn't do this, he is going to destroy himself or continue, I say, to destroy himself.

Now, of course, John was another one, that if you will read that which is in the Bible, of some of the things that John taught, he would have never mastered life, nor would have Jesus, had they done what they were supposed to have been teaching. I will admit that the other disciples such as Peter and the rest of them did go into many negations and that is why they all went to their death in the various ways that they did—imprisonment and death. But John never taught many of those things that have been put in the *Book,* as that which is true. But then again, we've got to be ready to consider that which—from the time that Jesus, John, Peter, Paul, Mark,

Luke, Matthew and all the rest of these disciples were walking there, with Jesus, there was a different world. Then, of course, Jesus and his teachings taught an entirely different language, a language that was used very little at that time even.

Then let us take the expanse of years that the Bible was rewritten on paper by various ones. Never was it compiled and put together all through those years until approximately only four centuries ago. In fact, it was in the year of 1611 when the Bible was first compiled and put together as a book, four hundred years ago.

Now, Jesus and his disciples walked the plane of earth over two thousand years ago because of the calendar changes. Let us be honest with ourselves, and let us look at the conditions and changes of history. The backgrounds of the religions of that day were not the same four hundred years ago as they were—even the pre-Christian religions were not the same. Understand?

Look, beloveds, you are just expressing on this earth a very few years and you have seen, I am sure most of you, the great changes that have taken place in your religions in just those few years that you have lived upon the earth. That is, if you have gone into the temples, at all, you have seen these changes. So, you can imagine what has taken place in two thousand years. You can also imagine—some of you can't even hardly understand your own children, because they talk their own language now. They use the same words, but they mean an entirely different meaning than you, when you spoke to them. You see?

And so maybe—let us take a look. It's possible that these things put in the Bible, in their translation throughout the various years of retranslation, and the changes in the religious orders—the changes among mankind itself and the political backgrounds and so on, because the religions in the time of Jesus were also politically guided. In fact, they were, actually, at that time the politics. They were that, which was known as the church politics. They were the controlling faction of physical mankind.

So I'm explaining these things to you because I feel it is terrifically necessary, now, that you really and truly understand these things. Because your Bible having been put into a book for the first time, in print, in 1611 also caused a great deal of confusion in England in 1620. That's when the pilgrims left there to come to your country which is known as America now. And they left because of religious persecution, didn't they? You see? So, again when the Bible was set in print, then the leaders of the temples immediately began to create greater suppression, didn't they? Because now they had something in print that was supposed to be infallible. And now they could keep the pressure upon their followers.

Well, those in England that decided to leave were not going to take that persecution, that religious domination. So, they left and came to this country called America. Alright, but they never did escape it. You don't run away from anything. Because the British came over and eventually they had their hold, as well as the Spaniards, and as well, the Italians. Those that came into this country then attempted also to dominate the religious backgrounds, and to suppress those in this country called America.

Again, let us take another look at these things because they are very important to the future. The country of America was founded then, not under that which was called Christ or Christianity at that time, but was founded under God, and it was written in the Constitution of this country called America. You see? It was founded under God. And it was not called Christianity until many years later.

So again, if man will go back into their histories they will see what has taken place here and will not be so apt to blindly accept these conditions that are being foisted upon man in a manner that is constantly limited. He is constantly limited. It has taken away from you your freewill. If you step over one way or another you are eliminated. So, you are bound by these conditions and anytime that man becomes bound, he is not living according to his gifts out of the Father, because the Father gave it all, gave us dominion over it all, and here it is. And, He gave you the freewill to use it in any way that you willed to use it. And, now you are not doing so. You are bound by this. You are tied—but who has done this, God? No. God has nothing to do with this. Man has done it to himself. (Kuthumi)

(12-938)
But what did Jesus do as he was aware? He began to become more and more aware of this your third-dimensional world, and he found that things weren't always going smoothly? It is said that he went into the garden. Where was the garden? The garden was his own consciousness, into his higher consciousness. He'd go into that higher consciousness. He'd go into that higher consciousness and then he'd have a talk with himself. He wasn't bitter, he knew there were certain things that he didn't appreciate that were taking place. They were not *happening*. He knew that he had been the cause

of it being there. You see? But, in your physical world you say, "Well, this happened to me." But, you never stop to realize, that it didn't happen. You caused it, and you were getting the effects of that cause.

So, Jesus began to realize these things, and he would talk to himself and he would say, "Well wait a minute, now, I see this here." He would have a talk and those that sometimes came within hearing—they thought that he was talking to God, that he was crying to God for help, and so on, which he wasn't doing, he was only talking to his higher self, which is God within himself.

But, also if there were certain situations and conditions that he wasn't sure of how to cope with, certainly he would turn to the Father and say, "Show me." He wasn't crying to the Father to do it for him, because he knew that there was no way that the Father was going to do it for him. (Akim)

(13-904)

Now, then, I am going to touch to a little something else here because it has to do with lifting the self into this sort of an awareness. And what were the main principles of the teaching that your Elder Brother Jesus brought forth? What were his main characteristics of creating an awareness within you, that you might find your way into the development of yourself. Or that which you know as the self to a higher pitch of vibration, in order that you can function more beautifully in this which you call the physical world? Of course, as I look at it—and I look at each one of you as individuals, I cannot say and be honest with myself and say I'm looking at you and say you're but just a physical. If I say you are just physical, I am not telling you the truth, because I look at each one of you and I see you in the reality of you, that which is beyond destruction.

Therefore, what I am looking at, now, is you in your spiritual rebirth. You see? This was one of the great things that your Elder Brother Jesus brought to you and I, very constantly, about being born again of the spirit. In other words, he was trying to let you know constantly that you were not physical, but when you said, "I am one in the Father and the Father is one in me," you knew that's what you were. And, that's not only what you were, that's what you are. You see? So, basically then, he was teaching us how to live.

Then, the next thing he was trying to teach you was to know yourself. To constantly delve within your consciousness, within the very being of you—because, look, you see each one of you have been through so many incarnations that I'm not going to even begin to count what you've been through, because even in the past six thousand years I'm seeing all too many. Understand?

So, then, I know that I say to you, "Each one, every cell in your temple in order that mastery be reached, must be light." Understand? As long as there is any darkness in any cell, mastery cannot be achieved. Therefore, then, your Elder Brother was teaching us how to know yourself, how to get within and know yourself. Now, in this incarnation, lessons of the past learned can be a key to unlocking the doors of lessons yet unlearned in this incarnation. That is why knowing yourself more thoroughly, you then know what you have been searching for, in reality, and that is God.

Then, when you have found yourself fully in this mastery awareness you know, now, I am that which is the I AM. You see? And no longer is there any thought pattern functioning out of you that can even contain the least bit of separation from the mind throughout the temple—in every fiber, cell, bone and tissue of that temple. You see? (Orion)

(11-925)
This man (Jesus) taught you—he was not giving you what you see on the surface there. This man was beyond that surface. He was a man that was living in reality. He wasn't living in the expression of death or he wouldn't have told his disciples, "Let the dead bury their own dead." When his disciple wanted to go to his uncle's funeral—he would have let him go, he would have said, "Well, go ahead." But he said, "Let the dead bury their own dead," because he was trying to show this man and his disciples and all mankind—even though Jesus had spent hours upon hours, hours upon hours in private lessons, as well as listening to him speak to the multitudes, and not any of it was being absorbed. This is disgusting, you know? I looked at this man, Jesus, and I thought, often times, why do you continue? No one is absorbing any of it. But, you see, it wasn't true. There was one, once in a great while, that did absorb. John, and also Paul, they were the only ones of the disciples to master life. But you see, not that they were special, but they did put what Jesus was teaching into action. (Kuthumi)

(12-981)
Are there any questions you would like to ask?

Participants: "Didn't we create ourselves out of the Father? How did I or her as a personality identity originate? If we gave ourselves that origination, then didn't we give ourselves life?"

No. You were always alive, always had life, but it was all in the Father. But then the Father gave you that identity outside of himself, and that identity that he gave outside of himself, he says this was known as the atom or Adam that you put in the Bible. Then the atom decided to split itself and took on the animal being, and then, from there on, man produced himself out of that. With never losing the identity, the identity always remained. It is forever. It cannot die. That identity can never die. But man brought this upon himself because he has been told constantly that he sinned for having taken the identity of the lower self.

Anyone else want to ask a question?

Participants: "Can you explain how an eye for an eye and a tooth for a tooth was put into the Bible, and how it was meant to be interpreted?"

An eye for an eye and a tooth for a tooth was created by religion. And in effect it was telling you that if somebody hurts you, hurt them back.

Participants: "Which is just continuing the cycle."

That's all. Which of course, is not what God is—that's what man is. The animal in man is doing this and he is thinking he is doing the right thing. In reality, if anyone would think just a little bit they would realize that that is not the way to function. So, whoever says to you that the Bible is all truth—this is a sad, sad thing.

Participants: "Sometimes you quote the Bible and its okay and sometimes you say that it isn't right."

That's right. But remember how we have always said it. We said, "The truth is there but it's sure messed up."

217

Participants: "What I want to know is—it's easy to recognize, you know, like from the King James version onward. It's easy to see all the changes there. What is the Bible? How do we have it today? Can you give me a real quick run down?"

You've got many, many bibles. You take even your Catholicism has its own bible. Then you have the King James version, and then you have the German, way back there in the German version. Then you have that which is the Jewish version. Then you have the Mohammedan's bible. Then you have, well, name it. And they're all different. Yet, in their substance, the true substance in every one of them is exactly the same.

And, as we've said time and time again, you could have the whole Bible in less than twelve pages. And it would give you everything of consciousness—that if you followed it to the best way of life—because it's just a few words that can cover everything; how to live, and especially these words, physician heal thyself. Do unto others, as you would have them do unto you. And, fear not life, for life is God. God is life—that is the energy that you are assimilating every day.

But, how am I assimilating those energies? I assimilate them with fear, I assimilate them knowing that every day I'm getting a little older. I assimilate them knowing that next year I won't be able to do quite as much as I was able to do this year. And, especially after I have reached the retirement age, oh that's the day I have to sit down. Because I just can't—I know I won't be able to, because I am already fifty now, and so fifty, my goodness, another fifteen years, I will not be able to do much. And so I live—maybe I don't say it, but in my own consciousness, that's where I'm living. No. I'm existing in that kind of thought pattern, and so what happens?

Pretty soon I get a little ache and I say, "Old age is creeping up." I get another little ache and I say, "Oh, my goodness I think I'm getting rheumatism." And pretty soon I am building up on these things, and what can happen? It has to fulfill what you want it to fulfill. Even though you say you don't want it, you're asking for it and so that's the way it is. You should be able to do everything that you've ever done, no matter when—not only that which you've ever done in your life, but better as the years go by. Why? Because, there's no lack of energy, and the experiences you've had should allow you to flow graciously, and creatively, and abundantly in all facets. (Akim)

APPENDIX

(13-548)
Now, are there any questions that you would like to ask?

> Participants: "Yes, I have a question. You mentioned, 'Thoughts of our youth' in this lesson. Are you referring to the biblical saying by Jesus, 'Lest you change and become as little children?'"

No. Because Jesus didn't say that, your church said that. Then, they put it in a book called the Bible. And also, it is said in your Bible that Jesus said that we were his sheep, and we were never his sheep. This, again, the temple put there, because they wanted to herd you. They wanted to keep you under suppression. They wanted you to be their sheep. You see? And they wanted to be the shepherd. They wanted to put that hook around your neck and say, "Come on, come my way." (Orion)

(12-753)
Are there any questions that you would like to ask?

> Participants: "We went into this body and we became a living soul. Then we are actually expressing through one of the gifts of life, are we not?"

Right.

> Participants: "I know we are doing it the hard way. And the fact that we went into this body, we now have to overcome the various little things that we have allowed ourselves to take on through our consciousness, allowed us, unfortunately, to forget what we really are in reality. So we have, unfortunately, I'm afraid, used it, have we not to make things more difficult for us?"

Well, definitely. Actually, when man took over this hu-body, immediately his thoughts were—because once he took it over he found himself as though he was trapped. Then, what happened? Just like your Bible says, "He sinned." You see? And, therefore, in his sin he said he had to experience death once. But man has been doing it over, and over, and over. Not only once, but continuously and he didn't have to experience death at all. But, he said he sinned, and so in that consciousness that's what he had done. It's just that simple.

Participants: "Thank you."

There is one that said, "Ye are born to die," and it is expressed even in your Bible. And who ever put such a thing there? The money changers! But your brother Jesus never taught it, and never did your brother Jesus ever tell you, you were born to die. But he told you, you were born to live, and you were born to the greater gifts, and the countless gifts of the Father, and, only through opening wide the door of life and expressing life, regardless of seeing, the death all around you and self destruction. If one would only stop to take a glimpse of that which you are seeing, and then try to pin it on a God of love, try to give all of that mess, that destruction and saying it is God's will. Your own father—physical father or mother wouldn't do that to you unless they were criminals. And yet, you would say that your God did it.

When you are hesitant to admit to yourself that I am the one that put my creative energies, my God-given powers and energies into these conditions and this is what I am getting in return, am destroying myself then blaming it unto my God. Then, I run when I have become so ill and so depleted within my temple. Now, I run to every false god that I can run to, to be healed. Doing everything excepting what my brother Jesus taught me; physician heal thyself.

In the Father's house is the answer to eternal life. We are going to enter that house and never to leave it. And, that house is here and now, and you, each one of you are the temples of His divine expression. Remember this and you will walk tall with greater energy and power then you ever walked through, out any of your past incarnations.

Participants: "I have one. I have been thinking about it for quite a while and I haven't been able to get the answer to it. Well, the question is, "What happened to Adam?" We know that he came down and took possession of the hu-animal and then eventually produced children. And, when he left the earth did he keep coming back? Or did he go back into the higher realms of spirit and reestablish his consciousness?"

He did come back, but eventually, of course, he did return to that which was his original expression. But not as the total man because after all he left those that we call cloned through the female hu-animal. And yet, of course, the consciousness of man, as the atom of life, is the same in all man, is the same in all males, all females, because once the cloning started you can't separate that which is the perfect man. We call them souls because that's exactly what they are on your physical earth. But yet, as we have spoken—as all of the great teachers of the past have spoken, yet said, "We are one." That is the consciousness, that is the Christ consciousness or the consciousness of the one living and eternal God in all man.

Participants: "Or the mind of God."

Yes, in all man. So, when we speak of, there is no separation, it is rather difficult for man to realize that there is no separation. Because, all of the confusion of the almost countless religious backgrounds or the countless thoughts in each one of the religious backgrounds seem to always cause man to be separated in thought—not in reality, but in thought. And, if you don't belong to what I call my church you are not my brother. This is brought on because of the lack of understanding, and, of course, through the lack of teaching truth. And, so, I say to you the Adam (or atom) of the conscious living image and likeness of God is not disturbed. It is absolutely as God established it.

And all we have to do is enter into that consciousness. We are in it, actually, but actually, not of it, because of our scattered forces, or scattered thoughts. But, once we gather that thought into the oneness, then you rise above that which you said has been the sin of man, by having taken on this animal body. But your Bible tells you Eve fed the apple. Understand? But you, with your own freewill—that is Adam, in his own freewill, his own consciousness, decided to experience this animal, entered within it and became confused in the density of what they call the lower self, the animal self, and the higher consciousness, which is the God within. It's very simple. Does that answer your question? (Akim)

Participants: "Yes, thank you."

EPILOGUE

I don't think it would be too much to say that my life has been enriched in many ways by these teachings, and that I felt honored to be a part of such a worthy project. A quote by Mark Twain comes to mind when thinking about these most important teachings and history of Jesus, "Truth is stranger than fiction, but it is because fiction is obliged to stick to possibilities; Truth isn't."

Look for my next book with the master teachers which I am currently preparing.

For consultations, speaking engagements and information on audio CD's, contact J. A. Wright at: JesusSpeaksBook@gmail.com

DISCLAIMER
The information provided
in this book is only
designed to provide interesting
and entertaining info on the
subjects discussed. This book
is not a substitute for medical advice
of physicians. For diagnosis
or treatment of any medical concerns
or problems, consult your physician.

22962080R00145

Made in the USA
Columbia, SC
03 August 2018